Reading *American*

Reading
American Horror Story

Essays on the Television Franchise

Edited by REBECCA JANICKER

McFarland & Company, Inc., Publishers
Jefferson, North Carolina

ISBN 978-1-4766-6352-4 (print)
ISBN 978-1-4766-2892-9 (ebook)

LIBRARY OF CONGRESS CATALOGUING-IN-PUBLICATION DATA

BRITISH LIBRARY CATALOGUING DATA ARE AVAILABLE

Front cover: Haunted Hotel © 2017 DpArtPhoto/iStock

Printed in the United States of America

*McFarland & Company, Inc., Publishers
Box 611, Jefferson, North Carolina 28640
www.mcfarlandpub.com*

For Lincoln.

Acknowledgments

I would like to thank the contributors to this volume for all their hard work, as well as to acknowledge the contributions they made to the contents of the Glossary.

As ever, my biggest thanks go to Lincoln for all his support and practical advice, as well as for watching countless episodes of *American Horror Story* over the last year.

Table of Contents

Introduction

In October 2011, a program entitled simply *American Horror Story* hit the small screen for the first time. Quickly building on its rapid success—in terms of both critical reception and of ratings—series co-creators Ryan Murphy and Brad Falchuk developed this fecund concept into a horror anthology franchise which now comprises numerous series dedicated to a diverse array of bloodcurdling and gruesome scenarios. From fictional visits to terrifying destinations like the *Murder House* and the *Asylum* through to the *Hotel*, meeting the members of the *Coven* and the *Freak Show* along the way, this high-profile television drama repeatedly draws on a range of troubled spaces and beleaguered communities to tackle issues pertaining to wide-ranging aspects of American history and culture.

Small screen horror, as Lorna Jowett and Stacey Abbott observe in *TV Horror: Investigating the Dark Side of the Small Screen* (2013), has gone from strength to strength in recent years (223–224). From long-running shows like *Supernatural* (2005–), through such lavish productions as HBO's *True Blood* (2008–2014) and Showtime's *Penny Dreadful* (2014–2016), to big screen spin-offs like *Wolf Creek* (2016–), the quantity and variety of horror texts available to contemporary television viewers has burgeoned. Yet, beyond helping to sate an increased appetite for consuming Gothic and horror within a domestic setting, *American Horror Story* has come to make its mark in other ways. *AHS* materialized in what Jason Mittell has described as a growth era for television (17). Indeed, much has been made of the show's novel approach to storytelling, which functions to separate it out from other horror narratives. Though it follows the basic mini-series model of a finite run of episodes that culminates in a finale with narrative closure, *AHS* differs because its weekly format aligns the show with ingrained TV programming practices. With its numerous stand-alone series—plus its notable recycling of actors—this is a show that enjoys a distinctive structure. Looking back over the five seasons to date, unity of theme renders each season as a distinct "text," and *AHS* thus seems to operate as an anthology *franchise* rather than an anthology *series*.

To speak of *AHS* is to index an intricate, self-reflexive and ever-expanding universe of horror scenarios derived from, and entrenched within, a long history of popular culture that seeks to make sense of the world by grappling with terror and gore.

Positioned as it is within a time-honored tradition of Gothic horror, *AHS* time and again offers its audience images, however warped, of the society that they themselves inhabit. Struggling families endeavor to start anew, troubled teens strive to carve out an identity for themselves, and people from all walks of life search for love and acceptance. Themes of romance and family, individualism and community, personal and professional success, all find their expression in the various seasons that make up the *AHS* narrative thus far. Wider social issues pertaining to gender, sexuality, disability, race, ethnicity and the treatment of minority groups, both in contemporary American society and throughout the nation's history, also feature on a regular basis. As such, the various horror stories portrayed by this franchise effectively lay before their viewers some very familiar subject matter presented with a creative twist: a twenty-first-century take on a traditional and popular genre. This volume of essays addresses the *AHS* phenomenon from three main angles, looking at the contemporary entertainment industry, at issues of representation and at hallmarks of the horror genre.

The collection begins by seeking to place *American Horror Story* within a wider context of the entertainment industry and of popular culture. In this way, Part One: Industry and Culture, contains essays on various aspects of television form and scheduling practices, as well as on ways of engaging horror audiences that go beyond the text itself. The first essay makes clear that, in shifting its geographical and temporal focus with each new season, *AHS* combines the pleasures of the anthology show with serialized storytelling to feature the same characters for a given length of time. Here, Lorna Jowett demonstrates how notions of the repertory company and of what Jeffrey Bussolini dubs "intertextuality of casting" (3) function both within the horror series itself, and within a broader TV landscape. Jowett stresses that *AHS* pushes strategies of intertextuality of casting in TV by having the same actor taking on similar or contrasting roles from season to season, and playing on their previous roles in other productions. Particular attention is paid to "older" female actors and the ways in which the multiple characters they play potentially challenge more conventional female roles and the industry's apparent sidelining of aging women.

In the second essay, Stacey Abbott makes a study of Gothic tourism, a growing trend within the contemporary travel industry whereby cities worldwide promote walking tours or tourist attractions that celebrate a history of the ghoulish, the ghostly, and the garish. Abbott discerns that *AHS* has many links to Gothic tourism, both by taking its audience on a journey through periods of macabre and disturbing American cultural and social history and also by featuring various types of Gothic tourism within different seasons of the show itself. Addressing the seasons to date, most especially Season Three, *Coven*, this essay shows how a focus on horror potentially serves as a critique of aspects of American history and culture while also wallowing in genre excess.

The third essay takes as its subject matter that which defines *AHS* as specifically American, analyzing the way that the program's narratives are structured to fit in with U.S. television scheduling. Derek Johnston investigates the use of seasonal celebrations as a way of expressing that national identity, with special emphasis on the importance of family. Noting that Halloween and Christmas both have long associations with the supernatural, Johnston argues that the former holiday is seen as a time of disruption to society and of horror, while the latter is presented more as a time of togetherness for the family. This essay proposes that the narrative structures of *AHS* combine with their use of the festivals of Halloween and Christmas to enhance the sense of this series as a particularly *American* horror story.

For Part Two: Issues of Representation, the scope becomes narrower as televisual treatments of gender, sexuality and disability are explored in greater depth. Here, contributors draw on gender studies, queer theory, monster theory and freak discourse to provide case studies of how specific seasons of *AHS* depict social mores and attitudes pertinent to these themes. Nikki Cox contends that gender in Season One, *Murder House*, is shown to operate under the constraints of the heteronormative social construction of gendered sexes in American popular culture. By adhering to this restrictive characterization, Falchuk and Murphy illuminate fixed images of gender and thus make a prominent statement about the motivations of the quintessential American family. The program's representations of men as lovable failures, and women as greedy and vengeful, demonstrate clear imbalances of power. For Cox, *Murder House*'s representation of gender, in suggesting the existence of intrinsically gendered characteristics, demonstrates the ineffectiveness of American society to overcome such stereotyped images of men and women, reflecting what she terms a static dichotomy of male and female.

With a focus on Season Three, *Coven*, Kyle Ethridge draws on queer theory and the emergent field of monster theory to examine the relationship between the contemporary figure of the witch and the key themes of desire and violence in order to consider what this complex economy might convey about wider cultural attitudes. As Ethridge explains, monsters inhabit odd and often contradictory spaces, and their relationship to desire is no less odd. Building on existing discourses of both contemporary monsters and queerness, this essay analyzes an array of the show's witch protagonists—including novitiates such as Madison, Zoe and Queenie, in addition to established witches like Cordelia and Myrtle—in terms of their individual dealings with desire and violence inside the Coven.

The sixth essay offers a case study of Season Four, *Freak Show*, which is distinctive in the *AHS* franchise in that its elements of horror are decidedly less supernatural than those found in other seasons. Observing that historical freak shows featured the display of non-normative bodies for the entertainment of able-bodied audiences, Carl Schottmiller argues that *Freak Show* turns disability into a hypervisible spectacle even as it simultaneously erases the real life effects of ableism through assimilationist rhetoric. However, case studies of characters reveal that, while the show revolves around social constructions of disability, its primary political critique is actually the elevation of the status of white gay male oppression through the subordination and normalization of ableism.

The final section, Part Three: Genre Tropes and the Horror of History, turns attention to horror conventions and issues of genre. The first essay in this section is concerned with how *AHS* treats that most Gothic of devices, namely that of haunting. In analyzing *Murder House*, Rebecca Janicker utilizes the concept of liminality, a term derived from social anthropology, to explore the fundamental "in betweenness" of haunted places and experiences. Rooted in the Gothic, the haunted house motif works to conjure up a powerful engagement with history as the human residents of the Murder House are obliged, often unwittingly, to interact with the ghosts that bring to life its troubled past. Focusing on Dr. Ben Harmon, this essay shows that, through the liminality of haunting, this protagonist learns much from his time in the house, and that this process is enhanced further by the formal properties of serial television drama.

Broadening the investigation into genre, the next essay makes a case study of a rather more contemporary horror trope in examining the alien abduction narrative. Philip L. Simpson observes that the alien abduction subplot in Season Two, *Asylum*, was greeted by many fans and critics alike with varying degrees of disbelief, puzzlement, and even anger. However, Simpson notes the importance of this season's primary temporal setting in the tumultuous decade of the American 1960s when traditional and countercultural values fought for dominance. *Asylum's* primary avatar of progressivism, Kit Walker—unjustly committed to Briarcliff for the murder of his wife and two other women—is subject to societal suspicion because of his interracial marriage to an African American woman. As Simpson shows, Kit's choices constitute an expression of Otherness alien to his particular location in 1960s America and render him an appropriate magnet for the alien abductors.

The ninth essay in this volume scrutinizes *American Horror Story's* treatment of narrative and aesthetics to consider the series' relationship to established televisual boundaries of genre. Here, Emma Austin follows initial arguments put forward by Linda Williams in the latter's piece, "Film Bodies: Gender, Genre and Excess," to explore the re-constructions of genre put forward by the production context of *AHS* as a whole, before moving on to examine the intersections of melodrama and horror. From this, using notions of the grotesque and the liminal, Austin considers the nature of the horrific patterns of representations present in the show, questioning whether it can be understood in straightforward terms as a horror text, or rather as a postmodern re-presentation of horrific tropes.

In the tenth and final essay, Conny Lippert proposes that the contemporary pervasiveness of Gothic texts, as well as of American culture, lets us all, to some extent, partake in the American dream and particularly in American nightmares. *American Horror Story* is a show that appears firmly rooted in American popular culture. It thrives on intertextual references, allusions, and homages, and the frequent inclusion of regional folklore and history serves to increase the show's saturation in its national context. Asserting that it is Season Three, *Coven*, that permits a glimpse of a truly "American" horror story, Lippert explains how this season engages with two of America's most fundamental Gothic tropes—witchcraft and slavery—to reconfigure the nation's traditional Gothic themes by positioning them within a contemporary context.

Overall, the aim of this book is to demonstrate that *American Horror Story*, with its ever expanding anthology of seasons and its continued capacity to shock, scare and intrigue, is a horror franchise that taps into social concerns, yields insights into preoccupations and practices of the television industry and makes a fresh contribution to the field of twenty-first-century horror.

WORKS CITED

Bussolini, Jeffrey. "Television Intertextuality After *Buffy*: Intertextuality of Casting and Constitutive Intertextuality." *Slayage* 10.1 (2013): n. pag. Web. 16 January 2016.

Jowett, Lorna, and Stacey Abbott. *TV Horror: Investigating the Dark Side of the Small Screen*. London: I.B. Tauris, 2013. Print.

Mittell, Jason. *Complex TV: The Poetics of Contemporary Television Storytelling*. New York: New York University Press, 2015. Print.

Williams, Linda. "Film Bodies: Gender, Genre and Excess." *Film Quarterly* 44.4 (1991): 2–13. Print.

PART ONE

Industry and Culture

American Horror Stories, Repertory Horror and Intertextuality of Casting

Lorna Jowett

AHS is a particularly rich series for examining the layers that structure serial drama on television in the twenty-first century. Various critics, commentators and indeed viewers have noted that as the television landscape expands in the digital or post-digital era, serial narrative and ongoing development have become key strategies for retaining audiences of "quality" TV drama. Most viewers are now familiar with the concept of the season arc—a plotline that develops over the course of one year's run of a given series—while many series also incorporate standalone episode narratives within the ongoing arc. From naturalistic, socially-aware crime series like *The Wire* (2002–2008), to long-running fantasy horror like *Supernatural* (2005–) all kinds of television drama now organizes itself around distinct narratives or thematic concerns in each season, allowing for consistency in terms of the premise of the drama, the main characters (though this can also be subject to change), but also offering something new and different to avoid characters and storylines becoming too predictable.

As a medium, television can be familiar and routine, offering daily, weekly, seasonal and yearly schedules, and although the prevalence of timeshifting and on-demand technologies might undermine this sense of predictable, regular repetition, many viewers inevitably still find that they watch the same things at the same time of day, irrespective of when it is broadcast. Yet routine familiarity works against television as an art form, suggesting it is formulaic, repetitive and lacking in innovation and originality. "Quality" or "cult" television especially, has countered this by positioning itself as different, distinctive and even challenging, appealing to viewers' cultural and subcultural capital, tastes and values to sustain levels of engagement that result in loyal audiences who pride themselves on being discerning and selective in a market that has historically been seen as aimed at the lowest common denominator. Thus Tosha Taylor, in an article on sexuality in *AHS: Murder House*, notes that "Such frank depictions of sexuality, especially when pertaining to practices considered deviant, are still relatively unusual on American television, and perhaps because of that, *AHS* certainly caught viewers' attention" (136–137). Likewise, the "low" associations of a genre like horror have been eroded by the popularity of the genre within the "quality" or premium cable television market. As Christine Cornea notes, contemporary TV drama series have "taken those characters" typical of a range of genres "and added a depth and complexity and degree of reflexivity that foregrounds the work of the performer" (11). *AHS* positions itself as doing something distinctive not simply in terms of genre, "quality" and authorship but in terms of its cast and their acting ability: here its position as an "anthology" series with a "repertory" cast is examined, as well as its inclusion of many older female characters, and actors.

AHS *and Anthology Series*

AHS is commonly described as an "anthology series," tapping into the reputation of classic anthology shows like *The Twilight Zone* (1959–1964) or *Hammer House of Horror* (1980), which viewers may be familiar with through their enjoyment of the horror and fantasy genre. Such TV shows tended to fit models of production at the time, when single play drama held a certain amount of status as showcasing both writers and actors (see, for example, Lez Cooke or Stan Beeler). Some episodes are known beyond those who might call themselves horror or science fiction fans. *The Twilight Zone's* creator and presenter, Rod Serling, made a point of employing what he saw as serious genre writers such as Richard Matheson and Ray Bradbury to give viewers "quality" material. In today's television industry single plays and even miniseries are rare and the economic model favors ongoing drama series that can use and reuse sets, actors, writers, directors and other crew. Ensemble casts can be enlivened with guest stars, writers and directors are often reemployed ensuring a certain level of consistency without stagnation.

AHS takes features of both the contemporary serial drama and the anthology show, combining them into an "anthology series." This was not apparent when the series launched: the first season focused on a particular house, and the family who had recently moved into it. Using the house as a location, episodes charted not just the disintegration of the present day family but also recounted the stories of previous inhabitants, many of whom had died in the house and continued to haunt it, unable to leave. In doing so, Season One already combined a season arc with more episodic narratives. Its plot, as Taylor argues, "is neither simple nor completely linear," given that the series uses "flashbacks juxtaposed against present-day events" to "[recount] the history of an Edwardian-style home in the Los Angeles suburbs, colloquially known as the Murder House due to the violent ends its inhabitants tend to meet" (136). Thus the series includes the stories of various characters, present and past, some alive, many already dead, until eventually "the subplots of each of these characters converge, the ghosts band together under a common goal—of killing Vivien [Harmon] and stealing her newborn children" (Taylor 136).

The announcement that Season Two would be set in the 1960s and its location would be an "asylum" (Briarcliff Mental Institution, Massachusetts) changed the game further. Season One thus became *Murder House* and subsequent seasons have been badged *Asylum*, *Coven* (present day; New Orleans), *Freak Show* (1952; Jupiter, Florida) and *Hotel* (present day; Los Angeles, with an epilogue dated 2022). By moving the geographical and temporal setting of the show and shifting its focus with each new season, *American Horror Story* combines the pleasures of the anthology show with serialized storytelling featuring the same core characters for a given length of time. While some structural elements are changed every season, *AHS* has cast many of the same actors across its seasons, playing with a particular form of continuity and disruption.

Naturally, this can be seen to fit into television's structures of repetition and variation. Calling the series *American Horror Story* indicates that it will engage with certain genre conventions, tropes and narratives and each season draws on a range of intertexts from horror and other genres. *Freak Show*, for instance, visually and thematically echoes Tod Browning's film *Freaks* (1932), while *Hotel* consistently references both *The Shining* (Stanley Kubrick, 1980) and *The Hunger* (Tony Scott, 1983). The theme music of Season One (adapted for each subsequent season) is reminiscent of *The Texas Chain Saw Massacre* (Tobe Hooper, 1974), the titles are presented in a font similar to those used by Charles Rennie Mackintosh, Scottish artist, designer and architect, and in *Asylum* and *Freak Show* musical numbers reimagine familiar songs ("Life on Mars"). This kind of intertextuality is not necessarily unusual in contemporary television drama, nor in genre: televisual storytelling is inherently intertextual. Yet *AHS*, for some, teeters on the edge of becoming empty pastiche rather than "clever" referencing and innovative repackaging. "The series' almost constant evocations of prior cultural products, whether self-consciously or not," Dawn Keetley argues in an article focused on Season One, "reinforces the central thematic of the show—that we are lapsing into a deathless realm of barren reiteration" (101). It is unclear from Keetley's article whether she thinks this is detrimental to the overall effect of *AHS*, which, in any case, takes up a different "central thematic" in its next season, but her choice of words suggests it.

However, what arises from the subsequent seasons and particularly from their casts of actors, is a more specific form of intertextuality that enriches the series for regular viewers: intertextuality of casting. Again, this is not a practice particular to *AHS*: many television producers and creators have "favorite" actors as well as other regular collaborators (writers, directors, cinematographers, special effects people and so on). The nature of serial television drama in the current climate generally involves an ensemble cast, allowing for a range of possible stories and viewpoints, as well as potentially providing actors with a less frenetic shooting schedule, if they do not appear in every episode. Likewise, networks and series often hire from a stable of writers and directors, whether, as the BBC frequently does, employing one director to do a block or a certain number of episodes in a given season, or by keeping a "writer's room" even where individual authors might be credited with specific episodes. Television, as well as being intertextual, is also inherently collaborative, despite revitalized interest in auteurs and creators who can provide certain branding or attract a presold audience.

Given that television is notorious for allowing "minimal rehearsal time" (Pearson 167), one advantage of having an ensemble cast for an ongoing serial drama is that they will work together, collaboratively, almost by default, developing their characters in relation to each other and in relation to the overall tone and direction of the series. Casting also functions as a "hook" both in preproduction and in promotion. Attracting certain actors to a project might enable its producers to convince other actors to join it. And—returning to the notion of intertextuality of casting, as posited by Jeffrey Bussolini—certain actors bring intertexts, and potentially audiences, with them. "Intertextuality of casting," Bussolini explains, "refers to the often intentional crossover of actors and actresses between and among different shows, and the way in which bringing along recognizable faces and styles serves to cross-pollinate televisual texts and create a larger televisual intertext" (3). This "larger televisual intertext" might be television horror, for example, or "quality" television, signaled to viewers by the appearance of certain actors who regularly work in specific genres, or in television drama that is considered to be original, innovative or more challenging than mainstream programming.

Increasingly, television drama has reached a level where it can attract movie actors and/or directors (J.J. Abrams, Matthew McConaughey), or showcase home-grown television talent (Bryan Cranston, Idris Elba). One interviewer, discussing *AHS: Coven*, asks Angela Bassett whether she would normally have taken a role on television:

> Had you thought about doing a television show before this, or was this show and character too good to pass up, regardless of the medium?
>
> BASSETT: It was more so the latter. It was just too good. Everything about it was perfect. The place, the timing…. I'm available for good characters and good writing. If it's on television, okay, but I can be a little tentative, especially if it takes me out of the country [Radish].

Both the question and the answer to it suggest that taking a role in television for an actor like Bassett is out of the ordinary, and her roles in *Coven*, *Freak Show* and *Hotel* may bring her talent to audiences who have not seen her work in cinema. Similarly, viewers familiar with her (award-winning and more niche) film roles might be persuaded to watch *AHS* to see her. (Her answer also indicates the many other external factors that impinge on casting.)

What Bussolini points out, though,

> is not simply that it is pleasurable to chart the careers and trajectories of artists (though it may be!), but that this casting serves in important ways to shape the "Verses" of the artworks at hand and that the conscious choice of such casting offers an artistic tool in creating a televisual text (while the unconscious and conscious association of actors and styles across discrete texts creates a larger field well-recognized by viewers) [3].

At times, as his article demonstrates, such intertextuality of casting is even marked in the current televisual text, with visual or verbal nods to an actor's previous role/s that viewers may pick up on (and thus have their sub/cultural capital reinforced and validated). For instance, it can certainly be argued that the role played by Jessica Lange in *Murder House* draws on and references some of her previous performances (most notably, perhaps, Blanche DuBois in *A Streetcar Named Desire* [Glenn Jordan, 1995]).

Yet, Bussolini argues, "even without being explicitly marked in dialogue, costume, or style, the presence of actors well-known for other roles brings with it notes and flavors of the prior roles that add texture to the new scenario, at least in part" (21). This includes the possibility of casting against type, or at least casting an actor in a role that differs from the role they may be best known for. *Freak Show* included Michael Chiklis as strongman Dell Toledo, a role that might initially seem to recall his lead role as charismatic, hyper-masculine corrupt cop Vic Mackey in police drama *The Shield* (2002–2008). Yet as Dell's story unfolded this sense of conventional strength was undermined by his failed relationships with female sexual partners and with his son, by his position as physically normal in a family of "freaks" (Dell is the only one in his family to have "normal" hands rather than "lobster claws") and by his closeted homosexuality. The potential for internal intertextuality also presents itself in this type of anthology series. Characters may repeat or reimagine relationships between the actors' previous incarnations, such as

Evan Peters and Taissa Farmiga whose characters were romantically paired in *Murder House* and then again in *Coven*. Likewise, when interviewed about his role in *Hotel*, Finn Wittrock alludes to a kind of karmic "payback, specifically in terms of what Dandy did to Matt's character on 'Freak Show'— Dandy dismembered him. So Matt and I may or may not go head to head over Lady Gaga" (Saclao).

The remainder of this article examines intertextuality of casting in *AHS* from two angles. The notion of the regular cast as a "repertory" company is explored, though the role of guest stars within this is also discussed. Finally, the focus on female actors and characters, especially for older women, in *AHS* is interrogated in more depth, looking at how the series repeatedly addresses female experience and women, rather than girls. Both are necessarily limited in the examples that can be drawn from the series, which has completed five seasons (and begun a spin-off *American Crime Story*, 2016[1]) at the time of writing. Yet these areas are vital to any discussion of the complex ways intertextuality and casting operate in contemporary television drama. Bussolini suggests the term intertextuality of casting "describes both a compositional style and a practice of viewing, interpreting, and engaging" with the televisual text (54).

Repertory Horror

Again like other television drama series, *AHS* combines a regular ensemble cast playing core characters with guest stars and recurring roles. It also offers a combination of well-known film and TV stars, respected actors and celebrities. Thus it has featured Oscar-winners Gabourey Sibide and Kathy Bates, television actors from other "quality" or cult series and/or films (Frances Conroy, Zachary Quinto, James Cromwell, Neil Patrick Harris and Lance Reddick), theatre and Broadway actors (Sarah Paulson, Denis O'Hare and Cheyenne Jackson) and celebrity guest stars (Naomi Campbell and Stevie Nicks playing herself in *Coven*) as well as Lady Gaga (as a main cast member) in *Hotel*.

The range of actors featured in *AHS* is, therefore, likely to appeal across a wide demographic, and casting announcements form a key part of promoting each new season. Many actors have received awards and nominations for their role/s in the series, and some have become much more widely known because of it. Therefore, trailers and promotion for the new season have tended not just to focus on some of the bigger names, such as Jessica Lange, but also on certain actors considered integral to its success, like Sarah Paulson and Lily Rabe. The casting hype reached a peak when it was confirmed that Lange would not be appearing in *Hotel*, but Lady Gaga would be joining the cast (see, for example, Tracy Phillips). Lady Gaga is mentioned in Taylor's article on *Murder House*, with reference to other performers who have incorporated BDSM as part of their act and persona, so it is perhaps not entirely surprising that she should eventually appear in the series herself.

Careful attention is clearly paid to casting each season, and writer and co-creator Ryan Murphy often cites particular performances by the actors that inspired him to want them in particular roles. *AHS*' explicit and challenging content (sexual as well as generic) may be both a disincentive and a lure for actors: Taylor mentions one interview, for instance, where Murphy "cites Dylan McDermott's willingness to perform a scene in which his character weeps profusely whilst masturbating as one of the reasons for the actor's casting" (137). Taylor is making an argument specifically about sexuality within the series, yet this demonstrates an investment by Murphy and the series in actors who can rise to the challenges of *AHS*' material and produce convincing performances according to the tone set by a given scene. Another example cited by Taylor is the performance of Zachary Quinto and Teddy Sears as gay couple Chad and Patrick: "Both men give camp performances … tempering masculine sexual prowess with feminine gestures to the point of caricature in a manner that recalls classic television depictions" (148). Here, Taylor does not allude to the fact that Quinto publically came out in 2011 and has often championed gay rights and LGBT causes, though this adds yet another layer of intertextuality to his character—and even the way he plays that character—in *Murder House*.

Denis O'Hare discusses the challenges in a series like this: "I always feel like I'm going to fail and every year you go, 'Oh God.' And this year especially when [Murphy] told me what it was, I really did sort of take a pause. I said, 'I'm scared to death, but all right, I'm excited. I'm in.'" He adds, "You don't want to be doing the same thing over and over again. I know I don't want to do the same thing. It's good to be scared" (Halterman). Likewise, McDermott, who appeared in *Murder House* and again in *Asylum*, notes that "for actors it's a dream come true" ("What is American Horror Story: Asylum?") to be in a series that allows actors to take on different roles. Thus while Sarah Paulson admits that for an actor a continuing part in a TV series is the "jackpot" (Television Academy) there are downsides to taking on such a role long-term. "It is not only the fear of typecasting or the chance of a film career that causes actors to leave long-running series," suggests Roberta Pearson, "it is sheer boredom" (168). McDermott's role in *Asylum* as Johnny Morgan, son of serial killer Bloody Face, is set in contrast to his previous role—Ben Harmon, middle-class father and cheating husband. "Ryan was really interested in me playing someone with blue collar origins" explains McDermott ("What is American Horror Story: Asylum?"), suggesting that those responsible for producing the series are consciously paying attention to how roles in different seasons might impact on each other. In the same way, Connie Britton relates how she was convinced to take the part of Vivien in *Murder House* because Murphy said she would be doing very different things to what she had been doing for the last five years (Television Academy). Thus while Lange talks about the actors being interested during the second season "to watch who played what…. Creating new characters" ("What is American Horror Story: Asylum?"), these new characters are also imbued, for the actors and for the viewers, by the previous roles inhabited by the same actor, either in *AHS* or elsewhere, as well as (as suggested in relation to Quinto) by the public persona of the actors themselves.

For celebrity guest stars, the public persona may take precedence, as when Stevie Nicks plays herself in an episode of *Coven* ("The Magical Delights of Stevie Nicks"), and again in the season finale ("The Seven Wonders"). Following a series of references to her and her music by Misty Day (Lily Rabe), it was a satisfying experience to actually see Nicks—a real person from the world of the viewer—interacting with the characters who had become familiar over the season and, of course, singing some of her well-known songs. Those familiar with Murphy and Brad Falchuk's back catalogue of TV series, recognize from *Glee* (2009–2015) that Murphy is himself a Stevie Nicks and Fleetwood Mac fan, and her work featured in this previous series. This complex folding together of real life and fictional celebrity, performance and fandom is unpeeled in a range of articles about Nicks' appearance in the series. Naturally, Nicks, Murphy and Rabe were all asked about the appearance. "I was very attracted to *Glee*," Nicks admits, "and to Ryan and Brad's writing of misfits. They write about people who don't fit in." This chimes with Murphy's own recollection of how he conceived the idea of Misty being a fan, which led to Nicks actually appearing in *Coven*:

> When we got to this witch idea, I thought, if you're Misty and you have grown up alone and you don't know any other witches, there's one witch you probably would know and that's Stevie Nicks…. So I called Stevie Nicks and first I said, "I want to use you in the show" [Busis].

Another layer is added when Murphy mentions that Nicks was initially reluctant because some people thought she was a witch. "[P]eople who are in the Wiccan community had given her a hard time thinking she was a witch and she got a lot of scary fan letters," he explains. Then, in addition, Rabe confesses that she is as big a fan as her character in Coven, admitting, "If I meet her, I actually think I might die on the spot" (Busis). Thus to have Nicks play herself, initially offered as a kind of bribe to superfan Misty demonstrating what she could experience routinely if she were the next Supreme (Nicks even gives her trademark shawl to Misty as a good luck gift), operates at various levels of inter/textuality. When Nicks performs Fleetwood Mac's "Seven Wonders" before the witches compete in trials to see who will be the next Supreme it is like an ultimate form of fan service.

This kind of blending of reality and fantasy is not a one-off for the series: *Coven* features historical characters Marie Laveau and Delphine LaLaurie (see Glossary), while *Hotel*'s Halloween episode "Devil's Night" has real life serial killers Jeffrey Dahmer, John Wayne Gacy, Richard Ramirez, Aileen Wuornos and the "Zodiac Killer" (see Glossary) convene in the Hotel Cortez for a dinner party with the hotel's owner, James Patrick March. In this sense, *AHS* fits and perhaps even extends the model of intertextuality that Bussolini sets out in relation to the work of Joss Whedon: "Whedon, as well as his carnival of collaborators, is effective artistically to a large extent because he instantiates a polyphonic and dialogic craft" (11). The way the actors often cite what Murphy asks them to do, and how exciting it is echoes this careful crafting of intertextuality in terms of casting as well as on other levels. The collaboration operates in terms of the repertory "company" too. Quinto talks about working with great people, mentioning Paulson in particular, while Lange discusses enjoying playing beside Conroy ("What is American Horror Story: Asylum?"), and Bates cites working closely with Gabourey Sidibe as something that attracted her to *Coven* ("Enter the Coven").

Older Women

Coven is perhaps the most obvious season of *AHS* to engage with issues of gender and race/ethnicity but the series overall frequently, consciously and consistently deals with diversity on various levels across sexuality, disability, race and ethnicity, as well as age and gender. Down's Syndrome actor Jamie Brewer has featured in more than one season, first as a Down's Syndrome character in *Murder House*, then as witch Nan in *Coven*, and next as ventriloquist's dummy Marjorie in *Freak Show*. She has talked about how she was particularly invested in taking the role of Addie in *Murder House*, but also about the opportunity this role afforded her at the start of her career (Television Academy). *Freak Show* also featured several actors with particular conditions, another way it connects intertextually with Tod Browning's film *Freaks*. Jyoti Amge, Ma Petite in *Freak Show*, explains that she had no reservations about taking this role, though, because in the show "no one is a freak" (Entertainment Tonight). Angela Bassett's roles as Marie Laveau, Desiree Dupree in *Freak Show*, and Blaxploitation star Ramona Royale in *Hotel* have all earned her nominations for NAACP Image Award for Outstanding Actress, while *Freak Show* itself was nominated. Taylor's article on *Murder House* discusses its foregrounding of sexuality and sexualities, and out gay actor Denis O'Hare, interviewed before shooting *Hotel*, says:

I do think it's a positive thing that we, as characters, can show up now and we can afford to be good gay people or bad gay people or stupid gay people or murderous gay people or psychotic gay people. We're not representing a race or a group. We are simply like everybody else and that's a positive development, I think [Halterman].

However, the aspect focused on next is the intersection between age and gender. The pressures of the television and film industries mean that roles for older women are often limited, stereotyped or comedic. Older female actors may find themselves without roles that challenge them and exploit their hard-won, carefully developed and nurtured talent. Bates, Paulson and many others praise the way Murphy in *AHS* writes for women and invents characters who are, as Paulson says, "complicated women and strong women and weak women and just all kinds of women" ("Enter the Coven"). Similarly, Lange talks about Fiona Goode as a character "that goes from A–Z… So it allows me to play just about everything that's out there to play" ("Enter the Coven") while Bassett identifies feminism and ageism as two key themes in *Coven* ("Enter the Coven"). Given that the third season features three regular female actors over 60 at the time it was first broadcast (Conroy, Bates and Lange), as well as Bassett (55 when *Coven* was broadcast) and guest roles for Stevie Nicks (65), Patti LuPone (64), Mare Winningham (54) and others, it serves to highlight the usual lack of dynamic and complex older female roles in U.S. television.

The emphasis in Western media and society on body image for women (and, increasingly, men) results in marginalization of older female actors in a way that does not operate to the same extent for male actors. Moreover, a focus on youth and youthful body image informs traditionally limited roles for female characters in popular media. Dafna Lemish and Varda Muhlbauer suggest that "Glorification of women's external appearance as the most central characteristic of a woman's essence" is a result of "the media's overemphasis on the portrayal of women as sexual beings whose central function is relegated to being objects of male sexual desire and pursuit" (169). Lemish and Muhlbauer's study of "stereotypes of older women prevalent in the media" found "three recurring types: the controlling mother; the plain, uneducated, but good housewife; and the bitch-witch older woman" (170). Arguably, all three of these "recurring types" appear throughout *AHS*, though it certainly delights in presenting variations on the latter. In this sense, the series fits Cornea's observation of how "the activity of performance becomes more crucial and noticeable, as generic modes are deliberately juxtaposed and melded and as the performance of genre character types becomes increasingly palpable" (10) in contemporary takes on screen drama.

The version of masculinity conveyed by a character like Dell Toledo in *Freak Show* has already been mentioned, and male characters in *AHS* often find their sense of conventional masculinity is challenged, attacked, undermined and revised. This may be because the series consistently foregrounds female experience, including, perhaps particularly, the experience of older women. In doing so it showcases the talents of older female actors who might otherwise find it difficult to secure TV roles that stretch and celebrate their considerable talent. That said, changes in the industry—or, more accurately, lobbying for change in the industry—as Lemish and Muhlbauer point out, have effected some movement:

> The growing presence of women in many media-related professions, as well as the devotion of several mature celebrity-actresses to issues of gender equality (including acting such roles, as well as directing and producing movies themselves), have resulted in innovative images of older women, mainly in the film and television industries [172–173].

As Maricel Oró-Piqueras notes, "the body that starts showing signs of aging may be perceived as 'the other' since there is a mismatch between what the woman feels and the role she is expected to perform in society" (21). Such disjunction is amply portrayed in *AHS* by older female characters, where scenarios and storylines also deal with perceptions of older women as "other" to younger female characters "who fear aging as the tombstone that will distance them from social visibility" (21). This "social visibility," of course, is visibility primarily through the male gaze. *AHS* certainly challenges the invisibility of older women, either by drawing attention to it narratively (Kathy Bates' character Iris in *Hotel*, particularly "Room Service," is just one example), or aesthetically through genre conventions. As several scholars have argued (see Vivian Sobchack's chapter "Scary Women" in *Carnal Thoughts*, for instance) the aging woman can be perceived as grotesque or monstrous. Janani Subramanian observes that this is

> most famously seen with actresses like Gloria Swanson in *Sunset Boulevard* (1951), Bette Davis and Joan Crawford in *Whatever Happened to Baby Jane* (1961), Tallulah Bankhead in *Die! Die! My Darling!* (1965) and even Anne Bancroft as Ms. Dinsmoore/Miss Havisham in Alfonso Cuarón's *Great Expectations* (1998) [116].

In a horror TV series, though, this presentation can take on a slightly different tone.

As horror television, *AHS* engages frequently with the grotesque and the abject, and admittedly this is often via its older female characters. Yet this might simply be because it *has* so many older female characters. Younger and male characters also undergo abject experiences and are presented in similar ways. This engagement with the body, the abject and the grotesque can either maintain or challenge traditional notions of the proper feminine body. "*AHS* manipulates female bodies in artificial and often violent ways that encourage the critique that Sobchack claims other horror texts often disavow"; Subramanian notes of *Murder House*, "the use of special effects to regress the aging process or inflict grotesque wounds on female characters highlights the emotional pain of femininity, aging and domesticity" (115).

Lange's pivotal roles in the first four seasons of *AHS* have attracted considerable comment, as have Kathy Bates' contributions to the series; both engage with this dual representation of physical aging and emotional pain. Lange's performance in her roles conveys a mixture of vulnerability and ambition: even the strong-willed Supreme witch Fiona from *Coven* is shown to be at the mercy of physical aging and illness when a new Supreme arises. Lange's first character in *Murder House*, Constance, is potentially a controlling mother, or even a witch bitch, yet—as performed by Lange—she also foregrounds the "pain and violence associated with domesticity and motherhood" (Subramanian 115) and not necessarily in ways involving the supernatural hauntings that affect other characters in the Murder House. In addition, while Lange's previous roles inform this character, so too does her status and physical presence as an embodied older woman, which in turn reflects back on the industrial context that sidelines women who become "too old" to get serious roles. "It draws attention," argues Subramanian, "to the 'out of sync' nature of older femininity and its representations; the alternation between digitally altered younger Lange and 'real' Lange makes visible the displaced nature of older actresses in Hollywood in general" (116) and she goes on to quote Linda Williams on how "female stars 'considered too old to continue as spectacle-objects nevertheless persevere as horror-objects'" (116).

Subramanian touches on the way that "horror-objects" within a horror genre context are also, inevitably, "spectacle-objects," attracting the gaze, if not in the way conventional female characters/actors might be expected to do so. Within the horror genre, the "horror-object" or monster has also always attracted a certain amount of sympathy (Frankenstein's creation offers an obvious example), and in contemporary horror often takes a lead role as a sympathetic subject (the reluctant vampire being one such popular trope). Certainly Keetley points out that *Murder House*, and Lange's character Constance in particular, mediate "specifically early twenty-first century anxieties surrounding the aging mother" (94). Referring to the title sequence, which shows twin boys and Jamie Brewer's character Addie, Keetley notes: "Both multiple births and Down's Syndrome are more common outcomes for mothers who are older, and the rates of both multiple births and Down's Syndrome births have been rising in the US and the UK" (94). Lange's performance of Constance, then, taps into anxieties about birth, as well as anxieties about parenting children who do not fit society's norms, in ways seemingly designed to engage viewers' sympathy as well as, or perhaps even excusing, potential criticism of her as a parent.

Lemish and Muhlbauer note that while the increasing numbers of older female characters on screen "demonstrates 'embedded feminism,' as older women are portrayed as having it all: wealth, beauty, sex, control" this is not, yet, moving outside of conventional parameters of femininity. A "closer look at these screen images reveals that older women are allowed to represent all of the above qualities as long as they abide by three criteria: They must be White, rich, and remain beautiful and desirable to men" (173). Lange may fit this model, despite the often complex nature of her characters' femininity, though Bates is not, in terms of U.S. television norms, "beautiful and desirable to men." However, given Bates' casting as firstly a sadistic racist (in *Coven*) and then a bearded lady (in *Freak Show*), the actor's distance from such norms is signaled by the characters she plays. Her roles foreground endurance; whether this takes the form of clinging to old values (*Coven, Freak Show*) or putting up with friends who exploit her (*Freak Show, Hotel*) Bates' characters are survivors, pitting their strength against the odds. Here, though, I focus on Conroy and Bassett, who also fail to fulfil these three criteria.

Conroy's character in *Murder House* is the elder of two embodiments of housekeeper Moira O'Hara. This seems designed to play off her role as Ruth Fisher in HBO drama series *Six Feet Under* (2002–2005), which was praised for its representation of complex aging femininity, partly because it unapologetically included sexual activity. Myrna A. Hant describes Ruth as "an exceedingly complex woman, layered with inadequacies, uncertainties and struggles," (16) while Kristyn Gorton argues that she, like other older female characters on television, articulates a tension between "care and desire" that is, between their role as carers for others, and their desire to act for themselves. Given that *AHS*'s Moira appears to women as a uniformed and respectable older woman (Conroy) but to men as a seductive young beauty in a fantasy maid's outfit (Alexandra Breckenridge), both the complexity and the tension of domesticity and desire embodied by Conroy as Ruth are apparent in the character.

The young version of Moira is characterized by embodied physicality and sensuality, displayed for men, and this version consistently tempts Ben Harmon in the present day. Conroy's portrayal of Moira thus dwells, in contrast, on her embodied and "respectable" older femininity, but adds a further, less conventional, element of physicality by the way filming emphasizes rather than minimizes Conroy's discolored eye. This physical imperfection is even accounted for in the diegesis when a flashback shows Moira being shot in the eye by Constance after Constance finds her husband forcing himself on Moira ("Murder House"). Casting director Eric Dawson talks about the way Ryan Murphy works with actors and casting, citing Conroy's eye "being written into the story" in *Murder House* as one example (Laws).

While generally the cast praise the writers and Murphy for creating such complex roles that challenge their talents, in the beginning all was not smooth sailing, according to Conroy. She recounts one story of shooting a scene with Jessica Lange where their two characters have a tense altercation:

It was the end of the day, and we were tired, and when we were rehearsing it and I was screaming at [Jessica] off-camera, one of the men on the crew said something inappropriate like, "Granny's letting loose now." I said very quietly that I was about to rip his head off. When we ended the night, they all applauded us because they saw that the scene was a real bitch to do. But that was the moment where I had a very violent reaction. I had to temper myself and just say, "Don't ever talk to an actor like this again, ever, when they're rehearsing something that's so intense." You don't ever want to go there [Goldberg].

While Conroy here does not comment directly on the sexist, ageist undertones of the remark she reports, it does seem to inform her "very violent reaction" to it. Given *AHS*', even in this first series, conscious foregrounding of older female characters and their complexities, this comment seems even more inappropriate and insulting than it might normally.

Another of Conroy's characters, Myrtle Snow in *Coven*, seems to be deliberately established as a response to Fiona's more conventional, sexualized femininity, exploiting Conroy and Lange's differing careers and personae as actors to deliver a critical commentary on society's expectations around femininity. In terms of *AHS*' repertory company, the dynamic between Myrtle and Fiona also revisits or references the clash between Moira and Constance in *Murder House* that Conroy describes above. Both Conroy and Lange admit they enjoy working together on the series, and Murphy also confesses he deliberately puts them together as actors and as characters:

I also love love it when Franny and Jessica have scenes together because they love doing them and I love it when they hate each other and they're rivals as they were season one. When we were coming up with the idea [for Myrtle's character], I sort of thought about this woman who if your rival is Jessica Lange and you're so tormented as Myrtle is by Fiona's character, I think you just totally go this crazy route and literally reinvent herself. Like I love that she's come up with this completely different voice other than what she had when she was younger [Stack].

Acting on television, as several scholars observe, has moved from a theatrical or histrionic style to a more naturalistic style, partly as a result of changes in technology and production (see Richard J. Hand, for example) and this means that *AHS* can credibly employ emotional realism within its fantasy/ horror context. Yet, the series' nature as horror—a genre invested in spectacle, emotion, excess and affect—also allows, and possibly even calls for, a more histrionic or theatrical performance style. "Performance in most television drama," Pearson observes, "is suited to the intimate, close-up, domestic nature of the medium—cool, low key, realist" (180). Yet Pearson goes on to argue that "the epic quality of some science fiction or fantasy programmes … requires the greater intensity of a theatrical performance mode" (180–181). In this article, Pearson discusses some of the "challenges" inherent in the science fiction genre for actors who might be performing wearing elaborate wigs, make up or prosthetics. Some of this applies to the horror genre too and although Hand laments that advances in technology mean that in contemporary horror "there is less focus on the performance practice of the actor: in other words, they may be less 'stagey' than their antecedents but they are also less *theatrical*" [original emphasis] (56), this does not seem applicable to more recent developments in television horror and especially series like *AHS*.

Conroy's recurring role in *Asylum* as angel of death, Schachath, for example, might constitute a challenge in that when the angel gives someone the "kiss of death," digitally-produced immense black wings (which Conroy is not physically wearing or manipulating) emerge from her back. Playing such a character also challenges the boundaries of naturalism and fantasy. Actors playing angels in cinema and in television have done so using a range of styles adapted to the particular production. Here the angel wears period clothing, including a hat and veil, and, according to her position and dialogue within the diegesis, Schachath only comes when called but can then offer her kiss of death on demand to those who call her. "I don't judge," she tells Sister Jude ("Dark Cousin"). Such a clearly symbolic role requires careful handling to appear convincing, even allowing for the heightened, melodramatic or theatrical elements of *Asylum*. Conroy performs Schachath as an empathetic being, despite her forbidding physicality, and when Lange's Sister Jude/ Judy calmly accepts her kiss of death in the season finale "Madness Ends," this forms a peaceful resolution to Jude's tempestuous character arc across the season.

In each season, Conroy has played very different characters, as Murphy admits. "Maybe of all of them, she's the one we require to do the most drastically different thing. She every season has done a different voice, a different physical look" (Stack). The allocation of these roles to Conroy is a tribute to her talent as a character actor, and other cast members often mention her ability or "genius" (Television Academy) despite her being a less well-known "name" than others.

Angela Bassett does not fit what Lemish and Muhlbauer identify as acceptable criteria for older female characters simply because she is black. As recent debates around awards in television and film highlight, roles allowing actors of color to excel and reach award-winning heights are few and far between. On winning the Outstanding Lead in a Drama Series Primetime Emmy in 2015—the first time it had been won by a black woman—Viola Davis made the point that "the only thing that separates women of color from anyone else is opportunity," (BBC) something echoed by Idris Elba in his address to UK Members of Parliament in 2016 (Channel 4). Bassett talks about being attracted to *Coven* by the thought of playing Marie Laveau, aligning this part with her previous roles in biopics like *What's Love Got to Do*

With It (Brian Gibson, 1993), *Malcolm X* (Spike Lee, 1992) and *Panther* (Mario Van Peebles, 1995) and *The Rosa Parks Story* (Julie Dash, 2002). Talking about her meeting with Murphy prior to being cast she says:

> New Orleans is one of my favorite cities, and I knew something about the historical figure of Marie Laveau, so I was excited about that, and I think he could see that in me. I don't think the country, as a whole, is familiar with her, but in the city, she was a very powerful and important figure who still lives on [Radish].

In this sense, Bassett indicates her interest in representing a "powerful" female character, as well as in raising awareness about the diverse history of New Orleans and African American culture. *Coven* certainly deals extensively with issues of race and racism, most obviously through Delphine LaLaurie's "education" in twenty-first century race relations by Queenie (Gabourey Sibide), but also in how race and inequalities around race and gender factor into Marie and Fiona's power struggles.

As demonstrated by the NAACP nominations Bassett's roles in the series attract, all of Bassett's characters have conveyed strength in a world ridden with inequalities and oppression. Desiree struggles with being intersex as well as a black woman, a triple marginalization that is less visible in the environs of the carnival but results in a forceful character who is always prepared to act rather than accept her fate. Likewise, Bassett has talked about how Ramona's past as a Blaxploitation star again speaks to U.S. racial history and to the ways black women have become strong just by virtue of their situation. "They're all very strong minded, strong willed, under adversity," she says of her characters, "they all deal with adversity, whether it's race or whether it's how the world sees you" (in Stedman). This does not mean these characters are perfect: all *AHS* characters are complex and multi-faceted. Marie Laveau's willingness to sacrifice an innocent to Papa Legba in *Coven* leads to her taking a baby from a hospital, and although the series stops short of actually depicting its sacrifice, she subsequently drowns Nan in a bathtub with Fiona's help ("The Magical Delights of Stevie Nicks"). When Desiree instigates the tarring and feathering of Penny's abusive father in *Freak Show*, for example, it causes many more problems, and even the sense of revenge being satisfied is unbalanced by Maggie's reaction ("Blood Bath").

It is elements like these that lead actors and viewers alike to describe *AHS*' characters as complex and challenging. Murphy is enthusiastic about the kind of acting talent attracted by this depth:

> The material is always so baroque and the people who are attracted to it are usually actresses who like really emotional extremes. Kathy is known for that. Jessica is known for that. Angela is known for that. Also more than that we're fans of all those women. So I feel we're writing scenes tailored towards what we as fans would love for them to do [Stack].

Upping the Game

In one of several blogs about television acting, Gary Cassidy and Simone Knox underline how "the close linking of actor to character risks … sidelining, if not diminishing, the actual work undertaken by an actor for a part." The anthology series structure of *AHS* almost seems designed to minimize this risk; rather the series showcases actors who return to its repertory company by providing them with new and challenging roles each season. Many of Murphy's comments also point to the way that writing might be influenced by particular actors and their specific talents. Writer and producer Jennifer Salt also notes how writing for a skilled cast helps "create an energy" for her, and other writers (Television Academy). This reinforces the sense of a "company" who collaborate closely across cast and crew, a production model that valorizes and prioritizes collective effort.

In turn, this presents further challenges to the inequalities within the industry and its dramatic representations. Lemish and Muhlbauer observe that "The hegemonic discourse that reinforces women's rivalry undermines the possibility of women's bonding, sisterhood, and friendship that allow the collective building of social and political power," adding that such "discourse pits older women, as a tremendously valuable resource of experience, wisdom, and skills, against young women rather than as supportive of them and transferring social capital that might strengthen younger generations of women" (171). In this way, they argue, media representations shaped by such discourse reinforce "the de-valuation of older women and the perception that they are not only non-productive and expendable, but also destructive and dangerous to society's stability and well-being" (171). In terms of the social capital or "old boy's network" that drives the television industry, *AHS* presents challenges in that Bates often relates how she got the job on *Coven* through her friendship with Lange. This situation, she adds in at least one public appearance, also helped Bates at a crucial time after her series *Harry's Law* (2011–2012) had been canceled and she had undergone a double mastectomy: joining *Coven* "was like coming back to life," she says (Television Academy). Thus the behind-the-scenes collectivity of *AHS* can operate as support and inspiration for actors, rather than reinforcing female competition. Likewise, its abundance of roles for women, especially older women, also reduces any sense of destructive competition among actors. As Bassett notes, being in a "Group of women…. On display and together" has positive effects instead: it "really ups your game" ("Enter the Coven").

The success of *AHS* is, then, fairly typical of contemporary "quality" television, in terms of its production context, its sense of being an authored text, the stories it tells and the ways it tells them. Producer Alexis Martin Woodall may be over-stating the case when she says that no one but Murphy is "doing this on television" (Television Academy), yet it is clear that *AHS* is not just extrapolating current trends in television form and content, but in providing roles for older female actors that result in complex, critically-acclaimed and fan-favorite performances and characters, in turn challenges norms of industry practice as well as of dramatic representations.

NOTES

1. *American Crime Story* features *AHS* actors such as Sarah Paulson and Connie Britton, forming yet another layer of intertextuality of casting.

WORKS CITED

BBC News. "Viola Davis' Emotional Acceptance Speech." *BBC News*. BBC, 21 September 2015. Web. 16 January 2016.

Beeler, Stan. "*The Twilight Zone*." *The Cult TV Book*. Ed. Stacey Abbott. London: I.B. Tauris, 2010. 55–58. Print.

"Blood Bath." *American Horror Story: Freak Show. The Complete Fourth Season*. Writ. Ryan Murphy. Dir. Brad Buecker. Twentieth Century Fox, 2015. DVD.

Busis, Hillary. "Stevie Nicks to Guest on *American Horror Story: Coven*." *Entertainment Weekly*. Entertainment Weekly, 12 November 2013. Web. 16 January 2016.

Bussolini, Jeffrey. "Television Intertextuality After *Buffy*: Intertextuality of Casting and Constitutive Intertextuality." *Slayage* 10.1 (2013): n. pag. Web. 16 January 2016.

Cassidy, Gary, and Simone Knox. "What Actors Do: Adam Driver in *Girls*." *Critical Studies in Television Online*. 7 January 2016. Web. 16 January 2016.

Channel 4 News. "Idris Elba: Speech on Diversity in the Media and Films." *YouTube*. YouTube, 18 January 2016. Web. 20 January 2016

Cooke, Lez. *British Television Drama: A History*. London: B.F.I. Publishing, 2003.

Cornea, Christine. Introduction. *Genre and Performance: Film and Television*. Ed. Christine Cornea. Manchester: Manchester University Press, 2010. 1–17. Print.

"Dark Cousin." *American Horror Story: Asylum. The Complete Second Season*. Writ. Tim Minear. Dir. Michael Rymer. Twentieth Century Fox, 2013. DVD.

"Devil's Night." *American Horror Story: Hotel*. Writ. Jennifer Salt. Dir. Loni Peristere. FX Network. 28 October 2015. Television.

"Enter the Coven."*American Horror Story: Coven. The Complete Third Season*. Twentieth Century Fox, 2014. DVD.

Entertainment Tonight. "American Horror Story's Ma Petite. Don't Treat Me Like a Baby." Online video clip. *YouTube*. YouTube, 25 November 2014. Web. 20 January 2016.

Goldberg, Lesley. "Emmys 2012: Frances Conroy Finds Life After Death in American Horror Story." 21 August 2012. Web. 16 January 2016.

Gorton, Kristyn. "Domestic Desire: Older Women in *Six Feet Under* and *Brothers & Sisters*." *Feminism, Domesticity and Popular Culture*. Eds. Stacy Gillis and Joanne Hollows. London: Routledge, 2009. 93–106. Print.

Halterman, Jim. "Denis O'Hare on His *AHS: Hotel* Character and the 'New Frontier' in LGBT Roles" *Xfinity*. 2 September 2015. Web. 16 January 2016.

Hand, Richard J. "Captured Ghosts: Horror Acting in the 1970s British Television Drama." *Genre and Performance: Film and Television*. Ed. Christine Cornea. Manchester: Manchester University Press, 2010. 38–58. Print.

Hant, Myrna A. "Television's Mature Women: A Changing Media Archetype: From *Bewitched* to *The Sopranos*." *CSW Update Newsletter*. 1 January 2007. Web. 16 January 2016.

Keetley, Dawn. "Stillborn: The Entropic Gothic of *American Horror Story*." *Gothic Studies* 15.2 (2013): 89–107. Print.

Laws, Zachary. "*American Horror Story: Freak Show* Casting Director Eric Dawson." Online video clip. *YouTube*. YouTube, 11 June 2015. Web. 17 January 2016.

Lemish, Dafna, and Varda Muhlbauer. "'Can't have it all': Representations of Older Women in Popular Culture." *Women & Therapy* 35.3/4 (2012): 165–180. Print.

"Madness Ends." *American Horror Story: Asylum. The Complete Second Season*. Writ. Tim Minear. Dir. Alfonso Gomez-Rejon. Twentieth Century Fox, 2013. DVD.

"The Magical Delights of Stevie Nicks." *American Horror Story: Coven. The Complete Third Season*. Writ. James Wong. Dir. Alfonso Gomez-Rejon. Twentieth Century Fox, 2014. DVD.

"Murder House." *American Horror Story: The Complete First Season*. Writ. Jennifer Salt. Dir. Bradley Buecker. Twentieth Century Fox, 2012. DVD.

Nicks, Stevie. "Stevie Nicks Spills *American Horror Story* Secrets." *Rolling Stone*. Rolling Stone, 13 December 2013. Web. 16 January 2016.

Oró-Piqueras, Maricel. "Challenging Stereotypes? The Older Woman in the TV Series *Brothers & Sisters*." *Journal of Aging Studies* 31 (2014): 20–25. Print.

Pearson, Roberta. "The Multiple Determinants of Television Acting." *Genre and Performance: Film and Television*. Ed. Christine Cornea. Manchester: Manchester University Press, 2010. 167–183. Print.

Phillips, Tracy. "'*American Horror Story: Hotel* Goes Gaga with a Starry Cast and Plenty of Little Monsters." *Bio*. 6 October 2015. Web. 16 January 2016.

Radish, Christina. "Angela Bassett Talks *American Horror Story: Coven*, Filming in New Orleans, Whether She's Willing to Return for Another Season, and More." *Collider*. 29 January 2014. Web. 16 January 2016.

"Room Service." *American Horror Story: Hotel*. Writ. Ned Martel. Dir. Michael Goi. FX Network. 4 November 2015. Television.

Saclao, Christian. "Finn Wittrock Teases *American Horror Story: Hotel* Role: 'I'm definitely not a good guy'" *Design & Trend*. 22 July 2015. Web. 20 January 2016.

"The Seven Wonders." *American Horror Story: Coven. The Complete Third Season*. Writ. Douglas Petrie. Dir. Alfonso Gomez-Rejon. Twentieth Century Fox, 2014. DVD.

Sobchack, Vivian. *Carnal Thoughts: Embodiment and Moving Image Culture*. Berkeley: University of California Press, 2004. Print.

Stack, Tim. "*American Horror Story*: Ryan Murphy on the Latest *Coven* and 'the most shocking thing we've ever done'—EXCLUSIVE." *Entertainment Weekly*. Entertainment Weekly, 31 October 2013. Web. 16 January 2016.

Stedman, Alex. "*AHS: Hotel*: Angela Bassett on Her Relationship with Lady Gaga's Countess." *Variety*. Variety, 21 October 2015. Web. 16 January 2016.

Subramanian, Janani. "The Monstrous Makeover: American Horror Story, Femininity and Special Effects." *Critical Studies in Television* 8.3 (2013): 108–123. Print.

Taylor, Tosha. "Who's Afraid of the Rubber Man? Perversions and Subversions of Sex and Class in *American Horror Story*." *Networking Knowledge* 5.2 (2012):135–153. Print.

Television Academy. "An Evening with the Women of American Horror Story." *Television Academy*. 20 March 2015. Web.16 January 2016.

"What Is American Horror Story: Asylum?" *American Horror Story: Asylum. The Complete Second Season*. Twentieth Century Fox, 2013. DVD.

Haunted History
American Horror Story
as Gothic Tourism

STACEY ABBOTT

In the third episode of the first season of *American Horror Story* ("Murder House"), Vivien Harmon discovers that her new Los Angeles home is the culminating stop on the *Eternal Darkness Tours of Hollywood,* a fictional Los Angeline open topped bus tour of murder locations. Reportedly inspired by the actual *Dearly Departed Tours* (http://dearlydepartedtours.com/), Eternal Darkness takes its customers on a guided visit to the locations of the city's infamous and often grisly murders including the home of O.J. Simpson and the alley where 1950s actor Sal Mineo was stabbed, believed to be the victim of a hate crime. Like the real *Dearly Departed* "Tragical History Tour," Eternal Darkness focuses upon recounting in detail the history of notorious true crime within the city. Once at the Harmon house, dubbed the "Murder House," the tour guide Stan recounts the macabre events that took place there, while also straying into the realm of the fantastic and the supernatural, when discussing the film's original residents Dr. and Mrs. Montgomery, the couple who built the house and died in a murder/suicide. After explaining the events that led to their "tragic" deaths—which included a history of back alley abortions, failed medical experiments, the kidnapping and murder of their son and Dr. Montgomery's Frankensteinian attempt to bring his son back to life, leading to Mrs. Montgomery killing her husband and herself—the tour guide culminates his story by stating "legend has it that the ghost of Nora Montgomery still haunts these very halls" ("Open House"). The presence of this tour within the diegesis of the first season of *American Horror Story* highlights the interconnection between tourism, horror and television that is the subject of this essay.

The Eternal Darkness tour features in four episodes of the show's first season ("Home Invasion," "Murder House," "Open House" and "Afterbirth")

27

and appears in the DVD extra "The Murder House Presented by Eternal Darkness Tours of Hollywood." In this manner, the series pays direct homage to Gothic tourism, a growing trend within the contemporary travel industry, with cities all over the globe promoting attractions that celebrate a history of the supernatural and the macabre. These attractions entice audiences into an engagement with history through the promise of the ghoulish, the ghostly, and the garish, drawing upon atmosphere, performance and, occasionally, costumes and effects. Like Gothic tourism, *American Horror Story* also explores a macabre form of history through its seasonal horror narratives which are largely set in the past, or which feature lengthy flashbacks. In many ways its storytelling structure has much in common with Gothic tourism, taking its audience on a journey through periods of macabre and disturbing American cultural and social history. In so doing, it draws from a legacy of folktales, both fiction and non-fiction, but also constructs a mythology of twentieth-century American Gothic folklore through the series' narrative structure which serves as a composite of over a century's worth of stories surrounding death, violence, ghosts, magic, murder and mayhem. The series is aware of its connection to Gothic tourism, as each season directly references this trend. In addition to the presence of the Eternal Darkness tours in Season One, Season Two begins with a couple taking a self-directed walking tour of an abandoned asylum; Season Three includes a visit to one of the most haunted houses in New Orleans; Season Four explores the commercial exploitation of disability and physical difference within the Freak Show and the American Morbidity Museum; and Season Five is set within a haunted hotel, which becomes the subject of a TV documentary on hotel hauntings ("Be Our Guest").

The aim of this essay is to consider how the television show negotiates, alongside Gothic tourism, the relationship between history, storytelling and entertainment. In particular, through close analysis of Seasons One to Three—*Murder House, Asylum* and *Coven*—it considers the significance of place and location to the negotiation of horror and history, in many ways taking its audience on a televisual ghost tour of America's Gothic past. Exploring the relationship between tourism, television and the heritage industries, a key focus of this research is to understand what horror brings to our engagement and experience of history and how *American Horror Story* is building upon traditions established through Gothic tourism as a means of developing a new tradition of TV horror.

Ghost Tours and Gothic Tourism

Emma McEvoy defines Gothic tourism as "the act of visiting, for the purposes of leisure, a location that is presented in terms of the Gothic," specifically "the Gothic that came into being in the mid-eighteenth century, the narrative stamp of which came about with the publication of the first Gothic novel" (3). With this in mind, she explains that Gothic tourism "is intimately connected with Gothic narrative, its associated tropes, discourses and conventions" (5). A classic, and quite literal, example would be *Dracula* tourism, in which readers of the book attempt to experientially engage with the text by visiting its locations. As Stijn Reijnders explains, "as early as the 70s, a growing stream of foreign tourists began to visit [Transylvania], specifically interested in locations from the novel" (232). Despite the fact that Stoker had never been to Transylvania and some of his descriptions were fictionalized, including the location of Dracula's castle where "no castle originally stood" (Reijnders 232), fans of the novel began to travel to Romania to follow—or recreate—Jonathan Harker's journey. In the process, fans "appropriated Bran Castle [a castle located south of the region described by Stoker] as 'their castle'" (Reijnders 232). In this manner, these Dracula tourists integrated their experience of the story with an experience of a very specific landscape, capturing what Reijnders describes as "the lieux d'imagination" in which "Dracula tourists describe the desire to come 'closer to the story' and to make a 'connection' through a symbiosis between reality and imagination" (245). Dracula fans, therefore, experience a favorite Gothic text by interacting with a specific space.

This Gothic approach to travel and sightseeing is, in many ways, an off-shoot of a much bigger trend which is "dark tourism," an increasingly popular strand of the contemporary leisure industry, described by Julian Holloway as "the commodification of, travel to, and experiencing of sites and places associated with death, dying and disaster" (620). Popular examples include tours of historic cemeteries and celebrity gravesites (High Gate, Père Lachaise, Hollywood Forever), first world war battle fields, second world war concentration camps and the growing popularity of Titanic tourism, including Titanic Memorials in Belfast, visits to the Fairview Lawn Cemetery of Titanic victims in Nova Scotia, and even submarine tours to the Titanic wreck for the super-rich (Pemberton 2015). The Jack the Ripper tour in London's Whitechapel area bridges the gap between dark and Gothic tourism, built around the locations of the real historic murders, but presented through Gothic performance and storytelling techniques that encourage participants to imagine the contemporary and rather every day locations—pubs, alleyways and parking lots—through Victorian Gothic gloom, as evidenced by the promotional outline on the homepage for the "The Original Jack the Ripper Walk"[1]:

> He came silently out of the midnight shadows of August 31, 1888. Watching. Stalking. Butchering raddled, drink-sodden East End prostitutes. Leaving a trail of blood and gore that led ... *nowhere*. Yes, something wicked this way walked, for *this is the Ripper's slashing grounds*. We evoke that autumn of gaslight and fog—of menacing shad-

ows and stealthy footsteps—as we inspect the murder sites, sift through the evidence—in all its gory detail—and get to grips, so to speak, with the main suspects. Afterward you can steady your nerves in The Ten Bells, the pub where the victims— *perhaps under the steely gaze of the Ripper himself*—tried to forget the waking nightmare [original ellipsis and emphases] [The Original Jack the Ripper Walk].

The tours draw upon the "cultural fantasies" and "imaginary landscape" that emerged in the 1880s in the media coverage surrounding the murders (Walkowitz 191), tapping into the Gothic atmosphere that was central to the media representation of these monstrous and salacious crimes as well as the urban locations within which they took place. As Judith Walkowitz explains "[a]t night, commentators [within the media] warned, the glittering brilliance of Whitechapel Road contrasted sharply, with the dark mean streets just off the main thoroughfare. Turn into a side street, one was 'plunged' into the 'Cimerian' darkness of 'lower London'" (194). The language of the Jack the Ripper walking tour is clearly designed to evoke the Gothic language of the labyrinthine city, immersing the participant within an imagined landscape that is superimposed over the real city streets.

The merging of Gothic and dark tourism is a feature of many ghost tours, yet another increasingly popular form of tourism that has blossomed internationally since the 1990s and through which we see a similar "symbiosis between reality and imagination" (Reijnders 245). In contrast to literary tourism, the ghost tour is not based upon literary sources but taps into the history of folklore and folktales associated with a specific area. Cities, towns and villages throughout North America and Europe repeatedly seek to capitalize upon a legacy of legends of ghosts, hauntings and macabre events as a means of enticing tourists to their door. Holloway argues that ghost tourism can take three different forms. The haunted hotel, where hotels "seek guests through claiming to be haunted"; ghost hunting, an overnight paranormal investigation involving séances; and ghost tours or ghost walks, "involv[ing] organized walks around cities and towns during which one takes in the sites of alleged hauntings, listens to ghost stories, and in some cases (as in Edinburgh), watches actors perform the narratives behind the spooky happenings" (619). Ghost tours are offered across the UK, including Edinburgh, London, York, Brighton, Manchester and Belfast, and the U.S. and Canada, in cities as diverse as Savannah, New Orleans, Salem, Ottawa and Toronto. During these tours, participants are led through the streets of a city, or in some cases a specific historical location such as Hampton Court Palace or the Carleton Jail in Ottawa, at dusk or after dark while the guide recounts stories and legends of ghost visitations and sightings, as well as the macabre histories of death and violence that may have caused the spirits of the departed to become trapped on the earthly plane, thus uniting Gothic and dark tourism. Examples of such stories include the Salem witch trials; the horrific deaths of the inhabitants of Mary King's Close in Edinburgh, who died as a result of the bubonic plague; the hanging of a potentially innocent man in the Carleton Jail; and the bodysnatching exploits of Burke and Hare.

The location of these tours in the original historic settings creates a spatial association between present and past that is enhanced by the, often highly, performative approach to ghostly storytelling undertaken by the guides. These excursions reframe the guided tour of historic locations through Gothic and horror conventions and in some cases, as Diane E. Goldstein explains, utilize "rattling chains, skeletons that pop out at you as you are walking, and buckets of water thrown seemingly from nowhere during particularly chilling stories" (195). Even the more restrained tours, which focus on the performance of the guide to generate the requisite haunted atmosphere, will often costume the guides in long flowing black cloaks using a lantern to light the way, and can opt to "lock participants into small dark places," (Goldstein 195) or, in my own experience, invite participants to walk alone through long corridors of supposedly haunted palaces, lit only by (albeit artificial) candlelight (an option on both the Kensington and Hampton Court Palace tours). Through these techniques, the ghost tour fosters an experiential engagement with history. As Holloway argues, "the aim is not to learn and dwell on the intricacies of the place (although most guides stress historical accuracy) but to enjoy and become engrossed in the extraordinary possibility in place" (621). The ghost tour, therefore, offers an immersive experience of history through the participants' movement through a specific space, imprinted with its own local Gothic past, overlain and enhanced by the horror storytelling techniques adopted and performed by the guide. *American Horror Story,* as I demonstrate, draws from the ghost tour its focus upon negotiating a relationship between history and space, through which a local folklore of Gothic horror emerges.

American Horror Story: Murder House *as Ghost Tour*

The very premise of the television series *American Horror Story (AHS)* is based upon the reworking of established Gothic and horror tropes surrounding the haunted house, abandoned asylum, freak show, haunted hotel, or other Gothic locations, as a specifically American tradition through the association of horror with history, both personal and national. These are *American* horror stories that are being told and in this manner the series has much in common with the television series *American Gothic* (1995–1996) and the film *An American Haunting* (Courtney Solomon, 2006), in which familiar tales of the Gothic and the supernatural are deliberately and self-consciously

Americanized through an evocation of setting and history. This is achieved in *AHS* through the show's repeated and signature use of flashbacks as part of its storytelling structure, in which the narrative is built around interweaving historical lines. For instance, Season One is largely set in the present as the Harmon family moves into their new Los Angeles home (described as a 1920s classic Los Angeles Victorian), but the pre-credit teaser begins in 1978 when two teenage boys enter into the decaying and abandoned house, only to be murdered by unseen assailants ("Pilot"). The episode subsequently jumps to the "present" to introduce Vivien Harmon, a woman who has recently suffered a physically and emotionally traumatic miscarriage, who finds her husband Ben having sex with a student. The episode jumps forward again as the couple and their teenage daughter Violet move to LA to buy the now renovated house, as part of a planned fresh start. Time is clearly fluid and as the series progresses, it repeatedly moves back and forth between the "present" and key moments in the house's ninety-year history, moving between the 1920s, 40s, 60s, 80s, 90s, and the 2000s. This structure is repeated in the subsequent seasons, each of which highlights the interconnection between past and present.

This history, however, is not only channeled along temporal lines but, in the tradition of the ghost tour, is also evoked through place. In Season One, the Murder House is the lynchpin that connects each time period covered by the narrative. In this manner, it is reminiscent of other haunted house films or television series such as *The Amityville Horror* (Stuart Rosenberg, 1979), *Marchlands* (2011) or *The Secret of Crickley Hall* (2012), in which events in the present are related to or are mirroring horrific events that have previously taken place in the same location. The house is significant as it is the setting of a mystery that must be solved in order to put the spirits to rest (*Marchlands*/*Secret of Crickley Hall*) or it is itself possessed by an evil spirit, which is subsequently projected onto the "man of the house" (*Amityville*).[2] Similarly, in *American Horror Story*, the house is seemingly marked by repeated cycles of death and murder, thus causing its nickname the Murder House, but as the series progresses it becomes apparent that these events are not cyclical in nature, destined to endlessly repeat, but rather a tapestry of seemingly unrelated, horrific crimes that have built up throughout the house's psychic history. Each episode features a flashback to another event or crime that underpins the house's past and which subsequently leads to the presence of another ghost (or ghosts) within the location. For instance, "Murder House" and "Open House" include flashbacks to the story of Charles and Nora Montgomery, while "Home Invasion" begins with the flashback to 1968 in which a serial killer gains entry to the house now inhabited by student nurses. In order to be invited in, the killer pretends to be injured and once inside, he brutally rapes and murders the two women. "Halloween, Pt. 1" includes flashbacks to 2010 and the story of the house's previous owners, Chad and Patrick, and the events that lead to their presumed murder/suicide—they were in fact murdered by the ghost Tate. "Halloween, Pt. 2" and "Piggy Piggy" take us back to 1994 and the events surrounding Tate's murder of his fellow students in a high school shooting and his subsequent death by police officer in his own bedroom, following their pursuit of him after the shooting. "Spooky Little Girl" opens in 1947 as budding young actress Elizabeth Short arrives at the house, now serving as home and office to Dr. Curan, a dentist who makes special arrangements for women who cannot pay for his services through traditional means. After he puts Short under with nitrous oxide, the sequence cuts to an empty field where a mother and her child find Short's dismembered and disfigured remains.

Each of these flashbacks is presented as a form of macabre ghost story, which, in the form of the ghost tour, presents the horrors that have been committed in the house or by its inhabitants to the television audience. "Halloween, Pt. 1" even goes so far as to bookend one of the flashbacks by having Tate, huddled over candles and a Ouija Board, telling Violet the tragic story of the death of Charles and Nora's son and his subsequent revival and transformation by his mad scientist father into an undead monster who still haunts the house's basement. Furthermore, like the ghost tour, these sequences are embellished in their re-telling through the adoption of performative Gothic conventions and tropes, which in the case of the television series involves using highly recognizable Gothic musical scores. The murders in "Home Invasion" are staged to the Bernard Hermann score to Hitchcock's *Psycho* (1960)—in particular the stabbing of the student nurse Maria uses the violin score for Hitchcock's shower scene. Similarly, the scenes that chronicle Dr. Montgomery's scientific experiments and his Frankenstein complex are set to the Gothic music from *Bram Stoker's Dracula* (Francis Ford Coppola, 1992) and Tate's attack in the high school uses the unsettling whistling music from Hermann's score to *Twisted Nerve* (Roy Boulting, 1968), a piece of music that was subsequently appropriated by Quentin Tarantino in *Kill Bill: Vol. 1* (2003) as the assassin Elle Driver stalks the corridors of a hospital preparing to murder the main protagonist Beatrix, aka the Bride, in her hospital bed. These musical scores enhance the Gothic effect but also highlight the construction of the series' Gothic overtones by calling attention to their previous associations. In so doing, *American Horror Story* situates itself as TV horror but within a long tradition of Gothic and horror story telling.

While the music highlights the association with earlier traditions of Gothic and horror filmmaking, the types of events depicted within these flashbacks call to mind true crimes, in the way that ghost tours so often associate hauntings with historic events. For instance, the murder of the student nurses by the fictional murderer R. Franklin in "Home Invasion" is based upon the actual murders of eight nurses in one night by Richard Speck in Chicago in 1966 (see Glossary). The feigning of injury in order to gain access to the house also alludes to the modus operandi of serial killer Ted Bundy (see Glossary). Tate's high school shooting is deliberately reminiscent of the Columbine Massacre, as well as other similar shootings. Finally, the Elizabeth Short murder is a fictionalization of the actual unsolved "Black Dahlia" case (see Glossary), a crime that has led to seven decades worth of media speculation, including James Ellroy's novel *The Black Dahlia* (1987). Like the ghost tour, *AHS* draws upon a monstrous legacy of random, serial, and mass murder to underpin its exploration of an American Gothic tradition associated within this one fictional house.

Similarly, each subsequent season is clearly and evocatively associated with a particular location; the asylum in Season Two, the city of New Orleans in Season Three, the freak show of Season Four, and the hotel in Season Five. Location is as much a character within these narratives as the protagonists and each setting is revealed to be a composite or layering of histories, made explicit by the ghosts who refuse—or are unable—to leave the location. As such the flashbacks are intrinsically linked to the histories of each setting, revealing (like the stories told on ghost walks) the histories that are embedded within the space. Furthermore, like *Murder House*, these seasons also draw upon a legacy of fictional and historic characters and events, such as Richard Patrick March in *Hotel*, based upon the nineteenth-century Chicago serial killer H.H. Holmes (see Glossary), and the gathering of now deceased serial killers who attend his Halloween Devil's Night Dinner: Aileen Wuornos, John Wayne Gacy, Jeffrey Dahmer, Richard Ramirez and the "Zodiac Killer" ("Devil's Night") (see Glossary). Twisty, the monstrous clown serial killer in *Freak Show* is reminiscent of Gacy's alter-ego, Pogo the Clown, while Kit and Alma Walker, the mixed race couple in the first episode of *Asylum* ("Welcome to Briarcliff") are inspired by real-life couple Barney and Betty Hill who in 1961, like Kit and Alma, claimed to have been abducted by aliens.

The narrative trajectory of *AHS* is, however, not simply told on linear lines, with each story in the present looking backward into the past. Instead the stories recounted in each series move from evoking the Gothic past through flashback to having this past emerge in the present in the form of a ghost (or ghosts) who haunts these locations. For instance, in Season One, the story of Nora Montgomery and her husband is first recounted when Vivien is on the Eternal Darkness tour ("Murder House"). As the guide begins his narration, the sequence cuts from a shot of Vivien looking at *her* house to a low angle crane shot of the house before cutting into an interior shot with the camera craning down the elegant staircase as Nora's voice is heard calling to her husband Charles, the sequence having not only moved from exterior to interior—mirroring the opening penetration of Charles Foster

Kane's majestic home, Xanadu, in *Citizen Kane* (Orson Welles, 1941)—but also present to past; a movement that also figures prominently in Welles's film. The entrance into the past is followed by a series of images of Dr. Montgomery inhaling ether, close-ups of pathology jars filled with animal specimens and body parts, and shots of Montgomery stitching a wing onto a pig carcass, accompanied by the aforementioned escalating Gothic musical score from *Bram Stoker's Dracula* which reaches a crescendo as Nora's voice once more calls to her husband with barely concealed frustration. This sequence visualizes the tour guide's horror-inflected voice-over in which he explains that Dr. Montgomery developed a "Frankenstein" complex when his practice fell on hard times, while the recognizable musical score highlights the Gothic overtones of the narration. The voice-over and musical underscore, however, both stop once the music reaches its peak and the scene that follows is a flashback that moves away from Montgomery's Frankensteinian experiments and depicts the sordid decline of Charles and Nora's marriage and her forcing him into performing illegal abortions in order to maintain their comfortable lifestyle. An abrupt cut brings the sequence back to the present as the tour guide's voice-over returns, explaining that "an estimated two dozen girls went under Dr. Montgomery's knife, thanks to his wife Nora." The tour guide has served as a bridge into the past via the flashback.

Later in the same episode, however, Nora appears in the present, turning up on the doorstep of the house, presenting herself to Vivien as a potential buyer. While her appearance in the flashback presents her as a cold and nagging upper class woman, frustrated by the downward direction of her standing alongside her husband's professional prospects, in the present she possesses a melancholic nostalgia for the house, the past and her child, as well as a disdain for the trappings of the present. She appears out of time although not out of place. It is as if Vivien's participation in the ghost tour, which concludes when she spots blood on her white trousers and fears another miscarriage, has called Nora—the perpetrator of infanticide—forth. In this manner, the series draws upon the Gothic tradition of the past erupting into the present, a repressed presence that cannot be contained. This trope recurs throughout the season as the number of ghosts escalates within the house, each vying for dominance and increasingly interacting with one another, and with the living. The series, therefore, makes literal the aim of the ghost tour in which participants hope to see a ghost. Where the ghost tour promises ghosts, *AHS* delivers them, in abundance.

This literalization of the ghost tour is further evidenced in the paratextual DVD feature "Murder House Presented by Eternal Darkness Tours of Hollywood." In this feature, Stan the tour guide brings a group on a ghost tour inside the Murder House, taking the participants through each room and recounting the horrible crimes that have happened there, thus reinforcing the show's association with Gothic tourism and ghost tours. While his narration highlights the gruesome and the macabre, it also alludes to the potential for haunting, pointing out that the "current owners were known to have fled the house in the middle of the night. Now they weren't the first to succumb to the evil that seems to ooze from every nook and cranny of Murder House." Furthermore, as he guides the group through the house, the feature cuts back and forth from an unsettling unattributed point-of-view to the perspective of a participant filming the tour with his video camera, in the form of a found footage horror film or ghost hunting television series, intermixed with a montage of clips from *AHS* that conveys the horrors Stan is describing. This feature serves as a precis of the series and calls attention to the manner in which TV horror and the ghost tour offer similar Gothic pleasures, teasing us with the potential revelation of ghosts, the salacious delight in the macabre, and the frisson of the possibility of a supernatural encounter.

American Horror Story: *Touring Asylums and Covens*

Having established a relationship between TV horror and Gothic tourism in the first season of *American Horror Story*, the subsequent seasons have alluded to this heritage in linking horror with history. Season Two, *Asylum*, uses the trappings of Gothic tourism to serve as the audience's entry into the past that will be the primary focus of the story, which is largely set in the 1964. The pre-credit teaser to the first episode, "Welcome to Briarcliff," is set in the present and follows a newlywed couple as they arrive at the now abandoned sanatorium Briarcliff Manor, the last stop on their self-directed haunted honeymoon, in which they have visited the "twelve most haunted places in America," to have sex in each location. In this manner, they are enacting a form of "legend-trip" which Mikel J. Koven explains involves "travelling to a specific location attached to a legend in the hopes of witnessing some kind of phenomena *as if in the legend itself*" [original emphases] (186). As Koven argues, the legend-trip is not simply about recounting the legend but also involves adding new experiences to the story associated with a particular location "by engaging and replicating the legend itself." In this manner, the honeymooners in *Asylum* are not just interested in the stories associated with the place, but in making their mark through exploration and sexual encounter. In effect, adding their own footnote to the location's narrative.

The episode evokes the legend-trip from its opening sequence, with a series of hand-held shots of macabre and decaying objects abandoned in the woods outside the hospital—a cross made out of twigs, a doll, a religious statue—while the sound of a camera shutter snapping and the voices of our honeymooners are heard off-camera. This opening is suggestive in its wooded location, the camera style, and the cross made out of twigs, of *The Blair Witch Project* (Daniel Myrick and Eduardo Sánchez, 1999)—a film that follows a group of students visiting a supposed haunted location in order to make a film about the legend of ghosts and witchcraft. As such the film similarly operates as a form of legend-trip, in which they attempt to document local folktales of witchcraft, but which fundamentally chronicles their own encounter with the supernatural and their resulting mysterious disappearances. Formatting the *Blair Witch* as a found footage horror film reinforces the legend-trip quality to the film as the filmmakers' supposed disappearance is explained in the caption that opens the film: "In October 1994, three student filmmakers disappeared in the woods near Burkitsville, Maryland while shooting a documentary. A year later their footage was found." The found footage record of what happened to them that forms the fiction of the film is presented as having added to this particular legend, which is reinforced by the paratextual material available in support of the film on the internet, including a timeline of mysterious events to have occurred on this location (*Blair Witch Project* Website).

The allusions to *The Blair Witch* within the opening of "Welcome to Briarcliff" present the couple as similarly attempting to pursue and document the supernatural, in their own way. As the couple enters the building, they read out facts about its macabre history, in particular the deaths of 46, 000 patients as a result of tuberculosis, the transformation of the hospital into a "sanitarium for the criminally insane" run by the church, where it was reported that, if you were admitted, you would never get out alive. Most significantly, they focus on the hospital's most famous resident, a serial killer known as Bloody Face. Finding graffiti drawings of Bloody Face (evidence of previous adolescent legend-trips), they pose in front of the drawing, inadvertently repeating his name three times, seemingly suggestive of the Bloody Mary urban legend in which calling her name three times in front of a mirror will invoke the spirit—or *Candyman* (Bernard Rose, 1992), the horror film that offers variation of this legend. As such this opening seems to be calling forth the ghosts of Briarcliff, an invocation that is seemingly answered when the husband's arm is ripped off when he sticks it through an access panel in a locked door, in an attempt to take a photo as evidence of the supernatural. This bloody attack concludes the pre-credit teaser and, once the credits are complete, the series moves to 1964 to chronicle a selection of events that contribute to Bloody Face's legacy, his association with Briarcliff, as well as numerous other macabre events that haunt the history of the asylum. This opening also serves to position the season within a history of folk and urban legends that underpin popular American Gothic.

Season Three's *Coven* further reinforces the association between horror, history and place but in contrast to the other series, which are set largely in a particular building that is haunted by the living and/or the dead, the setting of *Coven* is not focused on one specific edifice. Although the Garden District, Antebellum House that homes Miss Robichaux's Academy for witches is a central location, the setting that underpins *Coven* is New Orleans itself; stretching from the Treme to the Garden District, but especially focused upon the historical legacy of the French Quarter. Furthermore, where each of the other series overtly reference Gothic tourism within its diegesis, *Coven* draws its narrative explicitly from the stories that underpin the city's very real Gothic tourist trade, offering its own reworking of these local narratives and, in so doing, transforming a local history into one of national significance.

New Orleans is no stranger to Gothic and horror fiction set within its midst or evoked through its Gothic past, with authors such as Anne Rice locating both her Vampire Chronicles and Mayfair Witches series on the recognizable streets of New Orleans. Similarly Poppy Z. Brite, described by Richard Davenport-Hines as "an imaginative mix of Tom Waits and the Marquis de Sade," sets much of her Gothic subculture fiction in New Orleans which was her home in the 1990s (359). More recently, Alys Arden not only located her vampire narrative *The Casquette Girls* within a post–Katrina French Quarter, but drew its supernatural narrative about witches and vampires back to an infamous moment in the city's history, the arrival of the Casquette Girls from Paris. According to the story as told in the ghost tours, these were young women brought to the city as brides but subsequently linked to rumors and legends surrounding vampirism; legends that reputedly originated as a result of the coffin shaped boxes with which they transported their belongings and which gave them their name. The vampire television series *The Originals,* set in New Orleans, also devotes one episode to a retelling of this famous local story ("The Casket Girls").

More significantly, the city has not only generated a wealth of literary fiction but is also the source of a rich culture of folklore and folktales that fuels much of the city's tourist industry. Localized, largely, within the French Quarter, this folk culture surrounds a history of fictional and non-fictional associations within the city with ghosts, witches, vampires, murder, and voodoo. Books such as Troy Taylor's *Haunted New Orleans: History and Hauntings of the Crescent City* (2010), Victor C. Klein's *New Orleans Ghosts* (1996) and Kalila Smith's *Tales from the French Quarter* (2010) recount a rich heritage of folklore surrounding a history of violence, magic and hauntings. As Taylor explains in the introduction to his book, "[t]he dark side of New Orleans is as much a part of the city as chicory-laced coffee and beignets and is filled with the seductive imagery of voodoo, murder and ghosts. Only in New Orleans could darkness and death seem so appealing" (7). It is this dark side that fuels the city's well established Gothic tourism trade, with numerous companies offering walking tours of the French Quarter, including Haunted History Tours, Ghost City Tours, and French Quarter Phantoms, to name a few. The offerings of these companies include walking tours of the city's most haunted locations, Gothic literary settings, cemeteries, and a legacy of grisly events that have taken place within the city's history. They also chronicle the city's long association with magic, voodoo and the vampire. In particular, however, the stories of two women serve as center pieces to many of these tours. These are the stories of Madame Delphine LaLaurie—a wealthy and prominent socialite who with her husband became infamous for her cruel and barbaric treatment of their slaves—and the Voodoo Queen of New Orleans, Marie Laveau, a renowned practitioner of voodoo whose tomb in St. Louis Cemetery No. 1 still draws countless visitors every year (see Glossary). As Taylor explains:

> the tomb looks like so many others in this cluttered cemetery, until you notice the markings and crosses that have been drawn on the stones. Apart from these marks, you will also see coins, pieces of herb, bottles of rum, beans, bones, bags, flowers, tokens and all manner of things left behind in an offering for the good luck and blessings of the Voodoo Queen [53].

Like Laveau's tomb, Madame LaLaurie's house is also a significant tourist attraction within the French Quarter, not as a site of pilgrimage but curiosity at seeing what is often described as "as the most haunted house in the French Quarter" (Taylor 39).

It is to these two women that *Coven* turns in the telling of its Gothic tale out of New Orleans, established in the series' first episode "Bitchcraft." Opening with a location shot of a horse-drawn carriage going past the actual LaLaurie house in Royal Street, the sequence then cuts to an interior shot as one of the proprietor's renowned social gatherings is taking place. After having introduced Madame LaLaurie at the center of New Orleans high society, presenting her daughters to the city's eligible bachelors, the scene cuts to a title card situating the narrative within New Orleans 1834, followed by a series of extreme close-ups of LaLaurie applying human blood to her skin as part of a barbaric black magic beauty treatment, claiming "when the blood dries, my skin's supposed to be tight as a drum." Here we see the contrast between the public and private face of Madame LaLaurie—one smiling, refined and congenial, the other hard, primitive and brutal. It is also the beginning of the recreation of the legend of LaLaurie; a woman perceived as "cruel, cold-blooded and possibly insane" (Taylor 41).

The image of her smearing blood over her face also associates her with another legend: the monstrous serial killer Countess Bathory, a sixteenth-century Hungarian Countess who was reputed to have bathed in the blood of her victims in order to stay young. In this sequence, Bathory is reimagined for the Americas, not exploiting and murdering young peasant girls, but instead LaLaurie is infamous for torturing and mutilating her African American slaves. According to the stories that circulate both within popular publications and in the ghost tours of the city, when a fire broke out in the LaLaurie mansion, the fire brigade came and entered the house to put it out and check that all of the house's inhabitants had been brought to safety. In so doing, they came across a locked attic room, which they entered:

> Almost immediately their nostrils were assailed by the pungent odor of death. As their eyes became adjusted to the dark cavern-like chamber, they reeled and vomited from utter revulsion. The dim room held more than half a dozen chained and bound slaves. Some were dead. Others were in such a stage of torment and mutilation as to make death seem a human blessing [Klein 7–8].

The stories of LaLaurie's atrocities are central to the myth surrounding her, and *Coven* does not flinch from exploring this aspect of the legend, depicting this house of horrors in true Grand Guignol fashion. As LaLaurie enters the attic, preparing to torture Bastien, the house man who her daughter attempted to seduce, she walks past a series of slaves chained up in cages and all suffering different physical tortures: a man with his eyes and lips sewn shut and his mouth filled with faeces; a woman with the skin removed from her face, revealing the bloody skull beneath covered in maggots; and finally Bastien, the house man wrongly accused of rape, beaten, bloody, tongue cut out and tied in a crucifix position as a bull's head is placed over his own, transforming him into a living minotaur to suit LaLaurie's amusement. Through the use of hand-held cinematography, extreme close-ups and expressionist lighting, the sequence is visceral and nightmarish.

The attic torture chamber is so central to the myth and to the city's haunted reputation that the series repeatedly returns to it throughout the season both in flashback and in the contemporary setting, now transformed into a tourist attraction. For instance, in the same opening episode, the show's modern day characters, the Supreme witch Fiona Goode and her students, take a field trip through the French Quarter and end up on the tour of the LaLaurie house. Here the walking tours and aural storytelling about the house are transformed into a museum tour, which does not currently exist on the location. This re-imagining of the space, however, allows for a contrast between its "reality" and the commodification of the tour as introduced by the guide who explains as she takes the participants through the various rooms within the house: "The New Orleans Presentation Foundation is proud to present the haunted home tour of the notorious Madame LaLaurie." While the guide's narration focuses, like most of the ghost tours, upon the "abject horror" which took place in the attic, her narration replaces detail with dramatic flourishes, explaining that "the torture she inflicted on her slaves would spawn 179 years of hauntings." The details are, however, provided via the televisual format which intercuts the guide's narration with "flashbacks" to these monstrous crimes such as LaLaurie's daughter cutting out the pancreas of one of the slaves to serve as poultice for LaLaurie's skin. As the group walk through the brightly lit attic, filmed in daytime, the scene is repeatedly inter-cut with night-time, darkly lit extreme close-ups of mutilated bodies. The graphicness of these sequences emphasizes the potential for television to render visible and visceral what can only be implied via the ghost tour while also highlighting the degree to which television has been liberated from the constraint that once defined its approach to horror (Jowett and Abbott 10–15).

The most significant aspect of this tour and the series re-imagining of the local history is the integration of Marie Laveau within the LaLaurie story. While the two women's New Orleans timelines do overlap, there is no connection between the two within the local ghost tours or popular literature. In *Coven*, however, Laveau is revealed by the tour guide to be the lover of Bastien and as a result she uses her magic to enact a terrible revenge upon LaLaurie. The implication of the tour guide's narration is that Laveau murdered LaLaurie, although her body was never found. This ambiguity surrounding her "death" is in keeping with the lore surrounding LaLaurie as there are conflicting stories about what happened to her after her attic secret was revealed and, as the guide explains, "to this day no one knows the final resting place of Madame LaLaurie." Within *Coven*'s refashioning of the story, however, Laveau cursed LaLaurie with immortality and buried her alive within her own grounds. The show later reveals that Laveau herself is also still alive, a result of her voodoo magic and a pact with a spirit, which does conform to some rumors surrounding the Voodoo Queen's fate after her death. This deliberate and fictional integration of these two stories serves to consolidate a legacy of New Orleans ghost tours and folklore into one narrative in which both of these women emerge in the contemporary city, not as ghosts but very much alive.

This deliberate re-imagining of the city's folklore is reinforced by the fact that in addition to Laveau and LaLaurie, the series also integrates other key figures from New Orleans history and culture into its narrative matrix, both in the past and the present. In "The Magical Delights of Stevie Nicks" a Voodoo loa, or spirit, is introduced, who as portrayed by Lance Reddick is actually a composite of Papa Legba—a spirit intermediary between the other loa and humans—and Baron Samedi, the loa of the dead who presides over cemeteries and crossroads. The show uses Papa Legba's name but draws upon the visual imagery associated with Baron Samedi, in particular the top hat and the white skeleton paint on his face.[3] The series similarly integrates the "Axeman" of New Orleans true crime mystery into its narrative (see Glossary), a mystery that as Smith explains, blurred the lines between crime and gothic in its telling:

> In May of 1918, a year and a half long reign of terror struck the French Quarter leaving a trail of blood and mystery that remains unsolved today. Many residents of the city believed the killer to be some sort of supernatural creature, others merely a psy-

chotic serial killer with a taste for blood. The nature of the massacres indicated that the killer used an ax, giving rise to the media calling him the axeman [141].

In "The Axeman Cometh," the Axeman is revealed in the episode's opening, typing the letter to the people of New Orleans for which he was famous, in which he describes himself as "invisible ... a spirit and fell demon from hottest hell" and promises not to murder anyone "in whose home a jazz band is in full swing" (Smith 143–144). While the episode's opening scenes present an answer to the Axeman unsolved mystery, by suggesting that he was murdered by the Robichaux witches—thus explaining the sudden end to his killing spree—the contemporary witches inadvertently release the Axeman onto the unsuspecting city, now the actualization of his original claims of being a spirit. The inclusion of these "real" figures from New Orleans haunted history embodies, through the show's narrative, a form of return of the repressed, a subtext that underpins many Gothic texts. While the ghost stories as they are told on ghost tours similarly offer a release of the city's macabre history, it is a sanctioned release in which participants dabble in the supernatural. In *Coven,* that history is rendered horrifically visible in gruesome detail both in the past and in the present.

Furthermore, this re-imagining of the Laveau/LaLaurie folk history serves broader narrative purposes. First it presents a historically significant precursor to the racial tension that underpins the contemporary narrative, as the white witches and the African American Voodoo Queen come into conflict, by having Laveau, a free African American woman, liberate the slaves held by LaLaurie and punish this monstrous woman and her family. Secondly, it immerses the fictional characters within the series—the coven descended from witches—within the New Orleans folk culture and reimagines this local folk narrative as a national folk history. LaLaurie's monstrous torture and murder of her slaves is later paralleled with the legacy of male witch hunters introduced in "Head," when a white male witchhunter shoots all of Marie Laveau's staff and followers in a brutal shooting spree, intercut with footage of the abuse of civil rights protestors by white authorities, overlain with the Golden Gospel Singers sing "Oh Freedom." The juxtaposition of past and present acts of violence, both fictional and historical, conveys how *AHS* uses the conventions of the Gothic in its storytelling to chronicle the legacy of persecution, torture and murder that continues to underpin the American horror story and American history.

Conclusion

Having integrated Gothic tourism within its storytelling from its first season, *American Horror Story* brings the topic full circle in *Coven* by not only drawing and re-working its narrative from existing ghost tours but also by making the show itself a fixture in many of the ghost tours of New Orleans. The shooting of the series in New Orleans, as well as elements of its fictionalized narrative, are now a part of the Gothic tourist landscape of the city, highlighting the way in which both tourism and television take audiences/participants on a tour of the past in the hopes of bringing wonder, fantasy and horror into the present. Furthermore, *American Horror Story* takes the way in which the ghost tour explores horror and history through an experiential engagement with space in order to evoke and develop an American horror televisual tradition drawn from a rich tapestry of folk tales that integrate Gothic conventions and storytelling, ghost stories, true crime, cinematic horror, serial killing and all-too-familiar mass murders. Finally, the series, produced by FX during a period of liberalization of television, draws upon the ghost tour and Gothic tourism to provide a new framework and language for the horror genre on television, thus contributing a distinct strand for this new golden age of TV horror.

NOTES

1. It is of note that another company offers the "Original Jack the Ripper Murders Tour," which promises that "as the night falls, and the long shadows reach into the darker recesses of the streets of Whitechapel and Spitalfields, our Original Jack the Ripper Crime Scene Investigation sets out to join the Victorian police as they hunt history's most infamous serial killer through the crooked, cobbled alleyways of the Victorian abyss" (Jack the Ripper Tour: A Walk Worth Investigating). The emphasis upon Crime Scene Investigation invokes the popular television series *CSI* and thus further highlights the connection between Gothic tourism and American television.

2. See Lorna Jowett and Stacey Abbott for a discussion of *Marchlands* and *The Secret of Crickley Hall* in relation to TV Horror.

3. In Voodoo belief, Papa Legba is usually depicted as an old man dressed "in rags and leaning on a crutch and with a pipe" (Morris 196).

WORKS CITED

"Afterbirth." *American Horror Story: The Complete First Season*. Writ. Jessica Sharzer. Dir. Bradley Buecker. Twentieth Century Fox, 2012. DVD.

An American Haunting. Dir. Courtney Solomon. Allan Zeman Productions, 2006. Film.

The Amityville Horror. Dir. Stuart Rosenberg. American International Pictures, 1979. Film.

"The Axeman Cometh." *American Horror Story: Coven. The Complete Third Season*. Writ. Douglas Petrie. Dir. Michael Uppendahl. Twentieth Century–Fox, 2014. DVD.

"Be Our Guest." *American Horror Story: Hotel*. Writ. John J. Gray. Dir. Bradley Buecker. FX Network. 13 January 2016. Television.

"Bitchcraft." *American Horror Story: Coven. The Complete Third Season*. Writ. Ryan Murphy and Brad Falchuck. Dir. Alfonso Gomez-Rejon. Twentieth Century Fox, 2014. DVD.

The Blair Witch Project. Dirs. Daniel Myrick and Eduardo Sánchez. Haxan Films, 1999. Film.

Blair Witch Project website. http://www.blairwitch.com/mythology.html. Web. 20 March 2016.

Bram Stoker's Dracula . Dir. Francis Ford Coppola. American Zoetrope, 1992. Film.

Candyman. Dir. Bernard Rose. Polygram, 1992. Film.

Davenport-Hines, Richard. *Gothic: Four Hundred Years of Excess, Horror, Evil and Ruin*. London: Fourth Estate, 1998. Print.

"Devil's Night." *American Horror Story: Hotel*. Writ. Jennifer Salt. Dir. Loni Peristere. FX Network. 28 October 2015. Television.

Goldstein, Diane E. "The Commodification of Belief." *Haunted Experiences: Ghosts in Contemporary Folklore*. Diane E. Goldstein, Sylvia Ann Grider, and Jeannie Banks Thomas. Logan: Utah State University Press, 2007. 171–205. Print.

"Halloween, Pt. 1." *American Horror Story: The Complete First Season*. Writ. James Wong. Dir. David Semel. Twentieth Century Fox, 2012. DVD.

"Halloween, Pt. 2." *American Horror Story: The Complete First Season*. Writ. Tim Minear. Dir. David Semel. Twentieth Century Fox, 2012. DVD.

"Head." *American Horror Story: Coven. The Complete Third Season*. Writ. Tim Minear. Dir. Howard Deutch. Twentieth Century Fox, 2014. DVD.

Holloway, Julian. "Legend-Tripping in Spooky Spaces: Ghost Tourism and Infrastructure of Enchantment." *Environment and Planning D: Society and Space* 28 (2010): 618–637. Web. 8 May 2016.

"Home Invasion." *American Horror Story: The Complete First Season*. Writ. Ryan Murphy and Brad Falchuk. Dir.Alfonso Gomez-Rejon. Twentieth Century Fox, 2012. DVD.

Jowett, Lorna, and Stacey Abbott. *TV Horror: Investigating the Dark Side of the Small Screen*. London: I.B. Tauris, 2013. Print.

Kill Bill: Vol. 1. Quentin Tarantino. Miramaz, 2003. Film.

Klein, Victor C. *New Orleans Ghosts*. Metairie, LA: Lycanthrope Press, 1996. Print.

Koven, Mikel J. "*Most Haunted* and the Convergence of Traditional Belief and Popular Television." *Folklore* 118 (August 2007): 183–202. Web. 8 May 2016.

"The Magical Delights of Stevie Nicks." *American Horror Story: Coven. The Complete Third Season*. Writ. James Wong. Dir. Alfonso Gomez-Rejon. Twentieth Century Fox, 2014. DVD.

McEvoy, Emma. *Gothic Tourism*. Basingstoke: Palgrave Macmillan, 2016. Print.

Morris, Brian. *Religion and Anthropology: A Critical Introduction*. Cambridge: Cambridge University Press, 2006. Print.

"Murder House." *American Horror Story: The Complete First Season*. Writ. Jennifer Salt. Dir. Bradley Buecker. Twentieth Century Fox, 2012. DVD.

"Murder House Presented by Eternal Darkness Tours of Hollywood." *American Horror Story: The Complete First Season*. Twentieth Century Fox, 2012. DVD.

"Open House." *American Horror Story: The Complete First Season*. Writ. Brad Falchuk. Dir. Tim Hunter. Twentieth Century Fox, 2012. DVD.

The Original Jack the Ripper Walk. http://www.jacktheripperwalk.com/. Web. 20 March 2016.

Pemberton, Becky. "Diving into History: Luxury Submarine Tours Offered to Visit Titanic Wreck at the Bottom of the Atlantic … for a Cool $60,000." *MailOnline*. MailOnline, 14 April 2015. Web. 1 January 2016.

"Piggy Piggy." *American Horror Story: The Complete First Season*. Writ. Jessica Sharzer. Dir. Michael Uppendahl. Twentieth Century Fox, 2012. DVD.

"Pilot." *American Horror Story: The Complete First Season*. Writ. Ryan Murphy and Brad Falchuk. Dir. Ryan Murphy. Twentieth Century Fox, 2012. DVD.

Psycho. Dir. Alfred Hitchcock. Paramount, 1960. Film.

Reijnders, Stijn. "Stalking the Count: Dracula, Fandom and Tourism." *Annals of Tourism Research* 38.1 (2011): 231–248. Print.

Smith, Kalila. *Tales from the French Quarter*. Memphis, TN: Kerlak Publishing, 2010. Print.

"Spooky Little Girl." *American Horror Story: The Complete First Season*. Writ. Jennifer Salt. Dir. John Scott. Twentieth Century Fox, 2012. DVD.

Taylor, Troy. *Haunted New Orleans: History and Hauntings of the Crescent City*. Charleston, SC: Haunted America, 2010. Print.

Twisted Nerve. Dir. Roy Boulting. Charter Film Productions. 1968. Film.

Walkowitz, Judith R. *City of Dreadful Delight: Narratives of Sexual Danger in Late-Victorian London*. 1992. London: Virago Press, 2000. Print.

"Welcome to Briarcliff." *American Horror Story: Asylum. The Complete Second Season*. Writ. Tim Minear. Dir. Bradley Buecker. Twentieth Century Fox, 2013. DVD.

Seasons, Family and Nation in *American Horror Story*

Derek Johnston

Arguably, the title of *American Horror Story* sets out an agenda for the program: this is not just a horror story, but a particularly American one. This essay examines the way that the program uses seasonal celebrations as a way of expressing that national identity, with special emphasis on the importance of family to those celebrations. The particular seasonal celebrations focused on are those of Halloween and Christmas, each of which has associations with the supernatural. However, the use of the supernatural at those seasons is one which is particularly associated with the U.S., presenting Halloween as a time of supernatural incursion and horror, and of disruption to society and the normal order of things, while Christmas is presented more as a time of unity for the family. Where the supernatural emerges in American Christmas television, it is typically as a force to encourage togetherness and reconciliation, rather than as a dark reminder of the past. While these interpretations of these festivals have been broadcast abroad by American cultural products, not least American television, they have different associations and implications elsewhere. So the particular uses of these festivals is part of what marks *American Horror Story* out as American, as is the way that the program's narratives have been structured to fit in with U.S. television scheduling. This essay, then, argues that the structures of the narratives combine with their use of the festivals of Halloween and Christmas in order to enhance the sense of this series as a particularly American horror story.

This is not to claim that seasonality is central to *American Horror Story*, but it does play a part in the stories and contributes to the identity of the series. In this way the show is not unlike many other programs. Indeed, because this is not a major aspect of the program, but rather a more subtle and underlying expression of broadcast and cultural traditions, this is arguably more important than more obvious elements, certainly in relation to national identity. However, the very fact that *AHS* shares this practice with many other programs is significant in that the show is regularly positioned as being something different from the norm.

This essay shows that *American Horror Story* uses the seasonal markers of Halloween and Christmas in ways that relate to their wider usage in American culture, including the media. While it draws on episodes and narratives from across the run of the show, it pays particular attention to the first two seasons: *Murder House* and *Asylum*. Halloween and Christmas in *AHS* serve as festivals of inversion and subversion, but also ultimately of reversion to the status quo, in line with the claims of structuralist anthropologist Victor Turner (176–177). They allow the disempowered to hold power briefly, but only at the specific time allocated to them. They allow for the policing of social boundaries and mores, and they allow for celebration and relaxation and revelry, not always operating in harmony with each other. They ultimately reinforce the boundaries of the community and its identity as a community. However, in *American Horror Story*, the community is often an unwilling one, or at least somewhat resistant to unity, and the festivals serve as opportunities to highlight, and so potentially to heal, the fractures within those communities. In the same way these festivals serve in wider American culture as a way of bringing together communities, policing their boundaries and behaviors, and also having a party, while ultimately reinstating the normative power structures after the permitted inversions and subversions of the festival.

What Is American About American Horror Story?

It would be easy to say that *American Horror Story* is American simply because it is made in the United States for a domestic audience, with settings in the U.S. and mostly American performers. But the concept of American horror and the questions of national identity go further than that. They are part of the narratives with which the show engages, and their frameworks within American culture and concerns. They are part of the unstated preconceptions around ways of behaving, around the dressing of sets, the use of props and costumes, and around the incorporation of cultural concepts, including holidays and the relationship with the changing seasons. In other words, this is what Michael Billig has termed "banal nationalism," in which:

> In so many little ways, the citizenry are daily reminded of their national place in a world of nations. However, this reminding is so familiar, so continual, that it is not consciously registered as reminding. The metonymic image of banal nationalism is

not a flag which is being consciously waved with fervent passion; it is the flag hanging unnoticed on the public building [8].

These unconscious and unintentional reminders of the "Americanness" of *AHS* will go largely unnoticed by a U.S. audience, and the international spread of U.S. television also means that they will be sufficiently familiar to many international viewers that they are simply accepted there, albeit as markers of a familiar difference. There is not the sense that this is something local, but rather that this is what is normal for the U.S.

What Is "American Horror?"

As covered in the various essays in this collection, *American Horror Story* contains an inclusive view of the horrors of American life and society. If anything, the program is almost excessively, baroquely referential and inclusive in its raids on American horror culture, whether in reference to individual texts, to genres, or to general cultural fears. Since this essay argues that the use of seasonality in *AHS* is part of its particularly American approach to horror, it seems important to establish what "American horror" actually is. Of course, here the American aspect refers to the U.S. specifically, rather than Canada, Mexico, or any of the other nations in the Americas. It also refers to modern U.S. society, drawing more on European immigrant cultures than native cultures and traditions. Horror is both universal and culturally specific. The sensation of being horrified, the experience of fear, is known throughout humanity, with many of the main causes of disgust and fear being shared across cultures, such as death and decay and violence, but the specific causes of horror are more particular to individual cultures at particular historical times. The ways that U.S. commercial horror has operated in literature and in other media differ from the ways that commercial horror has operated in other cultures. However, as with so much of U.S. culture, American strength in the international entertainment industries has meant that the iconography of American horror is familiar worldwide. Nevertheless, when it comes to understanding and interpreting the specificities of American horror, critics have identified a number of key concerns which separate it out from other national expressions of the genre.

Central to these concerns is the idea that the nation is new, and lacks the connections to the past that European or other countries have. This ends up presenting the pre–Columbian history of the Americas as something ancient, mystical, and as potent a source of terror as the pagan history of Europe, a "gnawing awareness that America as a nation has been built on stolen ground" (Murphy 104). However, this view not only ignores the actuality of pre–Columbian history in favor of demonizing it, it also ignores most of the over-400 years of history that has developed since North America began to be permanently colonized by Europeans (which itself is to set aside the brief establishment of the Vinland colony in around 1000 CE).

What it does not ignore is the importance of certain historical events and the character of certain aspects of U.S. history. Where European, particularly English, Gothic would repeatedly present the Catholic Church as an old scourge, for the U.S. it is slavery that is the deep scar in the culture. As Teresa A. Goddu puts it, "Over and over again, American authors turn to the Gothic mode in order to disclose the ghostly origins of the nation as issuing from the oppressive social structure of slavery" (63). This is clearly particularly relevant with regard to *American Horror Story: Coven,* but is also part of the general idea that American horror deals primarily with the differences between ideals and pragmatism, whether those are the ideals of the new colonies, or of the Puritans, or the ideals of peaceful twentieth-century suburbs. In this conception, the horror of America is America itself.

One particular Puritan legacy to the American character can be seen in its relationship with the supernatural. The Puritan church saw attacks by supernatural forces as proof of righteousness. The Devil, it was reasoned, would not waste time on victimizing those who were already damned, but would instead concentrate on those who were good. As Cotton and Increase Mather wrote at the time, "it is a vexing *Eye-sore* to the Devil, that our Lord Christ should be known, and own'd, and preached in this *howling Wilderness.* Wherefor he has left no *Stone unturned,* that so he might undermine his plantation, and force us out of our Country" [original emphases] (Mather 74). This attitude not only kept the Puritan colonists alert to the possibility that any problems they faced may be the work of an evil supernatural force, but also reinforced their sense of being special: if we are being victimized by the Devil, then it must be because we are essentially Good (Madsen 22). When translated outward, this can be seen as an influence on the American culture of exceptionalism, and the recurring sense of the USA as an embattled nation facing constant, external threats from various sources, which may all be different aspects of an overarching, existential evil. *American Horror Story* certainly draws on this tradition, but by making supernatural and other "outsider" characters sympathetic, by presenting those opposed to the supernatural as unsympathetic, and by presenting a variety of characterization for supernatural and non-supernatural characters, it takes what can initially seem to be certainties and reveals the complications that underlie them.

Yet at different times American horror has taken on different characteristics as the dominant culture has changed. The haunted house, for example, can be related to the nation as a place haunted by its unknown, pre–Columbian history, particularly in the trope of the house built upon a American Indian graveyard (Bailey 57). But it can also be related to the horrors of the economy, becoming trapped in a building that cannot be afforded, as in *The Amityville Horror* (book Jay Anson, 1977; film 1979, 2005) or *American Horror Story: Murder House*, or with the house itself symbolizing class and economic difference, as in *The People Under the Stairs* (Wes Craven, 1991). The idea of possession itself carries a doubled implication, of ownership both legal and supernatural.

While American horror is not unique in placing the family at its center, there is a particular focus on the family and "family values" within the culture of the U.S., re-emphasized every year at Thanksgiving, when broadcast drama stresses the unity of the family as paramount. Within horror, the family can as frequently be a source of fear and disruption as it is a source of protection and happiness. We need only think of examples such as the cannibal families of *The Texas Chain Saw Massacre* (Tobe Hooper, 1974) and *The Hills Have Eyes* (Wes Craven, 1977), or the nonhuman representatives of the wealthy upper-classes literally feeding on the ordinary in *Society* (Brian Yuzna, 1989). Indeed, Tony Williams has seen the family horror film as part of an "important American cultural tradition of protest against domestic constraint" (Williams 27).

The family is centered on the home, and each season of *American Horror Story* is based around a family, albeit mostly a non-biological and highly dysfunctional one, brought together into a community. The community is the home that keeps them all together, whether it is a literal house, an asylum, a hotel, or a traveling freak show. Concerns with family, love, inheritance and reproduction occur across the series, indicating their central positions in the American psyche. These concerns around family, as something that binds together disparate people, are supported by the use of seasonal gatherings and festivities throughout the series.

Broadcasting Seasons, Calendar Seasons

As Karen Lury has stated, drawing on the work of Paddy Scannell, "At the grandest scale, television marks the passing of years, and of each year—television's relaying of seasons (Christmas, summer) echoes and confirms the passing of the real seasons for the television viewer" (98). This occurs in a number of ways. There is the regular cycle of the television seasons, with new episodes being broadcast at particular times of the year. These cycles are in part determined by other calendars, including sporting calendars, with major events such as the Super Bowl being fixed spots in the U.S. television year. However, this essay is concerned with the representation of the seasons in drama, and the ways that this practice connects to the experience of the viewer and their understanding of the calendar year.

Broadcast seasons operate closely with calendar seasons, but they are not tied directly to them. Jason Mittell notes that "Many series follow the time of year that episodes air, with specific episodes for holidays such as Christmas or Halloween, a specific time scheme that loses meaning when a show is watched in reruns or on DVD" (224). This is also an issue in that, while many ongoing dramas can be seen to approximate the calendar seasons of when they are broadcast, increasing the potential levels of connection between audience and characters, the vagaries of television scheduling can lead to a separation between the diegetic season of the show and the calendar season experienced by the viewer. This is particularly evident in the case of repeats, and also in terms of international exports of programs, where the broadcast occurs weeks, or even months, apart from the original broadcast schedule, or, as Mittell points out, when viewed later through DVD or another on-demand system. Hence a Halloween episode in the U.S. may be viewed at Christmas in the UK, or at any other point in the year.

However, the associations with particular seasons are strong enough and have been reinforced sufficiently through televisual traditions that they are not completely lost with the move to a different context. A Christmas episode may not be engaged with as strongly in the summer, but the viewer understands the context of Christmas and has an emotional engagement with and memory of the celebration of the festival, whether it is actually Christmas or not. Similarly, once it is realized that particular types of narrative are associated with particular times of year, the patterns of seasonal engagement within broadcast television allow seasonal episodes to be identified even when the outward trappings of the festival are not part of the episode's diegesis. In this way, once a UK viewer of U.S. television has realized that programs in supposedly rational or real-world genres, like hospital or detective shows, often include a touch of the irrational at Halloween, it becomes possible to identify the Halloween episode of a series whenever it is encountered in the calendar year, whether there are jack o'lanterns and trick-or-treaters on-screen or not (see Derek Johnston).

There are also two types of broadcasting seasons to be considered. The first is the organizational unit of the broadcast season: a group of episodes which are produced under an organizational contract; in the case of *American Horror Story*, each of these broadcast seasons tells a single story, whether that is *Murder House*, *Asylum*, *Coven*, *Freak Show* or *Hotel*. These broadcast seasons then form part of the broader broadcasting season, which may be identified as a summer season, an autumn season, or simply as a "new season." These broadcasting seasons tend, like the calendar seasons, to merge into each other rather than being clearly differentiated, but there are various markers that indicate the shift from one to another. These may be the presence of particular events, often tied to the wider cultural calendar, and may also be the presence of a few weeks of "filler" programming such as repeats and specials. Over all of this lie the financial calendars of the producers and broadcasters, into which their production budgets have to fit.

John Ellis has argued that "any [broadcasting] schedule contains the distillation of the past history of a channel, of national broadcasting as a whole, and of the particular habits of national life" (26). This last point in particular is central to the ideas covered in this essay. Essentially, the way that a nation has developed its interaction with the seasons will influence the way its broadcasting relates to and uses the seasons. Patterns of work and worship that have developed over centuries will have influenced when particular holidays are held and how they are marked. The history that has shaped the nation will influence when and how particular historical events are commemorated, so that the U.S. Thanksgiving and Independence Day commemorate events specific to the nation, and their cultural significance and opportunities for (re-)interpretation. The agricultural calendar will have influenced the academic and political and sporting calendars, which in turn will influence the types of programming eventually broadcast at different times of the year. The seasonal changes in weather will also affect programming: when the weather is dry, warm and pleasant, people are more likely to engage in outdoors activities away from the television, so broadcasters will tend to show repeats, and cheap imports, and other types of less expensive programming, saving their expensive new investments for times when they have the opportunity to attract larger audiences, sheltering from the weather.

This means that seasonal episodes will carry with them indicators of their original season. In part, this is carried out through fairly obvious on-screen signifiers, from the mentioning of time of year in dialogue, on-screen dates, to the foliage on trees, or the explicit or implicit celebration of a particular festival marked through specific decorations, actions, clothing or music. But, as has already been stated, the indicators of the festival can also be less direct, as when particular types of narrative become associated with particular festivals. Thus, when *Grey's Anatomy* (2005–) or *Hawaii Five-0* (2010–) or *Castle* (2009–2016) include an episode in which there appear to be zombies, it is almost certainly a Halloween episode, even if the characters are not themselves marking Halloween. Similarly, any episode which focuses to a greater, more explicit extent than usual, on the idea of family and the need to maintain and reinforce a familial unit, whether biological or not, is likely to have originally been scheduled around Thanksgiving or Christmas. In this way, particular narrative tropes and genres become associated with particular times of the year, and those times of the year become associated with those tropes and genres, in a self-reinforcing relationship.

Halloween

American Horror Story, as a horror series, does not have the same immediate signifier of a special Halloween episode that series such as the aforementioned *Grey's Anatomy*, *Castle* or *Hawaii Five-0* have, in the form of the
eruption of the abnormal into the mundane, as this disruption is a basic and
constant aspect of horror narratives. Yet Halloween plays an important role
within *AHS*, in large part because of the festival's role in American culture.
As Nicholas Rogers has argued, "if modern-day Halloween increasingly
celebrates difference, it also represents American-ness. This is especially
true for immigrants to North America, but it is also the case in countries
where American culture is aggressively marketed" (Rogers 9–10). Exported
around the world by American media, the North American Halloween has
become a marker of difference, of modernity, of commercialism, and all of
those other symbolic values attributed to the idea of the United States. It is
either embraced, or it is rejected as a foreign invader not compatible with
traditional culture and values (see, e.g., Salvador Cardús, Lothar Mikos, Larisa
Prokhorova, John Helsloot and Dejan Jontes in Malcolm Foley and Hugh
O'Donnell).

The U.S. Halloween of today developed from traditions imported from
Scotland and Ireland by immigrants in the eighteenth and nineteenth centuries. Where the original traditions were closely tied up with divination, the
holiday in the Americas focused more on the social aspects of the festival,
combining with the social aspects drawn from other immigrant traditions.
Indeed, Rogers argues that the festival became a way of celebrating disparate
Irish and Scottish communities and traditions, while also encouraging members of other communities to interact with and experience goodwill towards
the Scots and Irish populations (50–51). However, this did lead to the celebrations becoming known as an excuse for rowdiness, following on from
those earlier traditions in which members of the community, particularly
young males, would police the boundaries of the community and punish
those seen as transgressors through a series of tricks, such as overturning
outhouses, stealing gates, and shooting flame through their keyholes from
hollowed-out cabbage stalks.

In the late nineteenth and early twentieth century, this led to increased
attempts to police the carnivalesque rowdiness, and to create more formal
events and more polite and domestic, and commercialized, ways to celebrate
Halloween, with magazines such as the *Ladies Home Journal* or *Werner's
Readings and Recitations* offering advice on how to host a Halloween party.
Throughout the rest of the twentieth century, and into the twenty-first, Halloween in the U.S. has had a tension between the public and the domestic,
expanding out into street parties, themed club nights, and horror houses. At

the same time, concerns for children's safety have led to increased policing of and restrictions on trick-or-treating, an activity that used to present a way to build community connections by reinforcing neighborliness and marking out those perceived to be outsiders to the community. Halloween has also moved into broadcasting, being marked by seasonal episodes, such as the ones covered here, which can be seen as encouraging a passive observation of the festival in the safety of the home, rather than an active participation outside in the community.

Turner has interpreted Halloween and its believed pagan origins as the Celtic festival of Samhain as a social purgation, claiming:

> it would appear that…. Samhain represented a seasonal expulsion of evils, and a renewal of fertility associated with cosmic and chthonic powers. In European folk beliefs, the midnight of October 31 has become associated with gatherings of the hellish powers of witchcraft and the devil, as in *Walpurgisnacht* and Tam o'Shanter's [sic] near-fatal Halloween. Subsequently, a strange alliance has been formed between the innocent and the wicked, children and witches, who purge the community by the mock pity and terror of trick or treat and prepare the way for communitas feasts of sunlike pumpkin pie—at least in the United States. Somehow, as dramatists and novelists well know, a touch of sin and evil seems to be necessary tinder for the fires of communitas—although elaborate ritual mechanisms have to be provided to transmute those fires from devouring to domestic uses [original emphasis] [Turner 183].

This supposed connection of the modern Halloween to Samhain is the one that Travis relates to Adelaide in *Murder House* ("Halloween, Pt. 1"), explaining to his lover's daughter why people dress up at this time of year, while also informing the audience that this episode is set at Halloween and reminding them that this is a time when the dead can walk freely abroad. While there is dispute over just how closely Halloween is related to Samhain, particularly in the way that it is celebrated, the idea that this is a pagan survival is one that has found a strong root in popular culture. More significantly for *Murder House*, there is the idea of the festival as a purgation of society through supernatural means, shown in the way that the murderous, now-dead, Tate is confronted by the spirits of those that he had killed years before in a high school shooting, on the only night that it is possible for them to meet, as the places that they haunt are geographically separated ("Halloween, Pt. 2").

However, *American Horror Story* twists this trope, as there be no reconciliation and reinstatement of normality following this confrontation because Tate exists in forgetful ignorance of his guilt. As Ben, the psychotherapist whose purchase of the titular "Murder House" in order to reunite his family is the originating event of the series' narrative, tells Tate in the final episode of the season, "Afterbirth," Tate is a charismatic psychopath, whose murderous nature is untreatable by therapy, which is just a narrative that people use to make themselves feel comfortable. The same can be said of the spell that the medium Billie Dean had suggested the family use to exorcize the house, but which turned out not to work ("Birth"). This can be interpreted as relating to horror stories in general, blaming supernatural sources for the things that have been done by ordinary humans, and the way that the house represents a building up of history and stories in one place emphasizes the way that human history is an aggregation of narratives and events that cannot be escaped. If *Murder House* represents America in any way, it does so by reminding us of the murderous piling up of history, and says that the only reconciliation that is possible is one that sets the conflicts of the past aside and gathers together a new family to protect the future, which the show presents through a peaceful familial Christmas, albeit one of ghosts, as the glowering, resentful forces of past mistakes and horrors watch on ("Afterbirth").

As far as *Murder House* is concerned, its original transmission closely matched the dates inside the episodes. Larry's statement that he follows all seven days of Halloween, because it is the only time of year when he feels that he can walk around freely, considering his burns, not only connects to the traditional extended Halloween season, but incorporates it more closely into the schedule of the program. This integrates the two episodes set on the same Halloween night, but broadcast each side of the actual calendar Halloween, marking seven nights of celebration. Similarly, the season finale, which brings the central narrative of the season to an end with a celebration of Christmas, was originally broadcast on December 21. This paralleling of the viewer's calendar with the calendar within the program recurs to a certain extent across each season of *American Horror Story*, but with the focal fixed point where diegetic date and non-diegetic date most closely coincide being Halloween. *Asylum*'s "Tricks and Treats" was broadcast the week before Halloween, on October 24 2012, while its Christmas-set episode, "Unholy Night" was broadcast on December 5, with only one further episode before the season took a two-week break. The first Halloween-set episode of *Coven*, "Fearful Pranks Ensue," was broadcast on October 30 2013, with the following episode, "Burn, Witch. Burn!" also containing portions set during Halloween. Similarly, *Freak Show*'s two episodes entitled "Edward Mordrake" appeared on October 22 and 29, and were set at Halloween, but the familial reconstruction occurs at Halloween in the narrative, in the January 21 episode "Curtain Call," disrupting this overall pattern. The fourth episode of *Hotel* is "Devil's Night," broadcast on October 28 2015, in which ghostly serial killers take up an annual one-night residence at the titular hotel, although the episode set at Halloween, "Room Service," was first broadcast on November 4.

This demonstrates the problems with fitting a heavily serialized story, where the main plot occurs within a fairly tight time-frame, into the weekly-episode model of most broadcast television. The calendar time of the episodes can be made to generally align with that of the outside world, to meet specific points, but the movement of time at different paces in the fictional world and in the viewer's world disrupts the alignment. Nevertheless, Halloween presents the central calendar point of each season of *American Horror Story*, emphasizing the festival's centrality to ideas of horror entertainment in the U.S. It can also be seen to extend the Halloween season to the seven days that Larry mentions in *Murder House*, something that happened in various parts of North America during the nineteenth and early-twentieth centuries, as festivities around Halloween and Bonfire Night[1] combined into an extended fire festival. This is particularly so where the festivities straddle a weekend, which is when most people will feel that they have the time to set up or take part in some sort of party or celebration, at the same time enhancing the feeling of the festivities as breaking from the norm in that they take place outside the schedule established by the working or educational week.

As with the ghosts of *Murder House* only being able to leave the grounds of the house on Halloween, *Freak Show* presents Halloween as a time when the ghosts of the past return, with Edward Mordrake's haunting of freak shows on that night in order to find new members for his ghostly entourage. Similarly, *Hotel* presents Halloween as being a time for the gathering of the spirits of dead serial killers, an annual "booking" that emphasizes the sense of seasonal recurrence and repetition in these narratives. Halloween is also presented as a time for disguises, and a time for horrors to be abroad and accepted because others are in disguise. This mixes American traditions of Halloween: the social and the mythic. The mythic is the conception that this is a night in which supernatural beings actually do move abroad amongst mortals. The social is one which presents the night as a time to dress up and to have a party. It is a time for social mixing which reintegrates the community, as shown by the acceptance of horrific beings such as the ghosts of dead teenagers showing the wounds that killed them in *Murder House.* What should be horrific is accepted as merely good costuming and make-up by ordinary people.

But *American Horror Story* uses these accepted patterns and shows the party of Halloween to be underlain by or to contain the potential for horror, which has arguably been softened by commercialization and the making safe of the festival for children. In *Asylum*, masked and costumed children calling at the door of Lana and Wendy's house—as an early trick or treat on the night before Halloween—are followed by the invasion of the house by the masked and costumed serial killer Bloody Face ("Tricks and Treats"). The desire to be somebody else which is a part of the play of Halloween is turned to tragedy in *Murder House* with Adelaide's desire to be a "pretty girl" ("Halloween, Pt. 1"), with the mask that makes that dream real for her literally blinding her to the dangers on the road as she tries to join the popular girls, to fit in, with the result being that she is hit by a car and killed.

Halloween specials often present a disruption to the norms of a television series, with the supernatural frequently making an appearance in non-supernatural programming. With *American Horror Story*, the norms of the series are intentionally hard to define. While each series might have a central theme, this serves more as a central location in which to bring together a range of horror narratives, with each season in many ways presenting variations on themes that recur through the series as a whole, and through horror fictions more broadly. However, there is an element of this disruption in *Murder House*, where Halloween provides the possibility for the ghosts to roam abroad and travel beyond the grounds of the house. In *Freak Show*, the arrival of Edward Mordrake and his ghosts introduces a supernatural element not present in the rest of the season ("Edward Mordrake, Pts. 1 and 2"). Freak show lore states that performing on Halloween will summon the spirit of Edward Mordrake, a man with a second face on the back of his head who murdered his entire freak show troupe one Halloween before committing suicide, and who now returns to take a soul from any freak show that performs on that night. Knowing this, Elsa, the frustrated performer who had finally found her way to success in show-business, finally agrees to perform in a television Halloween special when she discovers that her dark past as a brothel dominatrix who had her legs severed in a torture film has been uncovered and that her new mainstream career was over ("Curtain Call"). This addition provides for the conclusion of the season's narrative, forming a dark reflection of Christmas in which Elsa finally finds contentment with her freak show family in the afterlife. However, what is more important about Halloween to *American Horror Story* as a whole is its association as the central "horror" holiday in the U.S., unlike Christmas, which is usually seen as a holiday for reconciliation and happiness.

Christmas

While Mark Connelly argues that, "For the English Christmas had always meant home. It was this quality that made the English Christmas different from its celebration anywhere else" (11), it is the American Christmas which seems to be even more focused on the joys of family. Connelly himself suggests that "Perhaps it is a reflection of the fact that the USA, sprawling so rapidly and on the crest of such a cosmopolitan wave, needed to stress the unity of the family as a microcosm of the wider family of the nation" (165). This unity of the nation/family came to be a key part of the winter season festivals, particularly focused around Thanksgiving and Christmas. This was aided by the way that the celebration of Christmas developed from being a time of revelry and carnival, in which "the social hierarchy itself was symbolically turned upside down, in a gesture that inverted designated roles of gender, age, and class" (Nissenbaum 8), and transformed into a domesticated celebration, in much the same way as would later happen with Halloween. As a result of this, and the growing connection between Christmas and the pleasures of consumption, American reviewers and viewers have tended to reject the darker aspects of Christmas narratives, such as *A Christmas Carol* (1843), and replaced them with the importance of family and reconciliation. Indeed, author and essayist Michael Chabon has described the English tradition of ghost stories at Christmas, when "it is apparently traditional to sit by a crackling yule fire and scare one's friends out of their wits. (And it would be hard to imagine anything more English than that.)" (111).

This would seem to suggest that there is something un–American about connecting horror to Christmas, and it is notable that *American Horror Story* marks Halloween in each of its seasons, but has only included a Christmas-set episode in its first two seasons. In doing so, it draws upon two existing uses of Christmas in relation to the supernatural in U.S. popular culture: familial reconciliation and the Santa-themed serial killer. The series rejects the English tradition of the Christmas ghost story found in the work of people like M.R. James, which uses the supernatural as a source of terror rather than reconciliation. It also, so far, has avoided a more recent development in Christmas horror, adopting and adapting the Germanic folkloric figure of Krampus, who was responsible for punishing the naughty while Saint Nicholas took care of the nice. The growing popularity of Krampus in North American popular culture includes episodes of *Grimm* ("Twelve Days of Krampus," 2013) and *Lost Girl* ("Groundhog Fae," 2013), as well as the films *Krampus* (Michael Dougherty, 2015) and *A Christmas Horror Story* (Grant Harvey, Steven Hoban and Brett Sullivan, 2015). This avoidance of this newer aspect of the U.S. Christmas points to the way that *AHS* draws on the longer traditions of American horror, depending upon long-standing associations which tie these traditions more closely to American identity than more recent developments and adoptions such as Krampus.

This essay has already noted that Christmas is used in *Murder House* to present a sense of a new start for the house, with the forces of past irrationality and mistakes glowering from outside the protected and protective circle of light around the family that has united to protect the future. Where *Murder House* uses Christmas as a setting for resolution and a, somewhat twisted, familial reconciliation, *Asylum* ties in to other Christmas horror media. In particular, *Asylum*'s murderous Santa (Leigh Emerson, "Unholy Night" and "The Coat Hanger") represents a loss of innocence and a disruption of the familial ideal that is supposed to be part of Christmas. The character's initial trauma is revealed to be that, while serving time as a petty juvenile thief, he was raped by prison warders who were going around the cells singing Christmas carols, wearing Santa hats. The character serves as a further link to the serial killer film, most particularly the Christmas serial killer film, going back at least as far as the 1974 Canadian film *Black Christmas* (Bob Clark). However, it draws more strongly on the U.S. film *Silent Night, Deadly Night* (Charles E. Sellier, Jr., 1984), where a killer who was abused during childhood dresses as Santa to enact what he sees as the justified punishment of the naughty. As with *Murder House*, then, we are presented with narratives in which the horrors of the past keep returning to haunt us, and the stories that we tell ourselves and each other are simply comforts to avoid facing the realities of life. Emerson may dress as Santa to enact his crimes, but he does so with the sense that he is telling the truth about the season: that there is no Santa Claus, only a man who can find his way into your house at night and judge you.

The use of Christmas in only two seasons of *American Horror Story* fits with the series' associations with wider American horror culture and television. In American television, the supernatural is not uncommon at Christmas, but it usually presents in one of three ways, two based on existing texts. There is the adaptation of Charles Dickens's *A Christmas Carol*, and there is also the variation on *It's a Wonderful Life* (Frank Capra, 1946). Finally, there is the narrative in which it turns out that there really is a Santa Claus. Each of these narratives presents a family-centered, happy version of Christmas and its relationship with the supernatural. The supernatural is presented through these as a means of reconciliation, particularly of reconciliation within the family, or it is presented as a way of rewarding "goodness" in the form of Santa Claus, who thus acts to reassure the protagonist that their choices have been the right ones. The same narrative can be found in the variations on *It's a Wonderful Life*. Meanwhile, *A Christmas Carol* holds out the possibility of redemption through mending the bonds of family, as Connelly pointed out (quoted above), and particularly by reinforcing familial and social bonds through engaging with the capitalist structures of U.S. society, i.e., by buying things.

American Horror Story does not present problems that can be solved by conspicuous consumption. Indeed, *Murder House* is particularly about the problems of becoming trapped by the collapse of the housing market, about the horror of having financially over-extended, about the futility of trying to buy happiness and family unity. The family's potential for future happiness, and their present unity, only comes about once they are completely separated from monetary problems, through death. Even then, they are tied to the house, which can serve as a reminder of the literal meaning of the word "mortgage": "death debt."

The inversion of the happy family Christmas that is presented by the killer Santa in *Asylum* is also an inversion of other Christmas Santa narratives.

This is not the real Santa Claus. This is just a murderous man with a Santa fixation, who is not in the end actually that bothered about whether people have been naughty or nice; he just wants to hurt and kill them. The figure of Santa is for him a representation of pain and horror, and it is this rather than any wider cultural concept of judgment that drives this characterization. In *American Horror Story*, unlike in *Smallville* ("Lexmas," 2005), *E.R.* ("City of Mercy," 2006) or *The Twilight Zone* episode "The Night of the Meek" (1960), there is no real Santa Claus; all there is is a man dressed up like Santa.

Asylum thus presents Christmas as a festival of familial happiness that is corrupted and disrupted by the actions of the killer, who destroys the nostalgic and romantic ideals of the holiday. Sister Jude similarly sees the "real meaning" of Christmas as being itself disrupted and corrupted by television, in the form of television holiday specials like *Rudolph the Red-Nosed Reindeer*, with no sign of Christ ("Unholy Night"). She sees this commercialization as being the work of the Devil, distracting people from faith; in this it contributes to one of the main themes of the season: corruption. As Mengele-esque ex–Nazi Dr. Arden (see Glossary) represents the corrupt medical science of the Nazis, as the demonically-possessed Sister Mary shows religion corrupted by evil, as the driven Monsignor with his dreams of the Papacy presents religion corrupted by personal ambition, as serial killer Dr. Thredson and his son—the two Bloody Faces—present corrupted mother-son relationships in their treatment of women, as the asylum itself presents the corruption of the ideal of care through the torture that so many of its patients undergo, so Emerson represents the innocence of Christmas corrupted.

While there are undoubtedly a number of reasons that *American Horror Story* has not returned to a Christmas setting, some purely related to the structuring of the narratives that have been created, if it did follow the pattern of other U.S. Christmas supernatural narratives, then this would have the effect of making the series more like a standard U.S. networked program. As with the other programs created by Ryan Murphy and Brad Falchuk, *AHS* has been positioned as something that breaches expectations, that does not do what would be expected of a U.S. horror program. However, as can be seen with the Halloween episodes, *American Horror Story* is already beginning to tend towards falling into normative patterns. This is partly because, as with the other Murphy/Falchuk shows, the series parodies existing cultural forms and expectations, and to do so it needs to represent them. However, Murphy and Falchuk's productions have a tendency to slip away from satirizing to end up adopting the form and characteristics of the genre that it is engaged with. This is perhaps most apparent with *Glee* (2009–2015), which regularly slipped back and forth between revealing the empty fantasy of the high school musical genre, and simply reveling in the fun of producing a musical each week, complete with unabashed moments of learning, happy endings and fantastic song and dance numbers that are not explained away as either fantasies or the product of extensive rehearsal.

Thus, with *American Horror Story*, to present a variation on either the U.S.-version of *A Christmas Carol* or *It's a Wonderful Life* would run the risk of slipping into the typical version of these narratives, and so making the series less "special." Here it is worth remembering the way that the series is positioned as a "quality drama," in part simply by its serial nature, its finite narratives, and its presentation on cable and subscription channels rather than on network programming. But one of the key characteristics of "quality drama" presented by Robert Thompson is that it is simply "not 'regular' TV" (13). Following standard tropes without giving them some sort of twist would therefore simply be "ordinary," and would detract from the claimed specialness of the series.

Even so, the way that Halloween has been treated on the program is tending towards the ordinary. This is still in quite broad terms, and the narratives deal with this by utilizing the cultural belief in Halloween as a time when the boundaries between the normal and the abnormal, or the natural and the supernatural are thin. The individual seasons engage with this in a variety of ways, but the establishment of a pattern, that there will be an episode which is set at Halloween in which things that are even stranger than usual happen, is a point in which the series is falling into a norm of broadcast drama in the U.S.

Conclusion

The uses of Christmas and Halloween in *American Horror Story* connect them to their wider uses in popular culture in relation to the supernatural. While Halloween recurs as a point of disruption in the reality of each narrative, Christmas is presented only twice, once as a time of familial reconciliation and the second time as a festival for the family that is corrupted and disrupted. In engaging with the popular cultural associations with these festivals in this way, they serve to tie the program more closely to that wider sense of American identity, in a way that is emphasized by these episodes being synchronized to the actual festivals on first broadcast, so that characters and viewers are experiencing Halloween or Christmas at approximately the same time. This is itself enhanced by particular aspects of Halloween and Christmas, such as trick or treating, or decorating the house, being shared by both viewers and characters. While many of these aspects of these festivals may be shared in other countries, the inflection of them is particular to the culture of the United States, and the reception of the program outside the U.S. will not be as closely linked to the diegetic time of the episodes. In this way, viewers outside the U.S. will not be so closely connected to the seasonal aspects of the series, emphasizing once again that these connections enhance the American-ness of *American Horror Story*.

The uses are also part of the way that the series falls into or utilizes the patterns typical of U.S. network drama, which include the close approximation of the viewer's calendar time with the calendar time within the show's diegesis. The risk of simply emulating the norm is shown in *Murder House*, as are the attempts to subvert these normal practices, presenting a happy(–ish) family Christmas, only the family are primarily united by death, are unable to escape each other, and know that they and new living tenants are still constantly threatened by the malevolent ghosts. This is not a resolution, just a new and possibly temporary equilibrium. Halloween in each season presents a disruption of the normal order of things, and a direct engagement with the cultural practices around the festival. This is not just the case of the episodes near Halloween having stories relevant to the time of year; this is a presentation of the season of Halloween within the show as being a special time of breached boundaries, which is specifically shown at the calendar time of Halloween, linking the diegetic and the non-diegetic, thinning the boundaries between the world on the screen and the world of the viewer.

This is a result of the other key tension within *AHS*. The program is trying to be something different, to present a twisted version of known tropes, or to bring them together in unusual ways, such as the combination of demonic possession, Nazi medical experimentation and alien abduction narratives in *Asylum*. But to do that, the show also needs to be in some ways ordinary, to highlight the standard ways of doing things in order to show that it is in some way modifying them, whether to surprise or to satirize. The series' very identity as a specifically *American* horror story is therefore reliant on it in some way using and displaying these expected characteristics, such as having a Halloween episode in which the dead are free to walk about and seek vengeance.

NOTES

1. November 5, in which Americans of English extraction would follow the English custom of celebrating the defeat of a 1605 Catholic plot to blow up the Houses of Parliament and King James I.

WORKS CITED

"Afterbirth." *American Horror Story: The Complete First Season*. Writ. Jessica Sharzer. Dir. Bradley Buecker. Twentieth Century Fox, 2012. DVD.

Bailey, Dale. *American Nightmares: The Haunted House Formula in American Popular Fiction*. Bowling Green, OH: Bowling Green State University Popular Press, 1999. Print.

Billig, Michael. *Banal Nationalism*. Thousand Oaks, CA: Sage Publications, 1995. Print.

"Birth." *American Horror Story: The Complete First Season*. Writ. Tim Minear. Dir. Alfonso Gomez-Rejon. Twentieth Century Fox, 2012. DVD.

"Burn, Witch. Burn!" *American Horror Story: Coven. The Complete Third Season*. Writ. Jessica Sharzer. Dir. Jeremy Podeswa. Twentieth Century Fox, 2014. DVD.

Cardús, Salvador. "Halloween: Tradition as Snobbery." *Treat or Trick? Halloween in a Globalising World*. Eds. Malcolm Foley and Hugh O'Donnell. Newcastle upon Tyne: Cambridge Scholars Publishing, 2009. 104–112. Print.

Chabon, Michael. "The Other James." *Maps and Legends: Reading and Writing Along the Borderlands*. London: Fourth Estate, 2010. 109–120. Print.

"The Coat Hanger." *American Horror Story: Asylum. The Complete Second Season*. Writ. Jennifer Salt. Dir. Jeremy Podeswa. Twentieth Century Fox, 2013. DVD.

Connelly, Mark. *Christmas: A History*. London: I.B. Tauris, 2012. Print.

"Curtain Call." *American Horror Story: Freak Show. The Complete Fourth Season*. Writ. John J. Gray. Dir. Bradley Buecker. Twentieth Century Fox, 2015. DVD.

"Devil's Night." *American Horror Story: Hotel*. Writ. Jennifer Salt. Dir. Loni Peristere. FX Network. 28 October 2015. Television.

"Edward Mordrake, Pt 1." *American Horror Story: Freak Show. The Complete Fourth Season*. Writ. James Wong. Dir. Michael Uppendahl. Twentieth Century Fox, 2015. DVD.

"Edward Mordrake, Pt. 2." *American Horror Story: Freak Show. The Complete Fourth Season*. Writ. Jennifer Salt. Dir. Howard Deutch. Twentieth Century Fox, 2015. DVD.

Ellis, John. "Scheduling: The Last Creative Act in Television?" *Media, Culture & Society* 22.1 (2000): 25–38. Print.

"Fearful Pranks Ensue." *American Horror Story: Coven. The Complete Third Season*. Writ. Jennifer Salt. Dir. Michael Uppendahl. Twentieth Century Fox, 2014. DVD.

Foley, Malcolm, and Hugh O'Donnell, eds. *Treat or Trick? Halloween in a Globalising World*. Newcastle upon Tyne: Cambridge Scholars Publishing, 2009. Print.

Goddu , Teresa A. "American Gothic." *Routledge Companion to Gothic*. Eds. Catherine Spooner and Emma McEvoy. London: Taylor & Francis, 2007. 63–72. Print.

"Halloween, Pt. 1." *American Horror Story: The Complete First Season*. Writ. James Wong. Dir. David Semel. Twentieth Century Fox, 2012. DVD.

"Halloween, Pt. 2." *American Horror Story: The Complete First Season*. Writ. Tim Minear. Dir. David Semel. Twentieth Century Fox, 2012. DVD.

Helsloot, John. "The Fun of Fear: Performing Halloween in the Netherlands." *Treat or Trick? Halloween in a Globalising World*. Eds. Malcolm Foley and Hugh O'Donnell. Newcastle upon Tyne: Cambridge Scholars Publishing, 2009. 155–169. Print.

Johnston, Derek. *Haunted Seasons: Television Ghost Stories for Christmas and Horror for Halloween*. Houndmills: Palgrave Macmillan, 2015. Print.

Jontes, Dejan. "Resisting Halloween in Slovenia: A Case of Anti-Americanism." *Treat or Trick? Halloween in a Globalising World*. Eds. Malcolm Foley and Hugh O'Donnell. Newcastle upon Tyne: Cambridge Scholars Publishing, 2009. 249–258. Print.

Lury, Karen. *Interpreting Television*. London: Hodder Arnold, 2005. Print.

Madsen, Deborah L. "Witch-Hunting: American Exceptionalism and Global Terrorism." *American Exceptionalisms: From Winthrop to Winfrey*. Eds. Sylvia Söderlind and James Taylor Carson. Albany: State University of New York Press, 2011. 15–29. Print.

Mather, Cotton, and Increase Mather. *The Wonders of the Invisible World, Being an Account of the Tryals of Several Witches Lately Executed in New-England, to Which Is Added a Farther Account of the Tryals of the New-England Witches*. 1693. London: John Russell Smith, 1862. Print.

Mikos, Lothar. "How the Pumpkins Conquered Germany: Halloween, Media and Reflexive Modernization in Germany." *Treat or Trick? Halloween in a Globalising World*. Eds. Malcolm Foley and Hugh O'Donnell. Newcastle upon Tyne: Cambridge Scholars Publishing, 2009. 113–130. Print.

Mittell, Jason. *Television and American Culture*. Oxford: Oxford University Press, 2010. Print.

Murphy, Bernice M. *The Suburban Gothic in American Popular Culture*. Basingstoke: Palgrave Macmillan, 2009. Print

Nissenbaum, Stephen. *The Battle for Christmas: A Cultural History of America's Most Cherished Holiday*. New York: Vintage Books, 1997. Print.

Prokhorova, Larisa. "Halloween in Russia: What Makes an Unwelcome Guest Stay." *Treat or Trick? Halloween in a Globalising World*. Eds. Malcolm Foley and Hugh O'Donnell. Newcastle upon Tyne: Cambridge Scholars Publishing, 2009. 145–154. Print.

Rogers, Nicholas. *Halloween: From Pagan Ritual to Party Night*. New York: Oxford University Press, 2003. Print.

"Room Service." *American Horror Story: Hotel*. Writ. Ned Martel. Dir. Michael Goi. FX Network. 4 November 2015. Television.

Thompson, Robert J. *From "Hill Street Blues" to "E.R.": Television's Second Golden Age*. New York: Syracuse University Press, 1996. Print.

"Tricks and Treats." *American Horror Story: Asylum. The Complete Second Season*. Writ. James Wong. Dir. Bradley Buecker. Twentieth Century Fox, 2013. DVD.

Turner, Victor. *The Ritual Process: Structure and Anti-Structure*. New York: Aldine De Gruyter, 1995. Print.

"Unholy Night." *American Horror Story: Asylum. The Complete Second Season*. Writ. James Wong. Dir. Michael Lehmann. Twentieth Century Fox, 2013. DVD.

Williams, Tony. *Hearths of Darkness: Family in the American Horror Film*. London: Associated University Presses, 1996. Print.

PART TWO

Issues of Representation

Static Femininity
Gender and Familial Representation in Murder House

Nikki Cox

American popular culture often promotes binaries to establish and maintain a framework of security which reinforces what we "know" to be true and factual. Mary Douglas (9) explains in *Purity and Danger* (1966) that our cultural conceptions of good and bad, clean versus dirty, sacred versus profane (Durkheim 37–38) order our lives and have a critical effect on our routines and ideology. However, human beings are more complex than the static dichotomies we find in American culture, especially regarding gender. Gender is a topic of much current debate, as individuals (e.g. Chastity Bono, Laverne Cox, Caitlyn Jenner) have publicly shared their struggles with identity: male versus female, man versus woman, masculine versus feminine, gay versus straight. These perceived dichotomies seem to leave no grey area. However, humans are not as unified and static as images might depict; rather, sex, gender, sexuality and self presentation are fluid (Fontanella, Maretti and Sarra 2554). Individuals are a combination of genetic material and cultural influence, nature and nurture. Biological sex is not gender; gender does not determine sexual orientation and representations of self have little to do with biological sex. These are all small parts of an individual's identity, but must not be aligned in any one way to be correct, or "normal."

This is all to say, there is no normal. There is no stable identity that any female or woman, male or man, or any self identifier for that matter, should hold. This essay utilizes *American Horror Story: Murder House* as a case study addressing the problematic assumptions and representations of gender in American popular culture. While I cannot claim to know whether the show creators Brad Falchuk and Ryan Murphy deliberately reinforced traditional gender roles, I aim to highlight precisely how problematic these representations are and how they accomplish their ideological work within the series. I begin by providing a brief overview of the show, as some aspects of the house's history or plot of the show provide relevant information pertaining to character development, or the lack thereof. I provide examples of both the male forgivable fool and female baby crazed villain, showing the unification of characteristics into stereotypes. And finally I address the importance of this gender dichotomy in American popular culture.

A brief overview of the plot will serve to clarify the issues at stake here.[1] For example, after psychiatrist Ben Harmon has an affair with a student, the Harmons move from New York to Los Angeles. Wife, Vivien, struggles to forgive him. In a last-ditch effort the family, with angsty daughter Violet, moves across the country for a fresh start. The family is hesitant to purchase the home when the realtor reveals the last owners were found in the basement dead, an apparent murder-suicide. Violet insists the family purchase the house, "Murder House." Since the building of the home in 1920 a total of twenty-four people have died in the house. Twenty-two ghosts remain in the home at the season's end. This means that twenty-four individuals with their own selfish motivations must maneuver through limited space and resources but endless time.

The house's history is complex. Each previous owner has their own unique set of problems, though there is a clear connection between the residents through time. As Janani Subramanian explains, each "family is psychologically and physically tormented by the house's 'moral rot and emotional ugliness' and the past and present intersect in twisted and vicious ways as the house's secrets emerge" (113). The house's dark history haunts the family. Each of the former residents, now trapped inside the house, torments the Harmons. Women unite pursuing the unified goal; a child. *Murder House* is an intricately arranged series of flashbacks and present day vignettes, presenting a twisted history and explanation of the hauntings. The characters provide a representation of clichés and stereotypes, which, while utilizing the experience of the supernatural, emphasize a social commentary on gender norms and the American family.

The motivations of each character, regardless of sex, are united in upholding materialistic American culture. Both men and women are driven by the goal of accumulation of social capital, a proper home and children, to demonstrate their roles as successful members of society. Yet there is a gendered angle here. Men are expected to provide for their families. In this powerful role as providers, men manipulate that power in wicked ways. Women's expectations are drastically different. Women are expected to produce and care for children. This archaic view of women's roles is shown to be a very real condition of modern womanhood in American culture. The season carefully reveals how each character's motivations relate to this commonly held goal of familial success. Michelle Zimbalist Rosaldo explains that "Social scientists have by and large taken male authority for granted: they have also tended to accept a male view that sees the exercise of power by women as manipulative, disruptive, illegitimate, or unimportant" (21). In *Murder House*, male authority is clearly demonstrated and female characters are depicted exactly as Rosaldo explains: "manipulative, disruptive, illegitimate, or unimportant." The role of women, represented through this stereotype, is made clear through the generalized representation through time demonstrated by interactions between characters from different periods in time.

The Mechanism: Murder House and the Supernatural

Murder House is filled with individuals generalized into two distinct genders. The interactions among the supernatural "ghosts" and the living residents are complicated. The "ghosts" that remain in the house are attached to the land. They are free to roam only on Halloween, then again are bound to Murder House as is seen in the two Halloween episodes. These ghosts range in not only their abilities, but their manifestations and characteristics. As explained by James McClenon in "Haunting and Poltergeist Cases: Constructing Folk Belief," hauntings typically follow progressive stages, are experience based and are a collective behavior process which shape the narratives of those who have the experience (61). Utilizing David Hufford's experiential source hypothesis, McClenon investigates hauntings as experiences, regardless of the legitimacy of their happening (Hufford 19). The experience occurs to an individual no matter how illogical or irrational the believed cause. In the case of *Murder House*, these experiences are never questioned. The living participate (Greenwood 29–32) in the present, interacting, both knowingly and unknowingly with these ghosts. These ghosts are not entirely apparitions, as they remain attached to a specific place (McClenon 61). Though the ghosts display classic aspects of poltergeist activity (61), they are vocal and capable of moving things. Ghosts are also capable of passing as living individuals. The dead help, guide and interact with the living without knowing or acknowledging their supernatural experience. This effectively blurs the most blatant and realistic dichotomy of life and death.

By utilizing this dynamic, the supernatural, Falchuk and Murphy create a scenario in which different periods of time can come face to face, interacting in a single moment. The supernatural accounts for not only simple interactions, such as Constance's daughter, Addy's friendship with the ghosts in the house, but also for the complex happenings of the entire group. The living and the dead become intertwined, united in their motivations and desires, separated by the limits of death and the realities of life. There is some variation in what ghosts can do. For example, some age, Moira grows old and Thaddeus becomes a larger monster. Still others never change, Nora remains a young woman and the twins are still children. Some ghosts need to be told they have passed on, others are aware they have died. Additionally, ghosts have the ability to kill the living, but are unaffected by any actions of the living aside from the rejection of their existence.

Early in the season the audience becomes aware of how complicated this "haunting" is when Ben's young patient, Tate, disguises himself in the latex suit to become Rubber Man. Believing Ben has put on the suit, Vivien and Rubber Man begin to have sex ("Pilot"). The audience experiences flashes of Ben sleep-walking at the stove and Vivien being raped by Rubber Man. It becomes apparent that ghosts will not simply scare the home's residents, but will intentionally manipulate and torment them. Further, examples such as Moira's differing appearance provide the vehicle for social commentary, demonstrating men's objectification of women and women's role as objects. Moira is introduced as an old maid, in a uniform, ready to be of service. She is clearly past her days of reproduction and therefore useless in the eyes of any man. However, when seen through the eyes of a man, Moira is young, dressed in a risqué manner, seductive in every sense of the word. This is addressed a multitude of times throughout the season. Moira insists, "I'm not naive to the ways of men, their need to objectify, conquer. They see what they want to see. Women, however, see into the soul of a person" ("Murder House"). She addresses the two very dynamic categories that are represented within the show, which are only made possible with her ability to shift between the two manifestations of women in her ghostly state.

Generalized Genders

Reinforcing a binary categorization, *Murder House* makes grand generalizations about the gender stereotypes associated with the typified American family. As Judith Butler argues, gender—and sex for that matter—is a performative act (8–9). Butler asserts in *Gender Trouble* (1990) that gender and sex are one and the same, as there is no sex acknowledged that is not associated with a gender. Therefore, sex is gendered, and gender is a performative act developed and controlled by cultural action. Utilizing Butler's assessment of gender, I argue that *Murder House* uses this gender binary to depict very specific stereotypes which represent two clear categories of performed gender. Each gender is preoccupied with the physical act of sex for radically different reasons.

Men are represented as overcome by sexual desire, completely ravenous for the physical act of coitus and unencumbered by their disloyalty, sin and mistakes. Sex is a position of power and representative of the vulnerability of females. As explained by Kimberle Crenshaw: "race, gender, and other identity categories are most often treated in mainstream liberal discourse as vestiges of bias or domination—that is, as intrinsically negative frameworks in which social power works to exclude or marginalize those who are different" (1242). The category of male or man is privileged over the category of female. The male, typically forgiven for his sins, is a lovable idiot who is never liable for errors, usually because they are justified, most commonly by the horrendous acts of his wife.

Women are depicted as dependent on reproduction and the manifestation of a complete and perfect family. This is a very "American" theme, perpetuated by the dream of the American family: husband, wife, children, dog, white picket fence. It is also important to note that women are depicted as to blame for the majority of the male failure. Women are represented by a group of callous, at times vengeful, female characters. With few exceptions, women here are painted as evil monsters with self-serving intentions. Womanhood is seen as inevitably connected to motherhood. A successful marriage is the ultimate measure of a person's success and worth. The male's preoccupation with sex is beneficial to women desiring children, but also connects their success to motherhood and in effect, men. This generalization leads to tension, as "ignoring the difference *within* groups (women) contributes to tension *among* groups" [original emphases] (Crenshaw 1242). Women become a unified group despite the reality of a multiplicity of roles. Identity is more than simply sex but is reduced to singular and static images of cultural expectations of gender.

Aviva Briefel explains that there are two modes of monstrous characterization: masochism and menstruation (16–20). Male monsters are typically either part of a sadistic rampage, or are self-mutilative, attributes which are intended to close off the audience from the monster, keeping the audience at a distance because of the violent outbursts on the screen. However, the distance between the male monsters and the viewers is not the same as with female monsters. Females' menstruation positions the audience uncomfortably close (Briefel 20). Male monsters are detached from the audience, portrayed from an emotional distance as cold or unfeeling. Women, however, are in positions forcibly close through emotive and uncontrollable physical processes of menstruation, birth and rape (20). In essence, the masochism versus menstruation argument explains the dominant and aggressive male which contrasts with the female villainized victim. Such generalizations about the abilities and motives of these individuals make a larger and more prominent statement about the American dream, the American family and the American social landscape as a whole.

Men: Sex and Power

While men are represented as stupidly loyal and consistently disappointing, this is only a superficial analysis. Beneath the subtle commentary lies a far stronger connotation about the power men hold over women. While they are lovable fools, they are also villains. Masquerading as well-meaning, men intentionally perpetuate misrepresentations of women's reality and mental health. For example, Ben Harmon, the current and only living male resident of the house, is dedicated to reviving his marriage. He is distracted though, by remnants of his own mistakes. Vivien, his wife, experienced a late term miscarriage, forcing her to give birth to a dead son. In the face of Vivien's grief, Ben feels isolated and alone. Acting out against his perception of abandonment, Ben has an affair with a far younger student. This is a common theme seen throughout cinema. Kathleen Rowe Karlyn investigates this occurrence in the film *American Beauty* (Sam Mendes, 1999).

Karlyn argues that there is an over-sexualization of young women which has been paired with the avoidance or villainization of the mother and career-woman figures. This representation of women is complementary to that of middle-aged white males experiencing midlife crises. The paired characterization of the sexualized young female with the middle-aged man is explained as a remasculinzation of the man, due to the emasculation that is typically directly related to a home life with an overbearing wife (Karlyn 69). In the case of *Murder House*, Vivien plays the collusive mother (74), unavailable sexually, emotionally detached and in effect, responsible for her husband's unhappiness, relieving him of the guilt of his adulterous affair. Ben, however, is the romantic hero/victim (79). He is the victim of his wife's abandonment, his actions justified, his emotions more important than his wife's.

Despite his affair, Ben and Vivien make one last attempt at fixing their broken marriage. The family moves into Murder House for a fresh start. While he is working on his relationship with Vivien, Ben remains selfish. He demands Vivien stop punishing him, when in reality she is struggling to find herself. Being a psychiatrist, Ben almost innately diagnoses his family. However, since moving into the house, Ben has been falling asleep and waking up in strange places. He never once questions his own sanity, or seeks help for his problem. Even though he is struggling with his own issues, Ben is given the authority and power to demean other's representations of self (Foucault, *The History of Sexuality* 67). He tells his wife that she has post-traumatic stress disorder and just needs medication. Later, he attacks Vivien's desperate attempts to provide for their unborn child by eating brain for its nutrients by manipulating her motives and calling her crazy. Eventually, he has Vivien restrained and hospitalized, believing that her rape was a fantasy. This specific example is crucial because Ben is acting out of his own hurt, he believes

Vivien must have cheated on him because she is pregnant with twins who have different fathers. When Vivien explains that she was raped, he refuses the response and immediately uses his position of power, both as a man and a doctor of psychiatry, to demean and belittle her by committing her to a mental evaluation.[2]

The diagnosis of women by men occurs immediately in the show. In Vivien's first scene she is in stirrups being examined by a male doctor ("Pilot"). He compares her to a house with a cracked foundation and tells her he can prescribe her medication that will make her feel younger, demonstrating the cultural obsession with youth and reproduction. When Vivien tells him she is not a house and refuses the medication, he asks her what she's afraid of. This scene is utilized again in the episode when Ben is alone with Moira, presenting as the young sexy vixen. He denies her advances, as he is attempting to repair his marriage. Moira then asks him: "What are you afraid of?" The show simplifies the fears of each sex: women fear aging and losing their ability to be mothers, men fear losing their control over women.

Ben struggles with monogamy throughout the season. Moira is consistently tempting him. When his mistress, Hayden, returns she longs for his affection. And when approached by Patrick, another former resident of Murder House, masquerading as a living person, Ben denies his advances, asserting his heteronormative sexuality. It is not simply sex Ben desires, but the conquering of women. Further, Ben's moral character is clarified when he learns that he has impregnated two women at the same time. One pregnancy is joyous: his pregnant wife represents a successful marriage. Ben calls this baby their "salvation" ("Home Invasion"). While the other pregnancy is shameful, his mistress's baby is a symbol of his infidelity and failed marriage.

When Vivien finally decides that she can no longer work on their marriage, she tells Ben he is "disgusting and disappointing as a man," but he is a good father ("Piggy Piggy"). Here, unlike with the women of *Murder House*, Ben's manhood is separated from his abilities as a father. This is a complete contradiction of the standards of female success. Women are failures as mothers and women, but Ben, and men in general, are allowed to fail at one, but succeed in the other. Men are granted the ability to enact multiple aspects to their identities, while women are stuck within a singular and static image, connected solely to motherhood and associated almost exclusively with negative character traits.

This can be seen in many other television shows. For example, in "I Have a Character Issue" *Breaking Bad*'s Anna Gunn explains how her "strong, nonsubmissive, ill-treated" character Skyler White, and in effect herself, are hated for being husband Walter White's antagonist. Gunn explains that the character refuses to "collapse in the corner or wring her hands in despair" and continues:

I realize that viewers are entitled to have whatever feelings they want about the characters they watch. But as a human being, I'm concerned that so many people react to Skyler with such venom. Could it be they can't stand a woman who won't suffer silently or "stand by her man?" That they despise her because she won't back down or give up? Or because she is, in fact, [a man's] equal? [Gunn].

Gunn mentions that other complex television wives are viewed similarly, for example, Carmela Soprano of *The Sopranos* (1999–2007) and Betty Draper of *Mad Men* (2007–2015). While Skyler and others are not represented as solely connected to reproduction as the women of *Murder House*, they are viewed by the audience as problematic, negative and bad. Female strength and power are reduced, their male counterparts celebrated despite their own character flaws.

In *Murder House* there is a unification of male character traits. Dr. Charles Montgomery, the original builder of the home, is a drug addicted dependent failure. Here, the representation of women, and justification for male failure is epitomized. Nora, Charles's wife, is consistently disappointed. Charles simply wants her approval, but gets nothing but grief from his cold, bitter and distant wife. Being well meaning, Charles agrees to a scheme developed by Nora to help "girls in trouble" by performing abortions (an interesting male juxtaposition with the female obsession with giving life). When the remnants of the couple's kidnapped son, Thaddeus, reemerge, Charles pairs his Frankenstein complex with animal parts in an attempt to fix his boy. His good intentions are met with grief and despair when his son becomes a monster. Charles's well-meaning actions are met with critical responses, Nora assures him she is proud before killing him, but his failure is met with his own demise ("Open House").

Another well-meaning fool, Larry Harvey, is hopelessly in love with Constance. Larry begins an affair with Constance, who is using Larry not only to boost her own self-esteem, but also to attempt to regain the Murder House following the collapse of Constance's marriage and family. Larry is married to Lorraine and the couple has two young daughters. Larry attempts to maintain his reputation as a good father by assuring Lorraine he will care for the girls, but clearly is no longer a good man, asking her to leave the family's home to move his mistress in. Lorraine responds to Larry's request by setting both herself and their two daughters on fire. Larry moves Constance and her children back into the house, and remains loyal to her despite her unwillingness to be compassionate to him. Later, Larry confesses that "I'm still alive, and I still love you" ("Smoldering Children"). Constance tells him: "That's your problem—I never loved you, I endured you for my family—even a boy (Travis, her young lover) was twice the man you are."

Constance's lover, Travis is the epitome of the cliché "young and stupid." Travis is a good boy, not yet a man. He is patient with Adelaide, Constance's daughter who has Down's Syndrome. However, he is unfaithful to Constance. Unwilling to compromise his future as an actor to start a family with Constance, the couple fights. This echoes Constance's past desire to be an actress. She had refused nudity and was forced to abandon her dream to care for her family. Frustrated, Constance kicks him out. He then sleeps with Hayden, Ben's former lover, before deciding to return to Constance because he loves her. He is a lovable fool, but also a mechanism of the show to demonstrate the male's loyalty to the female villain, as well as the female insecurity that comes with age and loss of reproduction. This maintains the continuity of the betrayal by men of women they love.

Constance's son Tate is a young, immature and jaded teenage boy, who happens to be dead. Tate feels both rejected by his father and ignored by his grieving mother. He is emotionally damaged and in need of approval and guidance. Tate interacts with Nora, while he is still alive, and forms a bond. He wants to help, representing that well-meaning aspect of the male character type. However, his attempts to provide Nora with a child show his violent side. Violence is the most prominent aspect of Tate's character. Before his death, Tate burns Larry and kills fifteen teenagers in a school shooting. Tate is shot by the SWAT team that storms into his room following the school shooting, and, as he reaches for a gun to kill himself, he is shot in a storm of bullets. Following his death, he kills both Chad and Patrick when their relationship falls apart and will unlikely yield a child. Tate rapes Vivien in an attempt to provide a baby to Nora. Additionally, Tate is completely willing and even prepared to kill anyone for Violet. However, following the typical characterization of men, Tate cheats on Violet when he rapes her mother. He is romanticized as a dutiful boyfriend, constantly trying to please the women he loves, but inevitably succumbs to his mental anguish by acting out in violent and aggressive ways.

Men are portrayed by characters that have unified character traits. They are dedicated and loyal to the women they love, but unafraid to cross boundaries of marriage, committed relationships and monogamy. Men are vilified by those women who are greatly affected by their actions, but men are ultimately justified by the representation of those women as impossible to please, difficult and vengeful. Women create a loophole for men to be unhappy, frustrated, unfaithful or aggressive. The male is capable of being a bad man but a good father. For men, their ability as a father is completely detached from their actions as a husband or individual. The male is a lovable fool who is continuously making mistakes, but justified in this because of his powerful ability to reign over the unforgiving and cold female.

Women: "moral rot and emotional ugliness"

Male representation would be incomplete with a female counterpart to demonstrate the complete dichotomy of gender. Women demonstrate the contrast to the forgivable oafish male by being coldly unforgiving. The female voice legitimizes this commentary on the American family and American dream. Subramanian argues that the women's physical form in *AHS* also reflects their characterization: "*AHS* is gothic television to the extreme, and its use of visual effects, while intended to frighten and disgust the audience, also make the show's female bodies in a way that liberalizes the 'moral rot and emotional ugliness' of domesticity itself" (114). Throughout the show, women are portrayed as needing the experience of motherhood to be successful women while maintaining the socially accepted standards of beauty. They remain aggressive, demanding, greedy and competitive despite their slim form, long hair and delicate features. Special effects make-up is employed to make visible their internal ugliness: Nora's gunshot wound; Old Moira's appearance; Hayden's death; the discovery of Violet's body; each of these is somehow separate from their typical physical appearance, with the exception of Moira. Half of the time, Moira is scantily-clad in an over-sexualized uniform with flawless makeup. While physical appearance plays a role in characterization, the shared, innate desire of Nora, Constance, Hayden and Vivien to be successful mothers is the most prominent trait and the motivating factor for the female's ugliness.

Nora, a greedy East Coast socialite, is consistently disappointed. She is impossible to please and consistently preoccupied by her desire for more. Nora tells her husband Charles he is a disgrace of a man. She complains about having only two servants and being "expected to do everything else" ("Murder House"). Baby Thaddeus is taken from the table as he cries and it is clear to the audience that Nora is a mother and wife in title only, her actions are clearly rooted in wealth, privilege and arrogance. As previously mentioned, Charles begins performing abortions to make extra money when the family has financial trouble. A vengeful boyfriend steals Thaddeus, returning him in pieces. Nora spends the next century longing for her child. Young, living Tate interacts with dead Nora as she weeps for her son. Though, after Nora takes Viven's dead baby, Nora is keen to hand the child off. Nora sits in the basement of the house, rocking the screaming child only to hand the baby to Vivien believing that she is a nanny. Nora watches as Vivien instantly calms the baby and says she will leave the baby with Vivien because she just doesn't have the patience to be a mother, mentioning that her mother wasn't good at it either. Moira comments that Nora doesn't have "a motherly bone in her body"; rather "she [Nora] just got stuck on that idea" ("Afterbirth"). But that idea consumes Nora entirely. As explained by Rosaldo, "Danger is perceived only when a woman fails to bear children, or when her husband or children have died" (32). Nora never stops desiring a child, and the label, she simply requires another to care for the baby. She was fed the idea that her own worth and value as a woman was deeply seated in her role as a mother.

Constance, a bitter old racist, is one the few living characters who longs for attention and once had dreams of being a star. She kills her husband, Hugo, after she catches him raping Moira. Moira has had consensual sex with Hugo once before, but when Moira later denies his advances, Hugo forces himself on her. Constance shoots Moira through the eye and Hugo three times in the chest. With her husband dead, Constance's children are her sole symbol of success as a woman. However, each of her children has a terrible "affliction": Adelaide has Down's Syndrome, Beauregard is a mutant, the third child is never discussed and Tate is physically perfect but suffers severe emotional disturbance. Having aged, Constance is jealous of younger women and has no compassion or sympathy for anyone but herself. She has lost her chance to be revered for her looks and is relying on her abilities as a mother to find success. She wants nothing more than a healthy child, especially since her marriage has failed. Constance is deeply resentful of her husband, and in effect men. She mentions to Moira that "men lie, it's in their nature" ("Open House"). Constance is a symbol of the remnants. American society so often perpetuates images of youth being beauty. Women who cannot reproduce are villainized, demonized and disregarded. The ugly old hag, the evil stepmother, the witch, these stereotypes have to do with the jealousy of older women who can no longer produce children, whose "singular" purpose has or no longer can be served. At one point, Constance angrily declares: "One day your time will end and they will be building on top of you, too" ("Open House").

Hayden is a young, bitter and vengeful woman, now incapable of reproducing because she is dead. She is manipulative, needy and weak. Hayden desires love and approval, as Charles did of Nora, but is vilified because Ben, like Nora, rejects Hayden's attempt to please him. Hayden takes advantage of Ben when he is most vulnerable. She became his mistress despite knowing he was a married man. And, because she wants his approval so much, she traps him by becoming pregnant. After the Harmons move to LA, Hayden initially contacts Ben to have an abortion. While waiting for Hayden in the abortion clinic, Ben receives a call that his family is in trouble. He abandons her, and Hayden leaves the clinic before the abortion is performed. Hayden is killed by Larry after vengefully returning and threatening to reveal their love child to Vivien, who is currently pregnant as well. Hayden tells Ben, "I'm not a whore Ben. I matter. I MATTER!" ("Murder House"). Her ghost becomes obsessed with the baby she will never have. She feels that it is unfair that Vivien is alive and having Ben's child. She confronts Ben, telling him they were "written in the stars," but Ben confesses that he was lonely, heart-broken and he used her ("Spooky Little Girl"). Ben doesn't love Hayden. Hayden remains trapped, in love with a man that does not want her, seeking revenge for her death and longing for the child she was denied.

Moira is a liminal character, both a villain and a hero, demonstrating the interpretation of woman by the male and female gaze. She manifests as both a wise old housekeeper and a young seductive vixen-maid. Young Moira is perhaps vengeful, her naive and compulsive mistake of an affair with Hugo having trapped her in the Murder House for eternity. However, her ability to manifest in both forms presents to the audience the moral intentions of each individual and further represents the motives of men and women. Young Moira manipulates and seduces men for her own advantage, utilizing her beauty and their weakness. However, old Moira is modest and wise, a confidant to Vivien. Moira misses her mother and despises that she is stuck in the house with people she hates. She reinforces the established gender roles; young Moira's purpose is solely to seduce and manipulate men, whereas old Moira is a partner to women, reminding women of men's power and force. Despite being a partner, Moira accepts and reinforces women's place in the home, when Vivien asks if she ever gets tired of cleaning other people's houses, she says that "we're women, it's what we do" ("Pilot").

Moira demands Vivien fight for her own voice. Moira's strong statements about men speak to the depiction of men in *Murder House* and the male-female dynamic of degrading or dismissing female emotions and pain. In the episode "Rubber Man" Moira asserts: "That's what men do. They make you think you're crazy, so they can have their fun." She continues: "Since the beginning of time men find excuses to lock women away. They make up diseases, like hysteria. Do you know where that word comes from?" When Vivien says "no," Moira tells her: "The Greek word for uterus. In the second century, they thought it was caused by sexual deprivation and the only possible cure was hysteria paroxysm. Orgasms. Doctors would masturbate women in their office and call it medicine." Moira identifies the power men hold over women through sex, which is the intersection of bodily discipline and population control, explained by Foucault's analysis of systems of power (*The Foucault Reader* 67).

In *Murder House* the issue of mental illness and the power of diagnosis are similar to male to female dynamics (*The Foucault Reader* 67). Vivien's character is introduced in a doctor's office discussing her menstruation, a key, as Briefel would argue, to establish herself as a monster that is closely related to the audience. There is no separation of the audience from Vivien's horror and no hesitancy from the male doctor about insisting on how she cares for her body. The doctor forcefully suggests medication to Vivien who resists, not wanting medication because she "just wants control of her body back" ("Pilot"). Vivien is the character most affected by the evaluation of men. As mentioned previously, Ben often attempts to diagnose her with post-traumatic stress disorder and delusion, eventually having her committed to a mental hospital believing her rape was a fantasy. Men continuously demean the mental stability and intellectual capacity of women. As the doctor hands Vivien a prescription for a drug to make her feel young he asks: "What are you afraid of?"

This introduction to Vivien provides a clear image of who she is as a woman. She fills the prescription, but does not take the medication. She acts within her role as a woman, subservient to male desire for young sexualized women; but is skeptical of her need to fill this role. Vivien's character is a staunch contrast to the other women portrayed in the season. She is a sweet and well-meaning mother to her daughter, Violet. Though, following the miscarriage and consequent birth of her dead son, Vivien has lost herself and consequentially abandons her role as a mother and wife. Ben carries on an affair with a young student, leaving Vivien to grieve not only the loss of her child, but of her marriage. She is vulnerable, soft and weak, as well as kind and compassionate. These traits are viewed, in comparison to men, as negative or lesser.

Vivien differs from most of the other female characters in that she is alive and pregnant. Vivien's fertility is key to her femininity. The loss of her son demonstrates the beginning of the decline of her fertility, and therefore, her value as a woman. This is echoed when her daughter reacts poorly to her pregnancy. When Vivien becomes pregnant, it is not only notable that her pregnancy is a challenge to the social norms of reproduction, as the twins she bears hold their own symbolic importance. As Dawn Keetley explains, due to:

> the literal association of twins with reproductive technologies and aging mothers.... Twins thus stand in for a series of literal anxieties about interwoven children and homes—about the future of the "American Dream"—that have plagued the United States in particular since the beginning of the recession (2007 through at least the end of 2012) [89].

The pressures within American society related to the contemporary economic collapse are represented in *Murder House*: "with its entrapping houses and multiple dead infants, *AHS* quite overtly registers contemporary fears about impending societal collapse brought about by the recent housing crisis in the US and the subsequent, sustained recession" (Keetley 92). Vivien's anxieties related to her pregnancy and the home are rooted in the American social landscape. The pressures of social order in the U.S. have taught women to be dependent on their ability to provide and domestically care for a successful family. Despite her villainization by Ben, Vivien remains as strong, powerful and determined as the other female characters are, but in a more respectable way. She fights for her marriage: when Hayden, Ben's mistress appears, Vivien battles her. She is struck with jealousy and insecurity as the younger woman attempts to belittle her.

Vivien is the victim of rape and loses her husband to a young mistress. She miscarries her son, loses her daughter to suicide, her newborn son to the ghosts of the house and the child of her rape kills her in childbirth. Despite her constant struggle, being attacked by both her husband's mistress and a group of crazed murders staging a reenactment of a historical murder, as well as consistently being tormented by the individual spirits that remain in her home, Vivien fights to survive. She remains kind and compassionate, but also strong and independent. In each loss she still manages to push through. Vivien becomes the heroine; the survivor rather than the victim.

Vivien is the character that represents the true capabilities of a woman. However, she still fits the role of the damsel in distress, consistently in need of help. Her weakness comes from loss, of both a child and a husband, connecting her success to her familial life and reproduction. Her insecurities are heightened when challenged by a younger woman and confronted about having a child at her age. And, despite Vivien's strong moral character, she is still cheated on and blamed. Her familial security is broken by her husband, who is somehow justified due to her actions as a wife, mother and more importantly a woman.

Production and Reproduction

Each of these characters, male and female, desires a successful family. Men desire the position of power associated with fatherhood and husbandhood. They are rarely held responsible for their own failures, blaming them on the actions of women. And, a man's ability as a father does not directly correlate to his manhood. Women, however not only are expected to bear children, but their abilities as a wife and mother relate directly to their success as a woman. *Murder House* reflects the complex social landscape of the American family: the ability of men and women to reproduce and contribute to society, both physically in the familial structure, and also socioeconomically in accumulation and production of goods. The desire for the American dream, a married couple with children and a home (Cantor 24), connects each of these characters. Ben asks Vivien to go see the house in LA with the hope of a new start. Constance asks Travis to marry her, then tells him about the home and family they could build together. The need to be successful in the eyes of others, to attain social approval, or maybe even superiority, drives these individuals to act in unthinkably awful ways.

This is indicative of a material-obsessed capitalist society. American culture is driven by accumulation, both of goods and of children. The underlying importance of the physical space of the home demonstrates the importance of outward appearance—that of normalcy in American society. Normalcy requires an identity that fits within the constraints of the categories accepted by society. Men are expected to provide for their families. With the responsibility of financially providing for their families comes the failure of responsibility to honor the vows of marriage. Further, the patriarchal organization of society endows men with the right to viciously demean, diagnose and dominate women. Women are expected to produce children and reproduce the idyllic home life of a typified family. The women of *Murder House* are epitomized by collusive mothers, struggling to accept their place in society, which hinges on their fertility. A man's potential for success is endless, while a woman's is numbered by the amount of ova she has.

Further, the home is symbol of the typical/normal family. For women in *Murder House*, their success lies in filling the physical space with offspring. Motherhood determines the success of a woman, connecting her to nature in the nature versus culture dichotomy. Strong women are those who can fulfill their roles as mothers. Women are not depicted as anything but vessels for reproduction and vengeful reactions to the lack of offspring. Unlike women, men are evaluated by their cultural contributions and detached from their fatherly responsibilities. American culture emphasized an accumulation of wealth that is deeply connected to a male's success. For example, Nora's worth is linked to her son Thaddeus whereas Charles's relevance lies in his profession and work; Charles is criticized for not providing Nora with enough stuff; and Nora is criticized for lacking the skills to protect and care for her child.

This theme continues: Ben's worth lies in his position of power, as a man, but also as a professor and psychiatrist. Ben is an accomplished man, and a caring father, while being morally horrific. Vivien, however, becomes aware of her loss of social collateral as her reproductive years end. Vivien is seen as emotionally unstable and even deluded due to the male's interpretation of her truth. And further, she is criticized for breaking up her marriage for her own well-being (and that of her unborn twins) because it effectively destroys the familial dynamic. Vivien conforms to the show's female niche in her devotion to her unborn babies, but seemingly ignores her eldest, Violet. Vivien becomes preoccupied with the babies, deeming Violet more a woman than a child, and relentlessly pursues their health over her own.

Violet shows the fragility of a young woman, drawn into a chaotic relationship with Tate, the show's epitome of evil. Violet is blissfully unaware of the depths of Tate's darkness and romanticizes his psychopathy. It is not until Violet becomes aware that Tate has murdered both his classmates and the previous owners of the home, viciously burned his mother's boyfriend and raped Violet's mother that she leaves him. But, Tate has taken Violet's virginity and propels Violet into womanhood. Violet's angst and confusion are answered with the potential of reproduction.

Nora and Charles are shockingly similar to Vivien and Ben. Ben's infidelity and Charles's failure in business dissatisfy their wives. Vivien and Nora are preoccupied by their children, emphasizing their role as a mother. While there are individual characters that can be distinguished from each other, their similarities are striking even through nearly a century's worth of time. Male success remains separate from a male's ability as a father. Success as a man demands that a male provide for his family, and, as both Ben and Charles fail, their domination of women increases. Ben begins to diagnose his wife, and Charles aids Dr. Curan in dismembering the "Black Dahlia" (see Glossary). Nora and Vivien remain dissatisfied with their husbands and become preoccupied with their own role as mothers. Men and women remain distant. While male and female characters relate to characters of the same sex outside of the constraints of time, men and women remain clearly separated by their social roles.

The emphasis on the dichotomy between men and women, and the representation of men as static and women as developing steadily more evil through their lifetimes creates categories that audiences conceptualize as representative of reality. Cultural images, such as beloved characters in television shows, are often adopted and even emulated by fans (e.g. the creation of memes and fan fiction). In the eyes of the audience, these characters are people, giving credence to the stereotypes in the series.

Although I did not engage in thorough audience ethnography, I assembled and analyzed a data set of internet commentaries, consisting of hashtags from the blog building site, Tumblr. I utilized *American Horror Story: Murder House*-related hashtags including main characters' names, relationships between characters and the show's title to produce media data (photos, gifs, gif sets, fan art, fan fiction, etc.) associated with each hashtag. I found themes which support my analysis such as sexualization and the popularity of young women. For example, when the term "Moira O'Hara" is searched, results mirror the assertion that young women are more valuable, or at least more popular, than older women. The search of "Moira O'Hara" produces thousands of posts of young Moira in risqué clothing seductively cleaning, exposing or even pleasuring herself with hundreds of thousands of notes (the number of "likes" and "reblogs" combined, which is representative of a post's popularity on the site). The older Moira is quoted as saying, "we're all just lost souls aren't we?" and receives just twenty notes. Additionally, the proportion of young Moira to old Moira posts is staggering: at any point on the results page it is about 5:1 young Moira to old Moira. Despite the older Moira being more prominent throughout the season, young Moira is over-represented on this social media site

This trend is also echoed in searches for "Tate Langdon" which result in romanticized images of the actor Evan Peters. Captions on photos and gifs justify his actions and his unhealthy relationship with Violet. Male characters are romanticized, but this is not a result of objectification. Men's wickedness is overlooked, or possibly ignored, while women are shown enacting their "bitchy" personas. Nora is shown saying: "You're a waste. Even looking at you I'm sick to my stomach," while Vivien's famous line to Ben "and you buried your sorrow in some 21-year-old's pussy" appears often. Even these bitchy quotes from women are not nearly as popular on the site as images of handsome Evan Peters as Tate Langdon. Criticisms of the show's characters are far and few between. In this preliminary data set it is clear that the audience's positive response meshes with and upholds the representations in the show. The most popular posts demonstrate those aspects of the show that the audience consumes without question: male dominance and female submission. Furthermore, bitchy female ugliness is almost naturalized. In sum, the show has incited neither critique nor social outrage in its audience.

Conclusion

The Sartrean (1958) principle of "Hell is other people" is reflected in this series. The homeowners prior to the Harmons were a gay couple, Chad and Patrick, who were far from immune to the distinct categories of an American marriage. Chad desires a loving marriage and family. He is domestic and preoccupied with children, while Patrick is deeply dissatisfied with his overly critical partner. Patrick sneaks off to partake in affairs and one night stands, even offering to perform oral sex on Ben. He tries relentlessly to distract himself from Chad's overbearing nature. The couple's demise is due to their inability to get along. When Chad and Patrick argue, coming to the realization that they cannot remain together, and they will not be adopting a child, Tate kills them both. Despite operating outside of the traditional sexes associated with these gender roles, this couple fulfills the static image of gendered roles for each of the partners. They become one another's hell.

During therapy, in relating what Ben takes to be the teen's dark fantasy of embarking on a killing spree, Tate reveals: "It's a filthy, goddamn, helpless world. And, honestly, I feel like I'm helping to take them away from the shit and the piss and the vomit that run in the streets. I'm helping to take them somewhere clean and kind" ("Pilot"). Death is thus believed to be a release from these awful things, but *Murder House* shows that there is actually no escape from these social institutions. Ghosts are utilized to facilitate interactions between former and current owners, between history and modernity, connecting seamlessly the motives of the past to that of the present. *Murder*

House demonstrates the repressive and demeaning qualities associated with gender and familial structure that are seemingly timeless. The similarities between Nora and Constance are so strong that a generalized stereotype of women fits them both, despite the eighty years that separate them.

The mechanism of the supernatural provides the vehicle by which Falchuk and Murphy demonstrate that the antiquated gender stereotypes of the turn of the century are still prominent today. Falchuk and Murphy have portrayed the reality of a continued struggle. We must recognize the importance of gender representation in popular culture as it can reinforce hegemonic forces, causing a naturalization of this ideology and a perpetuation through enculturation. Representing only strict gender binaries reinforces the perception of binaries as truth. Non-conforming genders, sexes, orientations and identities are ignored entirely, or forced to fit within the masculine and feminine character niches. Further, as Butler explains, this generalization reinforces "the pervasive cultural condition in which women's lives [are] either misrepresented or not represented at all" (2). While gender may be socially constructed, is has a deeply important significance within our culture (Crenshaw 1296). These static representations refuse to acknowledge the true depth of a human being.

NOTES

1. *American Horror Story* is a unique television series in that each season is an entirely new installment, a different horror story. This is important to recognize because the characters in *Murder House* remain static within the specific season; they will not develop or change. The season I have chosen is, thus, representative of the character's complete arc.

2. Michel Foucault famously describes the connection of dominance through the development, deployment and reinforcement of sexuality (*The History of Sexuality* 110). One aspect of the deployment of sexuality is the hysterization of women, "which involved the medicalization of their bodies and their sex, [and] was carried out in the name of the responsibility they owed to health of their children, the solidity of the family institution, and the safeguarding of society" (147).

WORKS CITED

"Afterbirth." *American Horror Story: The Complete First Season*. Writ. Jessica Sharzer. Dir. Bradley Buecker. Twentieth Century Fox, 2012. DVD.

Briefel, Aviva. "Monster Pains: Masochism, Menstruation, and Identification in the Horror Film." *Film Quarterly* 58.3 (2005): 16–27. Print.

Butler, Judith. *Gender Trouble: Feminism and the Subversion of Identity*. New York: Routledge, 1990. Print.

Cantor, Paul A. "The Apocalyptic Strain in Popular Culture: The American Nightmare Becomes the American Dream." *Hedgehog Review* 15.2 (2013): 23–33. Web. 13 January 2016.

Crenshaw, Kimberle. "Mapping the Margins: Intersectionality, Identity Politics, and Violence Against Women of Color." *Stanford Law Review* 43.6 (1991): 1241–1299. Print.

Douglas, Mary. *Purity and Danger: An Analysis of Concepts of Pollution and Taboo*. New York: Praeger, 1966. Print.

Durkheim, Émile. *The Elementary Forms of Religious Life*. Trans. Karen E. Fields. New York: Free Press, 1995. Print.

Fontanella, Lara, Mara Maretti, and Annalina Sarra. "Gender Fluidity Across the World: A

Multilevel Item Response Theory Approach." *Quality and Quantity* 48.5 (2014): 2553–2568. Print.

Foucault, Michel. *The Foucault Reader*. Ed. Paul Rabinow. New York: Pantheon, 1984. Print.

_____. *The History of Sexuality*. Trans. Robert Hurley. New York: Vintage, 1988. Print.

Greenwood, Susan. *The Anthropology of Magic*. Oxford: Berg, 2009. Print.

Gunn, Anna. "I Have a Character Issue." *New York Times Online*. New York Times, 23 August 2013. Web. 13 January 2016.

"Home Invasion." *American Horror Story: The Complete First Season*. Writ. Ryan Murphy and Brad Falchuk. Dir. Alfonso Gomez-Rejon. Twentieth Century Fox, 2012. DVD.

Hufford, David. "Beings Without Bodies: An Experience-Centered Theory of the Belief in Spirits." *Out of the Ordinary: Folklore and the Supernatural*. Ed. Barbara Walker. Logan: Utah State University Press, 1995. 11–45. Print.

Karlyn, Kathleen Rowe. "'Too close for comfort': *American Beauty* and the Incest Motif." *Cinema Journal* 44.1 (2004): 69–93. Print.

Keetley, Dawn. "Stillborn: The Entropic Gothic of *American Horror Story*." *Gothic Studies* 15.2 (2013): 89–107. Print.

McClenon, James. "Haunting and Poltergeist Cases: Constructing Folk Belief." *Wondrous Events: Foundations of Religious Belief*. Philadelphia: University of Pennsylvania Press, 1994. Print.

"Murder House." *American Horror Story: The Complete First Season*. Writ. Jennifer Salt. Dir. Bradley Buecker. Twentieth Century Fox, 2012. DVD.

"Open House." *American Horror Story: The Complete First Season*. Writ. Brad Falchuk. Dir. Tim Hunter. Twentieth Century Fox, 2012. DVD.

"Piggy Piggy." *American Horror Story: The Complete First Season*. Writ. Jessica Sharzer. Dir. Michael Uppendahl. Twentieth Century Fox, 2012. DVD.

"Pilot." *American Horror Story: The Complete First Season*. Writ. Ryan Murphy and Brad Falchuk. Dir. Ryan Murphy. Twentieth Century Fox, 2012. DVD.

Rosaldo, Michelle Zimbalist. *Woman, Culture, and Society: A Theoretical Overview*. Eds. Michelle Zimbalist Rosaldo and Louise Lamphere. *Women, Culure, and Society*. Stanford: Stanford University Press, 1974. Print.

"Rubber Man." *American Horror Story: The Complete First Season*. Writ. Ryan Murphy. Dir. Miguel Arteta. Twentieth Century Fox, 2012. DVD.

Sartre, Jean-Paul. *No Exit, and Three Other Plays*. New York: Vintage, 1955. Print.

"Smoldering Children." *American Horror Story: The Complete First Season*. Writ. James Wong. Dir. Michael Lehmann. Twentieth Century Fox, 2012. DVD.

"Spooky Little Girl." *American Horror Story: The Complete First Season*. Writ. Jennifer Salt. Dir. John Scott. Twentieth Century Fox, 2012. DVD.

Subramanian, Janani. "The Monstrous Makeover: *American Horror Story*, Femininity and Special Effects." *Critical Studies in Television* 8.3 (2013): 108–123. Print.

The Minotaur, the Shears and the Melon Baller

Queerness and Self-Mortification in Coven

KYLE ETHRIDGE

Ryan Murphy and Brad Falchuk's anthology series *American Horror Story: Coven* premiered in 2013 on the heels of the previous seasons *Murder House* and *Asylum*. Starring Jessica Lange, Kathy Bates, Angela Bassett, and Sarah Paulson, the show features a group of witches who create a new representation of witches in popular culture. Stories like "Hansel and Gretel" and myths like Baba Yaga depict witches as crones intent upon eating children, sustaining themselves through deals with demons, or otherwise creating chaos.[1] Contemporary witches, especially in popular culture, exhibit more human characteristics than these classical representations. It is at this intersection of the monster and the human that this reading of *Coven* emerges. Marking a definite shift in the depiction of monstrosity, *Coven* offers a new understanding and representation of witches in popular culture. These witches craft this new identity by changing how they embody desire and how they receive or deny sexual fulfillment.

The third season of *American Horror Story* follows a Coven of witches based in Louisiana. The first witches escape from Salem, arrive in New Orleans and set up Miss Robichaux's Academy for Exceptional Young Ladies. Madison Montgomery, Zoe Benson, Nan, Queenie, and, eventually, Misty Day become members of the Coven. Daughter of Fiona Goode, Cordelia Foxx runs the academy. Though the witches face many problems, one of the largest is that Fiona has been largely absent during her time as the Supreme, the most powerful witch and political leader in the Coven. Her absence and abuse of the position have led to an infiltration of the Coven by a witch-hunting organization, of which Cordelia's husband, Hank, is a member. The Coven also faces renewed strife with the local voodoo practitioners led by Marie Laveau (see Glossary). The witches eventually join with Laveau, defeat the witch hunters, and depose Fiona as the Supreme. In order to save the Coven and find a new leader, one of the witches must successfully complete The Seven Wonders; Cordelia completes the ritual and ascends. With the help of Myrtle Snow, a sister witch and mother figure to Cordelia, she ushers the Coven into the public eye, encouraging other young witches to step forward and join the school's numbers.

Coven appears at a time of renewed interest in monsters, both culturally and critically. Along with a number of supernatural beings in films, movies, video games, and other cultural artifacts, the witch has recently received renewed critical attention as well. In her 2013 article "The Year of the Witch," Pamela J. Grossman notes that "The archetype of the witch is long overdue for celebration" and that "Witches are midwives to metamorphosis. They are magical women, and they, quite literally, change the world" (para. 3). The notion of change and metamorphosis especially parallels the witches in this season as it shows a different aspect of witches: their humanity through sexuality and desire. This essay analyzes the witches' relationship to sexual fulfillment, how violence mediates this relationship, and how queerness catalyzes a new representation of witches. Throughout this essay, I especially focus on Queenie's representation as a witch in relation to her fatness, Cordelia's identity as a witch as mediated by her desire to be a mother, and Myrtle's ostensible failure as a witch.

Defining Queerness

Queerness is not new to the horror genre; numerous critics have noted the connections among queerness as a social, sexual, political, or gender position and the narrative functions of horror. In *Skin Shows* (1995), Judith/Jack Halberstam claims the relationship between queerness and horror is partially in its "ability to reconfigure gender not simply through inversion by but literally creating new categories" (139). Indeed, this tendency is evident in *Coven* as queerness works to create a new understanding and representation of witches. Additionally, Sue-Ellen Case notes that queer sexualities mark a paradigm shift "out of the category of the living" (200). Horror narratives provide a fertile ground for the dead, undead, or otherwise supernatural to thrive and revel in their queer bodies, sexualities, or genders. However, little has been said about *Coven* and its queerness apart from online entertainment blogs. *Slate* even went so far as to have a weekly "How Queer is *American Horror Story: Coven*?" series to "call the corners and charm the most recent episode of its queer meaning, whether brazenly obvious or bubbling just below the cauldron's surface" (Lowder and Thomas para.1). Throughout the show, different characters present a type of sexual and social queerness: from the Axeman's phallic axe and saxophone to Delphine LaLaurie's BDSM-like treatment of her slaves (see Glossary) and even Myrtle's social marginalization by her peers, the queer spectrum is fully displayed.[2]

Queerness is a powerful position, partially because it can be so difficult to define or identify. Richard E. Zeikowitz provides a helpful, functional definition of queer, however, saying it can "signify any nonnormative behavior, relationship, or identity occurring at a specific moment. It may also describe an alternative form of desire that threatens the stability of the dominant norm" (67). Though this definition is admittedly broad, it is nevertheless useful. As a means of subversion, queerness calls into question heteronormativity and can thus critique a number of social ideologies, resulting in social progress and a deeper understanding of desire and sexual fulfillment. Throughout this analysis, queerness acts as a means of questioning structures of normative desire and their relationship to the body.

Most all sexual orientations receive sexual fulfillment in some capacity. Queerness can refer to control over one's sexual desire or a suppression of sexual fulfillment, primarily through sublimation. Sigmund Freud recognized this denial of sexual fulfillment as a type of queerness in his psychoanalytic framework, saying desire can "be diverted ('sublimated') in the direction of art, if its interest can be shifted away from the genitals on to the shape of the body as a whole" ("The Sexual Aberrations" 22). Though originally intended to represent a redirection of libidinal energies towards art or other humanist efforts, sublimated desire, and therefore denied sexual fulfillment, often operates as a type of queerness. *Coven*'s narrative does not allow for sexual desire to be fulfilled while the Coven is in danger, which is for most of the season, so the witches must sublimate their sexual desires and deny sexual fulfillment. In doing so, the figure of the witch transforms from a figure of sexual wantonness into a powerful, focused witch with control over her desires and the ability to effect change. Punitive violence awaits the witches in *Coven* who choose to indulge in sexual fulfillment. Witches who suppress, control, or deny their sexual fulfillment evade shared violence but still suffer violence at their own hands. This violence, however, is not punitive but empowering.

The Oxford English Dictionary defines mortification as "the action of mortifying the body, its appetites ... [especially] by the self-infliction or voluntary toleration of bodily pain or discomfort" ("mortification"). The term often refers to the practice of self-flagellation in monkhood as a means of purifying the spirit for growth in a religious domain.[3] Though the witches do not operate in the same religious sphere as would a monk, there are some similarities between their actions. In both Eastern and Western religious traditions, religion "played a central role in the attempt to contextualize pain meaningfully" (Shilling and Mellor 526). Violence and pain share a causal link, similar to how the witches' devotion to the Coven is similar to religious devotion. When the witches redirect their libidinal energies onto the Coven itself (much like a religious cause) and deny heteronormative desire and sexual fulfillment, this queering or sublimation is signified by a literal transformation of their magic into physically self-mortifying violence and subsequent pain. Often this shift is preceded by violence occurring as a result of an attempt to gratify the flesh through sexual fulfillment. In order to best protect the Coven, the witches offer a sacrifice of their own bodies and deny sexual fulfillment instead of engaging in sexual acts with another person. Subsequently, the witches use this augmented and strengthened magic to protect the Coven.

Monstrosity

The main figure used in this analysis is the monster, a source of fear and dread throughout history for many reasons. One reason that the monster is feared is because it illustrates an offensive difference, much like queerness does in regards to sexual heteronormativity. In the introduction to *Monster Theory: Reading Culture* (1996), Jeffrey Jerome Cohen outlines his idea of the monster, defining it as "an extreme version of marginalization, an abjecting epistemological device basic to the mechanics of deviance construction and identity formation" and an "uncertain cultural body in which is condensed an intriguing simultaneity or doubleness" (*ix*). As such, monsters illustrate issues of marginalization in texts as representative of society and culture. They dramatize and perhaps explain problems that cannot be understood on their own terms, much like the horror narrative. Halberstam adds to this monstrous purpose in arguing that monsters "make strange the categories of beauty, humanity, and identity that we still cling to" (*Skin Shows* 6). This tendency is also apparent in the depiction of witches in *Coven* as their "beauty, humanity, and identity" as monsters are all called into question.

Monsters emerge from cultural anxieties and mean something more than themselves. Cohen explains: "The monster is born only at this metaphoric crossroads, as an embodiment of a certain cultural moment.... The monstrous body is pure culture" (4). They are born in specific cultural moments that inform their meaning. As such, monsters must be understood within their contexts. Cohen expands on this statement: "The monster's body quite literally incorporates fear, desire, anxiety, and fantasy (ataratic or fantasy) giving them life and an uncanny independence" (4). As a signifier of social problems, monsters allow critics and authors methods of interrogating various societal and cultural problems as well as issues of race, gender, or sexuality. The witches in *Coven*, while also informing issues of gender and race, are used to examine issues of sexuality as realized in queerness. Seen in conversation with the sexuality of witches, this shift in representation of witches interrogates contemporary understandings of the figure.

Though this analysis does not necessarily include gender as such, witches are traditionally female, so gender is inextricable from the witch. Barbara Creed's *The Monstrous-Feminine: Film, Feminism, Psychoanalysis* (1993) examines the connection between monstrosity and femininity as they appear in horror films. Creed claims that "all human societies have a conception of the monstrous-feminine," citing Freud's and Joseph Campbell's separate con-clusions that women can be considered monstrous for their ability to castrate men and their invulnerability to the same (1). She goes on to say that women are so feared because they are "physically whole, intact and in possession of [their] sexual powers" (6). In the context of a Western horror film or text, a woman cannot be castrated and therefore presents a threat to a man's ability to remove her power (i.e. her sexual organs). In denying the normative (and arguably patriarchal) impulse to have sex, the witches of *Coven* can embody a certain feminine power. Through this newfound power, the witches protect the Coven, preserving the group as a woman-centered community.

Stephen T. Asma's *On Monsters: An Unnatural History of Our Worst Fears* (2009) chronicles, among other things, a history of witches, including how they came to their power. During the arguably misogynistic period of the Witch Trials, women were perceived as being "more completely dominated by sexual lust" and therefore more open to sexual relations with demons that would in turn empower them with witchcraft (118). I should note that Asma himself does not hold this deeply misogynistic point of view. He is discussing the *Malleus Maleficarum* (1486) by Heinrich Institoris, which is a sort of man-ual for witch hunters. Asma says that "women's amorous condition makes them easy targets for demons who wish to find some way to influence affairs" (118). Here we see the relationship between witches and desire most clearly: women who are too licentious or lustful are most susceptible to corruption as they are more likely to enter into sexual relations with demons or the Devil himself. Asma discusses this perception further, saying women's "receptacle natures were always in need of filling, and this made them crave penetration" (118). Obviously, these understandings of women are fraught with misogyny, but many classic depictions of witches are characterized by their sexual appetite. By denying or punishing the sexual act of penetration, *Coven* resists this historical representation of witchcraft. No penetration occurs without punishment in this world. By marking a shift from the hyper-sexualized witches of the past, *Coven* seeks to represent witches as women in control of their sexual identity who are, in some ways, more powerful than classical or historical representations.

Edward J. Ingebretsen begins to connect monsters and violence in *At Stake: Monsters and the Rhetoric of Fear in Public Culture* (2001). Though this text is more an examination of humans who exhibit monstrous behavior, monster theory supports his approach, which includes the element of violence that is necessary for this study. He claims that monsters can illustrate examples of "violences physical as well as rhetorical, social expressions of astonishment, scandal, and insult, displays of sex as moral currency and economic exchange" (2). The language of moral currency here is especially significant as this rhetoric helps describe the system in *Coven:* the give and take of violence, sexual fulfillment, and queerness all overlap with one another, producing a system that both sustains and harms the witches in many ways.

In conversation with Ingebretson, Halberstam further connects queerness and violence. Though the latter locates rage and violence within the queer political movement, these conclusions can be applied to this (more or less) textual analysis as well. Halberstam says that "represented violence takes many forms, and some still have power to produce change" ("Imagined Violence/Queer Violence" 190–191). Violence has long been an agent of change in numerous contexts, and it is no different in *Coven.* Focused through queerness, violence helps to mark a shift in the representation of witches. Through displacing violence and mortification, *Coven* offers new representations of witches that diverge from the traditional depictions of them.

Queerness and Violence

In these next sections, I address how sexual fulfillment and violence are related, mainly through the characters of Madison Montgomery and Zoe Benson. This discussion helps to contextualize its opposite: denied sexual fulfillment and self-mortification. To develop my argument concerning violence and queerness, I turn to the characters of Queenie, Cordelia Foxx, and Myrtle Snow. Queenie's physical body mediates her relationship to desire. Additionally, her being fat parallels her status as a witch; both of these subject positions are marginalized and abject, which allows comparisons to be made between the two. Together, these categories influence how she experiences desire and sexual fulfillment. Next, Cordelia functions as a mother within the Coven, so her relationship to violence is mediated by her desire for motherhood. Finally, Myrtle ostensibly fails to successfully participate in the queer system of violence since she dies at the story's end. However, her failure should be understood on different terms than a character like Madison. Ultimately, her death benefits the Coven despite being a loss.

Madison and Zoe

Madison and Zoe most clearly illustrate the system of sexual fulfillment and shared violence. By Queenie's description, Madison "is a stone-cold bitch who loves hard drinking, big dicks, and trouble" ("Fearful Pranks Ensue"). Madison's characterization also corresponds with the archetypal witch seductress: beautiful, charismatic, and manipulative. Margrit Shildrick notes this Western historical alignment of women with "essential excessiveness," usually in sexual terms (31). Asma echoes this sentiment in his discussion of how witches were understood historically to corrupt the church by seeding sexual immorality while under the control of demons (116–117). Though his discussion does include instances of male witches as seducers as well, his previous discussion of female witches in relation to gender creates a space for the seductress figure to emerge. There are many literary and cultural examples of this figure as well, including Circe and the Sirens of the Greek tradition, Ravenna from the recent *Snow White and the Huntsman* (Rupert Sanders, 2012), and even the monstrous succubus figure.

In keeping with this archetype, Madison engages in sexual acts connected to violence. The first instance occurs when Zoe and Madison attend a frat party ("Bitchcraft"). After leading one of the fraternity brothers upstairs, Madison is drugged and raped. Though I do not mean to imply that Madison was "asking for it," this instance illustrates *Coven*'s attitude toward sexual fulfillment: Madison's relatively flippant attitude regarding her choosing a sexual partner and lack of concern for her well-being puts her in a position that results in her rape.[4] This act also leads to police interest in the Coven, which risks exposing the witches to the public. To punish those who raped her, Madison telekinetically flips the fraternity's bus. Madison later seeks to become involved with her neighbor, Luke Ramsey, only to be repeatedly denied by his mother, Joan. After being rebuffed, Madison lights the Ramseys' curtains on fire with her newfound power of pyrokinesis, marking another act of violence. Madison is eventually killed after instigating trouble into the already tumultuous relationship between Zoe and Kyle, one of the fraternity brothers who was killed in the bus accident and brought back through necromancy. Knowing that they are attracted to one another, Madison repeatedly tries to seduce Kyle to hurt Zoe. After having sex with him and eventually refusing to bring Zoe back after a lethal accident, Madison is strangled by Kyle, ending the cycle of sex and violence in which they had been involved for most of the show.

Perhaps more than Madison's, though, Zoe's relationship with sexual fulfillment illustrates the relationship between violence and desire. Zoe's unique power lacks a true name, but her sister witches call her a Black Widow: her power causes massive internal hemorrhaging in any sexual partner. As such, Zoe's sexual desire and fulfillment are already associated with violence: in the first episode, she and her boyfriend have sex for the first time, resulting in his death and her being sent to the academy, and Zoe later uses her power to kill Madison's rapist. The link between normative sexual desire and fulfillment is most clearly shown in Madison and Zoe. In instances in which normative desire appears, the violence is shared among the members of the relationship instead of being focused on the originator of the violence. In the following analyses, the second system of queerness and self-mortification is examined in contrast to Madison and Zoe.

Queenie: The Exploding Witch

In her work *The Weight of Images* (2014), Katariina Kyrölä examines the depiction of fat bodies within media. She notes that "'Fat' as a term is constituted through its (fairly recent) history of devaluation, through its opposition to the acceptable and the 'normal'" (7). Fat, then, parallels the construction of the monstrous and queerness as both of these terms derive their meaning from what is considered normal. Within *Coven*, Queenie is a "fat" character both in terms of her appearance and in how her character and backstory are developed. Though the fat body is not a one-to-one comparison to the monstrous body, the relationship among these concepts occupies the same theoretical space of the othered and marginalized body. Both fat and monstrous bodies are non-normative and thus share theoretical underpinnings similar to queer bodies.

Queenie's development as a fat witch begins in the second episode, "Boy Parts." In an expositional scene, Queenie reveals that, before coming to the academy, she worked at a fried chicken restaurant. Already, Queenie's backstory involves food—a relatively unhealthy food at that—further reinforcing racial stereotypes about her character as well. We first see her power when she harms a customer who accuses her of shorting him chicken in his combo meal. After he insults her, she submerges her arm in boiling grease, injuring the customer instead of her through her Voodoo-doll like powers. After this incident, she is sent to the academy to receive formal training for her powers. Madison undercuts the sincerity of the moment with a sarcastic comment, and Queenie retaliates, saying "Bitch, I will eat you!" ("Boy Parts"). Another connection emerges between Queenie and food: violent outbursts are coded with food and eating. She has likely internalized the societal stigma surrounding the fat body and weaponizes it against those who once mocked her. In "Bitchcraft," Queenie attacks Madison by stabbing herself with a fork and injuring Madison as a result. Madison's adherence to the Western and normative standards of beauty—and thus desirability—serve to contrast with Queenie, and their relationship carries this tension throughout the show.

Queenie's weight also directly affects her ability to be desired. Nan, the Coven's mind-reading witch, reveals that Queenie is a virgin, so Queenie responds with "I'm saving myself" ("The Replacements"). Her fat body is undesirable according to Western standards of beauty as embodied by characters like Madison or even Zoe. Queenie does not fit these normative standards, so it is difficult for her to find someone who desires her. With characters like Madison and Zoe as her competition, Queenie is "othered" in a sense by her fatness.[5] The body she inhabits is abject in this way and actively disallows her to fully participate in any part of normative desire or sexual fulfillment. We see that Queenie's desire has been denied for some time, and she attempts to find sexual fulfillment in other ways.

Queenie's encounter with the Minotaur illustrates the relationship between violence and desire. As punishment for the supposed rape of her daughter, LaLaurie turned Marie Laveau's former lover, Bastien, into the Minotaur. He is dormant until Laveau calls upon him to exact revenge on the Coven after Fiona comes to her hair shop to strike a deal for youth and beauty. The Minotaur attacks when Queenie and LaLaurie, who are working through racial and generational problems, are in the kitchen during Halloween. She goes into the garden house on the academy's property to investigate the attacker and, unaware of exactly where the Minotaur is, speaks to it: "You just wanted love. And that makes you a beast? They call me that, too. But that's not who we are. We both deserve love like everybody else. Don't you want to love me?" ("The Replacements"). Her tone here seems both pitying and pleading as she sympathizes with the monster's plight since both have abject, othered, or otherwise monstrous bodies. The Minotaur comes up behind Queenie, who begins touching herself sensually, and impales her in the side with his horns.

Though the Minotaur is not quite human, the dyadic pairing between Queenie and the Minotaur signifies a sexual relationship in this context. Since sexual fulfillment cannot be allowed while the Coven is imperiled, she is injured for attempting to engage in a sexual relationship with the Minotaur. This violence also parodies what Queenie intimately desires: the Minotaur impales Queenie with his horn instead of his penis. Additionally, Queenie's Voodoo-doll powers exhibit some sexual energy as an attempt to approximate her lack of sexual fulfillment. Queenie's use of foreign objects to penetrate herself seems already masturbatory. Her individual power reflects the nature of her body's inability to be desired and receive sexual fulfillment from another person. Her sexual fulfillment has already been denied before the fact by the subject position that she occupies, that of a fat woman in a normative society, so her power displays an effort to circumvent this fact. The encounter with the Minotaur signifies a foreclosure to and thus denial of sexual fulfillment. Becoming involved with the Minotaur would pose a threat to the Coven, so the punitive system at work in *Coven* prohibits this relationship through violent penetration. It is at this point, I suggest, that Queenie sublimates her desire and focuses it on the Coven.

Under the care of Cordelia and Fiona, Queenie eventually recovers only to abandon the Coven to join Laveau. As an act of revenge on Laveau, Hank attacks the hair salon where she is stationed, and Queenie's reaction to the assault evokes another aspect of Kyrölä's "fat-monstrous": the exploding fat body. Kyrölä locates within horror narratives the tendency of the fat body to explode and expand. She claims that fat "bodies change shape in a culturally condemned direction (swelling instead of reducing) and eventually self-destruct (literally or metaphorically)" (125). Already Queenie's body expands beyond what is culturally or aesthetically "normal"; she exceeds her borders and thus brings into question issues of categorization discussed earlier by Cohen and Halberstam. Later, her body undergoes a dramatic instance of exceeding by literally exploding.

It is in this explosion that Queenie completes the paradigm shift from normative desire to queer desire within the context of this analysis. As a last resort against Hank's attack, Queenie takes one of Hank's dropped guns to shoot herself in the head and kill Hank. The exploding body here transgresses the normative bounds of the body, allowing for Queenie's monstrosity to be fully realized both in terms of her being a witch and in her having a fat body. This point is also when her power is at its strongest. This instance of self-mortification strengthens Queenie to the extent that she is able to dispatch one of the Coven's largest enemies, which she was not able to do when she encountered the Minotaur because of her sexual attraction to him. Disregarding normative sexual attraction, albeit to a Minotaur, and focusing on the protection of the Coven, Queenie is able to become fully empowered and defeat Hank. Though it seems contradictory that Queenie kills herself in protection of Laveau, the change that her actions catalyze serves to strengthen the Coven: Laveau joins the ranks of the Coven and helps to protect them against the witch hunters, who ultimately become the largest external threat against the Coven. Once the witch hunters are neutralized, the witches can focus on finding a new Supreme.

Cordelia: The Mother Witch

Queenie's relationship to the system of queer desire and self-mortification is one of empowerment, a theme that also carries over into Cordelia's own relationship with this system and is mediated by her desire to become a mother. Though plenty could be said about her wanting to be a mother to make up for Fiona's lack of effective motherhood, I construct Cordelia's desire for motherhood in relation to the Coven and also to her being a witch. Much has been said on the relationship between motherhood and the witch. Shildrick examines this relationship by considering the witch's body itself in regard to motherhood, especially focusing on physiology of the pregnant body and its similarities to the monstrous nature of a changing and shifting body. She also focuses on the "monstrous births" of malformed children often viewed as the result of witch mothers (33). Additionally, Creed offers examinations of the witch as both mother and woman (more broadly) in her significant study of femininity and monstrosity, using both the *Alien* (Ridley Scott, 1979) and *Carrie* (Brian De Palma, 1976) films.

However, Cordelia remains unsuccessful despite repeated attempts to conceive, even with the help of a fertility specialist. She and her husband decide to resort to witchcraft to circumvent natural laws. During a relatively violent ritual, Cordelia pours black powder to form a spell circle at the corners of which she places a large egg. The lovers cut each other's fingers to draw blood and then drink it, the eggs crack to reveal serpents inside, and the powder catches fire as they have sex. The whole event is tied up in issues of desire, sexual fulfillment, and violence. The violence emerges in this coupling from the ritual itself: snakes, flames, and the drawing of blood are violent images or acts themselves, and Cordelia seems to be overcome with some supernatural presence while having sex with Hank, to the point that her face contorts and her eyes go black. Here, we see how violence and desire of any sort are bound up in one another. There are few instances in *Coven* when sex is not accompanied by violence in some capacity. Additionally, Cordelia's relationship to violence and desire is also mediated by a maternal impulse: she desires Hank in part because he is able to help her conceive a child. Cordelia's desire to conceive a child culminates in this violent ritual.

After being blinded by a witch hunter, Cordelia returns from the hospital to find that she has gained the new power of the second sight and, subsequently, that Hank has been cheating on her. Cordelia separates from Hank and realizes that she needs her second sight for the wellbeing of the Coven and the witches in it. In a way, she needs to become its mother. Fiona has all but abandoned it, so Cordelia become the Supreme *in absentia*. Eventually, a well-meaning Myrtle decides to help Cordelia regain her sight. After having her eyesight restored, Cordelia finds that she no longer has the supernatural second sight; further, she no longer feels as useful. She decides that she must remove her eyes to regain her power and become useful to the Coven again. Returning to her garden, she begins to think of ways to take her vision away again but finds that plant-based magic is ineffective. She must take more drastic means, so she picks up a nearby pair of garden shears to pluck out her eyes.

Cordelia has suppressed (or otherwise been denied access to) all heteronormative sexual desire and approximates conception through penetration with the garden shears. Though she does not literally become pregnant, her actions accord with the queer system of desire and self-mortification in this context. In her discussion of the film *Carrie*, Creed notes that "the body of each woman is marked by bloody wounds; the wound is a sign of abjection in that it violates the skin which forms a border between the inside and outside of the body" and that "Wounds signify the abject because they point to a woman's reproductive functions" (82). Though she takes up a largely more psychoanalytic project in her work than I intend to do here, Creed's discussion of wounds is important, especially in her linking them to "woman's reproductive functions." Cordelia's wounding herself in her eyes approximates her conceiving a child.[6]

In the paradigm of monstrous maternity, this "pregnancy" seems to be as close as Cordelia will get to fulfilling her desires. It helps her to become the mother-in-waiting for the Coven. Cordelia likely would not be able to have even followed this narrative arc if she had been able to conceive an actual child. The path of the monster laid out before her already denied her normative desire, allowing only for its monstrous counterpart to exist. Indeed, Cohen seems prescient of this situation when he articulates that the monster is the "harbinger of category crisis" (6). He further states: "the monster resists any classification built on hierarchy or merely a binary opposition" (7). The category of "mother" is troubled by the monster, thus creating the new formation that Cordelia inhabits.

Cordelia gives birth, so to speak, when she rises to the Supremacy. After the other witches try, fail, and even die, Cordelia successfully completes the Seven Wonders and becomes the Supreme. The scenes following her completion of the Seven Wonders, however, resonate with maternal energy and imagery of rebirth. Indeed, in the final episode, "The Seven Wonders," Cordelia awakes in her garden without any blemishes or trace of her former injuries.[7] The placement in her garden contextualizes Cordelia's own rebirth of sorts into the maternal figure that the Coven needs to thrive. After a dizzying series of camera spins, the camera stops on Myrtle, who says "Behold, the one, true Supreme," formally announcing Cordelia's ascension and rebirth ("The Seven Wonders"). The next shot is of the house, bustling with activity and Cordelia leading an interview in front of the hearth—an archetypally feminine and maternal space. Indeed, one of the last lines of her interview is directed at young women who might be witches: "There is a home and a family waiting for you" ("The Seven Wonders"). Cordelia has grown from Headmistress of the academy to the Supreme while also becoming a surrogate mother to Coven and its witches in the process.

The final scene of the series shows Cordelia, standing on the main staircase, welcoming the new class of witches to the academy with Queenie and Zoe flanking her at the bottom of the stairs. When one of the initiates asks

"What's a Supreme?" Cordelia does not answer but instead looks out and smiles over at the incoming group of young witches—the closest thing that she will have to children at this point. This transformation is necessary for the both the Coven and Cordelia: The Coven likely would not have survived without Cordelia's suppression of her normative desires, which allowed her to gain necessary powers. Moreover, Cordelia would never have become a mother in any regard without denying her normative desire for children. Indeed, in her dying moments, Fiona says to Cordelia: "You were always looking for another version of motherhood" ("The Seven Wonders"). Cordelia was able to navigate this economy of desire and violence successfully and emerge relatively victorious, much like Queenie. However, not all witches follow this path; others meet death.

Myrtle: The Failed Witch

Myrtle Snow does not successfully participate in the any system of desire and violence as they are constructed in *Coven*. Unlike Madison, whose hypersexuality leads to her death, Myrtle does not even enter the arena; rather, she is almost entirely outside of the constraints of this system. That is, she never exhibits any sexual desire. However, hers is one of the final deaths in the show. In order to understand why she dies, I look to Halberstam's *The Queer Art of Failure* (2011). In the context of *Coven*, success can be defined as suppressing normative sexual desire for the betterment of the Coven and ultimately surviving, but Myrtle fails for some reason. Indeed, Halberstam says: "Failing is something queers do and have always done exceptionally well; for queers failure can be a style" (*The Queer Art of Failure* 3). Myrtle's queerness is inextricably linked to her failure.[8] Growth is not possible without pruning, a metaphor that is especially apt as Cordelia relies heavily on herbcraft and since the final scenes begin in her garden. Myrtle is part of this pruning process, inasmuch as her death is beneficial to the Coven. In what may seem to be a counterintuitive turn, Myrtle's death is actually a success if she aims to produce a strong and thriving Coven.

Normative understandings of failure are largely negative: a set goal was not achieved, so the person has failed. However, when that failure is queered, the stakes change, and the payoff may be different. Halberstam's *Queer Art of Failure* looks mainly at artifacts of pop culture to find instances of failure but places them within a framework of queerness in order to reimagine their stakes. In the context of *Coven*, the application of this queer failure framework reveals another facet of the system at work in the Coven. Halberstam asserts that, in addition to its negative components, failure "provides the opportunity to use these negative effects to poke holes in the toxic positivity of contemporary life" (*The Queer Art of Failure* 3). Halberstam goes on to say that failure can also be seen "as a way of refusing to acquiesce to dominant logics of power and discipline and as a form of critique" (88). Myrtle's failure to perform in the other witches' system critiques the traditional representation of witches. Being from the previous generation, Myrtle is arguably out of place in the new Coven. The "dominant logics of power and discipline" (i.e. the old ways) have no place in this new Coven.

Throughout the show, Myrtle is presented as someone who shuns sexual desire in favor of supporting the Coven. If this is the case, one must ask why she does not remain in the Coven like Cordelia or Zoe. The reason for this is that Myrtle never has to overcome her sexual desire or that she never has to sublimate her desire into the Coven; it is already there. During a flashback detailing Myrtle and Fiona's history, Myrtle is contrasted with Fiona, who is largely her foil throughout the show. After Fiona kills Anna Leigh Leighton (the reigning Supreme during Fiona's time in the academy), Myrtle seeks to exact justice on Fiona for her actions. Fiona continually lies about what happened, causing Myrtle to say: "I'm a Guardian of Veracity in the Vernacular. I know when a lie's being told, and I protect the truth" ("Fearful Pranks Ensue"). Myrtle begins a rite that would make the object of her spell able only to speak the truth. She casts it on the butler who witnessed the murder, but he cuts off his own tongue rather than risk exposing Fiona.

This glimpse into Myrtle's character is revelatory: she is wholly devoted to the truth, a concept rather than a person. This sort of devotion is similar to a religious devotion to a deity, resembling a nun or a priest. Similarly, such religious figures take vows of celibacy that foreclose them to sexual fulfillment. If Myrtle is seen in this light, which I argue she should be, we see that she already denies her sexual desire and sublimates her libidinal energy onto the Coven and the truth that she believes should be a supporting pillar of the group. Since the show so explicitly explains other characters' sexual desires, the lack of a description regarding Myrtle's sexual history reveals an important absence. Myrtle's actions are always in favor of the Coven, so any violence she may cause is for the good of the Coven.

In an effort to maintain her status as the Supreme in the Coven, Fiona often lashes out at Myrtle, much as she did in her youth. The most significant example of this occurs when Fiona manipulates others into believing that Myrtle was the one who killed Madison. The punishment for killing a sister witch is to be burned at the stake, so Myrtle is killed despite her devotion to the Coven. Myrtle's death creates a power vacuum in the Coven that Fiona eagerly seeks to fill. Through Misty Day's power of resurgence, Myrtle is brought back from death, marking a turning point for the trajectory of the Coven's growth. Myrtle then becomes a vital force within the Coven to orchestrate Fiona's fall and Cordelia's ascension.

After her resurrection, one of Myrtle's most significant actions towards protecting the Coven is, ironically enough, violence taken against her fellow witches. Following Cordelia's assault by a witch hunter, Myrtle invites the other members of the council over for an afternoon tea. Cecily Pembroke and Quentin Fleming believe Fiona's story about Myrtle killing Madison and sentence Myrtle to death. In an effort to exact revenge and to help Cordelia, Myrtle paralyzes them and extracts their eyes with a melon baller to replace Cordelia's blinded eyes. Before she plunges the melon baller into Pembroke's eye, she claims that she intends to "help out the Coven, to help out my beloved Cordelia" ("Head"). She gleefully disposes of the bodies in acid afterwards. Myrtle betrays her own principles, leaving behind the truth she holds so dear and instead resorts to violence. Feeling justified in her actions, Myrtle helps the Coven in this regard: the members of the council are unable to see through her manipulation, and killing them thus purifies the Coven. Further, Myrtle did what she thought was most helpful for Cordelia in restoring her sight. She still supports the Coven while suppressing her own sexual desires that have been sublimated onto the concept of truth.

Myrtle also plays a large role in steering the future of the Coven through coordinating the ritual of the Seven Wonders. Shortly after the news conference that Cordelia holds to announce the Coven's presence to the world, Myrtle says to Cordelia: "You've planted the seeds, but in order to reap their harvest, you have to clear the rot of the past" ("The Seven Wonders"). Continuing with the plant metaphor, Myrtle realizes that the Coven cannot truly grow while she remains a part of it: she represents the past, the old archetype of the witch with which the Coven has too long been affiliated. There is cleansing in fire, so Myrtle decides to repeat the violence and punishment wrongly visited upon her at Fiona's request in order to pave the way for the Coven to grow under Cordelia's guidance. She effectively ends the conversation with "Now that you're in charge, my life's work is fulfilled.... I want my death to have some meaning" ("The Seven Wonders"). Her statement here seems to be aware of Halberstam's *Queer Art of Failure*, which goes on to say that "failure is unbeing" (23). This "unbeing" can be seen as her death, which begins to unravel old images of witches to create a new one. Myrtle offers to be burned at the stake again, so her death signifies not a total loss to the Coven but rather a chance for it to grow.

Myrtle's choosing to be burned, effectively committing suicide at the stake, is significant. Rather than being killed in some other way or just fading away as a scrap of the past, she operates within the historical witch narrative and reclaims two of the most infamous symbols in the history of witch hunts: the stake and the pyre. These were used heavily during most Western punishments for witchcraft, and they are especially powerful here, considering that the witches fled to New Orleans from the Salem Witch Trials. Geoffrey Parrinder notes witches' long history with violence, saying that "people accused of witchcraft were victims of the fears and superstitions of societies" (126). In addition to the more traditional and ultimately final witch burning, supposed witches were subject to torture by red-hot iron pokers or icy water (127). Positioned as a failure throughout the show, Myrtle is constantly ridiculed by her peers, her fashion sense is mocked, she seems out of touch, and she eventually dies because she is seemingly unable (or unwilling) to keep up with the times. Yet, her greatest "failure" is her voluntary death, and her suicide empowers her to explicitly break with traditional representations of witches. Myrtle is invaluable to the Coven, and it is through her ostensible failures that she helps it grow. All along, her queerness drives her desire to see the Coven prosper, and it culminates when she burns a second time with an echoing shout of "Balenciaga!" ("The Seven Wonders").

Conclusion

The witches discussed here all represent different aspects of the queer system at work in *Coven*. Queenie wants to be desired but cannot be because of her body, and her attempted sexual fulfillment results in her being impaled by the Minotaur's horns. She can only truly realize her potential as a witch when she fully sublimates her desire and sacrifices herself to protect the Coven. Cordelia's desire to be a mother literally cannot be fulfilled, and she eventually dismisses Hank as her object of desire. She then displaces her desires for a child, motherhood, and a husband as a means to sexual fulfillment onto the Coven itself, becoming a mother to it instead. This feat would not have been possible with a child or husband to draw her attention away from the Coven when it needed it most. Myrtle's desires and focus, though never sexual as such, are always on the Coven. Yet, this desire becomes all consuming and prohibitive of the Coven's growth. Myrtle must die for the Coven to flourish in the new age of witches. These denials of sexual desires and fulfillment become the key to both allowing the witches to achieve their full potential and for allowing the Coven to grow.

Though *Coven*'s position on sexual fulfillment and desire may seem draconian, it is necessarily dramatized in the show to illustrate its importance. The patterns regarding violence in a dyadic sexual pairing (i.e. Cordelia and Hank, Queenie and the Minotaur, etc.) warn against sexual fulfillment. The witches must keep themselves in check or face punishment in the form of violence towards them and risk death or harm to others (in the case of Zoe). The alternative is self-mortification, a taming of the body, which allows them to perform greater magic that ultimately protects the Coven. Though the show stops at the rebirth of the Coven, I suggest that the system of denying sexual fulfillment or punishing it would disappear as the Coven is no longer under the same danger that it was while Fiona was the Supreme or while the witch hunting organization threatened it. Normalcy would return to the Coven, allowing the witches to once more explore their sexuality—like normal humans. While explaining the academy's role to Zoe, Cordelia says: "I'm here to help you identify your gifts and teach you how to control them," but she is interrupted by Queenie, who says: "She means to suppress them" ("Bitchcraft"). Cordelia quickly corrects her to remind her that it is about control. Herein lies the message of the show: a lack of control risks the body's safety and by extension the Coven's. This message is a large departure from the wanton witch described by Stephen T. Asma.

This analysis has demonstrated an emergence of a new type of witch. As I have discussed briefly already, classical depictions of witches mark them as cannibalistic, violent, and often sexually charged women. While the witches in *Coven* do have some of these traits, the characters remaining at the show's end are strikingly human: they corrupt no churches, eat no children and strike no deals with demons. Instead, they navigate a complicated human terrain and struggle to find their place within it. The departure from the classic witch narrative in *Coven*, along with other contemporary witch and monster stories, signifies a shift in popular consciousness. Though violent witches still exist both in fiction, the construction and reception of these figures and monsters as a whole are largely different, especially in pop culture.

Keeping in line with Jeffrey Jerome Cohen's monsters as products of cultural fears, the humanization of monsters can be both comforting and troubling: the line is blurring, but current scholarship and culture seem to have problems finding which party appears on which side. Using witches to explore issues of queerness and violence is a powerful tool, but the question remains as to why monsters are used in the first place. Future studies may more fully explore the psychological aspects of humanity's fascination with monsters, but for now, we can rest knowing that humans might be more akin to monsters than previously thought, bridging the gap between the two seemingly exclusive categories.

Certainly, the witches of *Coven* are not the first of this new generation of monsters. Hermione in *Harry Potter* (novels and films) and Sabrina from *Sabrina the Teenage Witch* (1996–2003) both illustrate a similar new representation of the witch. However, the witches in *Coven* provide another example. The two examples above contemporize the witch by focusing the figure through puberty, adolescence, or by downplaying the role altogether. *Coven* does so by more explicitly focusing on the monstrosity of the witch and thus the figure's inherent queerness. Additionally, the target audience is largely different in *American Horror Story*, so the horror narrative can be utilized to explore these issues on more mature, adult levels than would be allowable for younger audiences. In this context, violence, sexuality, and desire can be used to illustrate or facilitate this transformation. Hopefully, *Coven* is not the last contemporary iterations of the witch. As the categories blur further, pop culture can further develop the witch, folding in issues of race, gender, class, or disability.

NOTES

1. In "The Sacred Taking," Fiona tells Myrtle to place her portrait where she had chosen, not in the basement next to "that disgraced Russian witch." Though not clear in the show, it is possible that she refers to Baba Yaga from Russia folklore, and the "disgrace" she talks about refers to the poor representation of witches as violent, cannibalistic monsters.

2. Fred R. Darkis, Jr., provides a more thorough examination of LaLaurie in "Madame LaLaurie of New Orleans," *Louisiana History: The Journal of the Louisiana Historical Association* 23.4 (1982): 383–399.

3. I understand that self-mortification closely parallels self-harm. I avoid this term because of the intentionality behind such actions.

4. Stemming from rape culture, victim blaming is the incorrect placing of blame for the rape onto the victim. Often, this comes in the form of such thinking as: "she was asking for it by wearing such a short skirt, drinking too much, etc." I wish to avoid that sort of mentality here and instead focus on the violence occurring in this situation rather than on the rape as such.

5. Queenie's being black and a woman can also be folded into this commentary, but that is outside the scope of this analysis.

6. Freud discusses eyes as part of his psychosexual analytics framework in his essay, "The 'Uncanny.'" In this essay, Freud explicates his idea of the uncanny, "that species of the frightening that goes back to what was once well known and had long been familiar" (*The Uncanny*, 1–2). He illustrates these principles through a discussion of E.T.A. Hoffman's "The Sandman," a story of symbolic castration and the uncanny fear of automatons.

7. Janani Subramanian examines the idea of rebirth more thoroughly in "The Monstrous Makeover: *American Horror Story*, Femininity and Special Effects," *Critical Studies in Television* 8.3 (2013): 108–123.

8. One can argue that all the witches in *Coven* are failures for not complying with heteronormative expectations of having a relationship with a man, having a child, or getting married. Being witches, though, they are already positioned strangely against these expectations. Myrtle fails even to meet the altered expectations of witches in *Coven*, which is how her failure rises to the top.

WORKS CITED

Asma, Stephen T. *On Monsters: An Unnatural History of Our Worst Fears*. Oxford: Oxford University Press, 2009. Print.

"Bitchcraft." *American Horror Story: Coven*. Writ. Ryan Murphy and Brad Falchuk. Dir. Alfonso Gomez-Rejon. FX Network. 9 October 2013. *Netflix*. 14 July 2015.

"Boy Parts." *American Horror Story: Coven*. Writ. Tim Minear. Dir. Michael Rymer. FX Network. 16 October 2013. *Netflix*. 20 October 2015.

Case, Sue-Ellen. "Tracking the Vampire (Excerpt)." *The Horror Reader*. Ed. Ken Gelder. New York, Routledge: 2000. 198–209. Print.

Cohen, Jeffrey Jerome. *Monster Theory: Reading Culture*. Minneapolis: University of Minnesota Press, 1996. Print.

Creed, Barbara. *The Monstrous-Feminine: Film, Feminism, Psychoanalysis*. London: Routledge, 1993. Print.

Darkis, Fred R., Jr. "Madame LaLaurie of New Orleans." *Louisiana History: The Journal of the Louisiana Historical Association* 23.4 (1982): 383–399. Print.

"Fearful Pranks Ensue." *American Horror Story: Coven*. Writ. Jennifer Salt. Dir. Michael Uppendahl. FX Network. 30 October 2013. *Netflix*. 25 August 2015.

Freud, Sigmund. "The Sexual Aberrations." *Three Essays on the Theory of Sexuality*. 1905. Trans. and ed. James Strachey. New York: Basic Books, 2000. 1–38. Print.

_____. *The Uncanny*. 1919. Trans. David McLintock. London: Penguin, 2003. Print.

Grossman, Pamela J. "The Year of the Witch." *The Huffington Post*. The Huffington Post, 15 July 2013. Web. 14 July 2015.

Halberstam, Judith. "Imagined Violence/Queer Violence: Representation, Rage, and Resistance." *Social Text* 37 (1993): 187–201. *CrossRef*. Web. 28 October 2015.

_____. *The Queer Art of Failure*. Durham, NC: Duke University Press, 2011. Print.

_____. *Skin Shows: Gothic Horror and the Technology of Monsters*. Durham, NC: Duke University Press, 1995. Print.

"Head." *American Horror Story: Coven*. Writ. Tim Minear. Dir. Howard Deutch. *American Horror Story: Coven*. FX Network. 11 December 2013. *Netflix*. 29 July 2015.

Ingebretsen, Edward J. *At Stake: Monsters and the Rhetoric of Fear in Public Culture*. Chicago: University of Chicago Press, 2001. Print.

Kyrölä, Katariina. *The Weight of Images: Affect, Body Image and Fat in the Media*. Farnham, Surrey: Ashgate, 2014. Print.

Lowder, J. Bryan, and June Thomas. "How Queer Is American Horror Story? Boy Parts Edition." *Slate*. Slate, 17 October 2013. Web. 25 August 2015.

"mortification, n." *OED Online*. Oxford University Press, September 2015. Web. 27 August 2015.

Parrinder, Geoffrey. "The Witch as Victim." *The Witch Figure*. Ed. Venetia Newall. London: Routledge, 1973. 95–124. Print.

"The Replacements." *American Horror Story: Coven*. Writ. James Wong. Dir. Alfonso Gomez-Rejon. FX Network. 23 October 2013. *Netflix*. 2 December 2015.

"The Sacred Taking." *American Horror Story: Coven*. Writ. Ryan Murphy. Dir. Alfonso Gomez-Rejon. FX Network. 4 December 2013. *Netflix*. 2 December 2015.

"The Seven Wonders." *American Horror Story: Coven*. Writ. Douglas Petrie. Dir. Alfonso Gomez-Rejon. FX Network. 29 January 2014. *Netflix*. 14 July 2015.

Shildrick, Margrit. *Embodying the Monster: Encounters with the Vulnerable Self*. London: Sage, 2002. Print.

Shilling, Chris, and Philip A. Mellor. "Saved from Pain or Saved through Pain? Modernity, Instrumentalization and the Religious Use of Pain as a Body Technique." *European Journal of Social Theory* 13.4 (2010): 521–537. *Sage*. Web. 4 December 2015.

Subramanian, Janani. "The Monstrous Makeover: *American Horror Story*, Femininity and Special Effects." *Critical Studies in Television* 8.3 (2013): 108–123. Print.

Zeikowitz, Richard E. "Befriending the Medieval Queer: A Pedagogy for Literature Classes." *College English* 65.1 (2002): 67. *CrossRef*. Web. 19 January 2015.

"Wir sind alle freaks"

Elevating White Gay Male Oppression Through Representations of Disability

CARL SCHOTTMILLER

Set in Jupiter, Florida in 1952, *American Horror Story: Freak Show* follows one of the last remaining troupes of freak show performers as they navigate the declining public interest in their business. This season is unique to the franchise in that its elements of horror are decidedly less supernatural than those found in other seasons. Whereas the other four iterations explore issues of spiritual haunting, demonic possession, and witchcraft, among other tropes from American folklore, *Freak Show* focuses on disability. To tell this story, the show's casting department hires more actors with disabilities than it has for any other season.[1] To cast the actors with disabilities, series co-creator Ryan Murphy seeks out individuals who want to be actors but lack regular job opportunities, as well as individuals without acting experience whose personal stories he finds "moving" (Dos Santos). Murphy hopes that, through their representation on the show, the "special-ability cast" gives "a voice to many people who don't have a voice" (Dos Santos). In both the show's narrative and casting, constructions of disability take center stage.

Freak Show's narrative explores how both the disabled performers and two closeted white gay men navigate issues of social marginalization in the 1950s United States. By choosing this subject matter, *American Horror Story*'s creative team presents a fictionalized account of freak show history that perpetuates a paternalistic understanding of disability, erases the diversity of disabled lived experiences, and frames white gay men as more marginalized than people with disabilities. To build this argument, I analyze episodes of *Freak Show*, as well as additional interviews with the show's creators and cast. First, I demonstrate how the show contributes to "freak discourse" through its "wir sind alle freaks" rhetoric. Next, I analyze the potentially progressive elements of the show's discourse in terms of how the casting and narrative align with a social model of disability. Then, I complicate this assessment by exploring how the show's creative team exploits the actors with disabilities and requires them to perform ableist stereotypes. Next, I analyze three examples of how the show's writers fail to approach disabled identities through an intersectional framework and, in so doing, further marginalize the histories of disabled trans women and people of color. Last, I demonstrate how the writers take greater care in presenting an historically accurate portrayal of how homophobia operates in the 1950s than they do with representations of disability. Through this analysis, I suggest that *American Horror Story*'s freak discourse ultimately privileges white gay men at the expense of other marginalized communities.

Freak Discourse on American Horror Story

While the display of non-normative bodies has a long history in Western cultures, freak shows were a specific, stylized form of Othering intended for profit and the amusement of audiences (Bogdan, *Freak Show* 10).[2] An organized exhibition of people with alleged and real physical, mental, or behavioral anomalies, freak shows were at the height of their popularity in the United States from 1840 to 1940 (10). Over the course of this history, a general typology of "freaks" emerged: Born Freaks (people who at birth had a physical anomaly that marked them as unusual), Made Freaks (people who did something to their bodies to make them unusual, such as adorning themselves with tattoos), Novelty Acts (people who had an unusual talent, such as sword swallowing), and Gaffed Freaks (people considered fakes or phonies, such as a four-legged woman whose extra limbs belonged to an additional person hidden from the audience) (8). Historically, freak shows involved a complex process of exploitation and subversion: some "freaks" gained fame, notoriety, financial stability, and control over their own acts and displays (Clare, *Exile and Pride* 89). More often than not, class-privileged white men took advantage of the performers, whose levels of volition varied according to their disability, physical anomaly, age, class, race, ethnicity, and gender (Gerber 47). Many "freaks" were enslaved people of color with no consent, and in some cases the showmen engaged in forms of chattel slavery (Reiss 20, 100–101). At the same time, many individuals within the "freak" subculture viewed nondisabled customers as rubes and exploited victims who were explicitly lied to, charged large sums of money for worthless items, and ripped off through pick-pocketing and/or inaccurate monetary exchange at the box office (Clare, *Exile and Pride* 90). By 1940, freak show popularity began to decline due to economic turmoil, modernization, competition from other forms of entertainment (such as television), and the medicalization of human differences that marked "freaks" as pathological specimens rather than wondrous curiosities (Bogdan, "The Social Construction of Freaks" 23; Gerber 43).

By developing a television season around this history, Murphy and series co-creator Brad Falchuk contribute to a long-established tradition of "freak discourse." Disability Studies scholar Rosemarie Garland Thomson theorizes freak discourse as a gauge for registering the different ways Western cultures interpret extraordinary bodies (Garland Thomson 2).[3] These interpretations necessarily differ according to the specific sociohistorical moments in which the extraordinary body exists. For example, during the height of freak show popularity a medical model of disability that frames "freaks" as deviant or pathological did not yet exist; instead, nondisabled people largely viewed "the disabled" as wondrous creatures who were not entirely human (Clare, *Exile and Pride* 97). In this formulation, a "freak" was not a quality within individuals or a fixed identity but rather a socially constructed category produced in order to differentiate "typical" from "atypical" bodies (Bogdan, *Freak Show* 3). My project builds upon Garland Thomson's scholarship by looking at how freak discourse operates on *American Horror Story* in this contemporary moment, while also recognizing how Garland Thomson's initial inquiry refers to a very different moment in time.

Through enfreakment, the process by which individual variations become stylized as cultural Otherness, freak shows turned an extraordinary body into a hypervisible text against which an onlooker's body read as "normal" (Hevey 54; Garland Thomson 10). During the exhibitions, showmen used the practices of costuming, staging, fictional histories, choreography, and marketing to enfreak four groups of people: disabled people (both white and people of color), nondisabled people of color from colonized countries (framed as "Cannibals" and "Savages"), nondisabled people of color from the United States (framed as "Natives" and "Exotics from the Wild"), and nondisabled people with visible differences (Clare, *Exile and Pride* 86). Racist and ableist[4] ideologies made the social construction of these groups into "freaks" possible, as freak shows capitalized on the eugenicist belief that cognitively disabled individuals and people of color represented a missing link between primates and humans (Clare, *Exile and Pride* 95). The public display of these marked bodies helped to create and strengthen the "typical" white onlooker's sense of white identity and white superiority, as the spectator projected "savagery" onto the person of color and reinforced the supposed distinction between "civilized" and "uncivilized" peoples (Clare, *Exile and Pride* 99). By gawking at the stylized presentation of "abnormal" bodies, freak show patrons reinforced ableist and white supremacist ideologies that marked disabled and non-white bodies as cultural Others (Clare, *Exile and Pride* 91).

Whereas historically freak discourses emphasized differences between the spectator and "freak," *American Horror Story*'s deployment of freak discourse uses the show's advertising, casting, and narrative to promote a universalist ideology that emphasizes shared humanity between "typical" and "atypical" bodies. The season's tagline, "Wir sind alle freaks" ("we are all freaks"), appears both on the official poster and as a hashtag to promote the franchise (West). This assimilationist rhetoric frames "freakishness" as an attribute of all individuals rather than as a stigmatized identity that results from institutionalized forms of oppression. Such aversion of freak discourse operates in part to bestow humanity upon impaired individuals by convincing able-bodied audiences to recognize and celebrate their own "freakishness." By this logic, if every member of the *AHS* audience is a "freak" then, simultaneously, no one is a "freak," and the marked identity supposedly loses its stigma. In universalizing "freakishness," the show's advertising attempts to blur the historically stark differentiation between "normal" and "abnormal."

In developing the show's freak discourse, Murphy in particular intentionally approaches the season's narrative through a more overtly political lens than in previous seasons. Actor Jessica Lange, who has a fascination with carnival culture, suggested the freak show topic to Murphy and gave him books to read on the subject (Stack). Murphy then, along with his team, began researching the history of carnival performers in the 1920s and 1930s (Weinstein). According to Murphy, setting the season within the context of the 1950s allowed the show to explore both the decline of freak show popularity that occurs in the late 1940s, as well as, "a time in [US] culture where different people of all different kinds of life start to stand up for their civil rights" (Stack). In creating this fictionalized account of freak show history, Murphy highlights discrimination against people with disabilities as the season's overarching element of horror. As Murphy says: "What happened to this group of people [the 'freaks'] is an American horror story," and he hopes that the show's audience will "take away a respect for what this group of people went through, which [Murphy] found to be very moving" (Weinstein). Rather than using freak discourse to emphasize difference between the disabled characters and the mainstream audience, Murphy hopes the show will reveal the horrors of ableist oppression and lead to a recognition of shared humanity.

Incorporating a Social Model of Disability

To Murphy's credit, the show's exploration of how U.S. society oppresses disabled individuals does in many ways offer a poignant political critique through use of a social model of disability. Within Disability Studies, activists and scholars differentiate between a medical model of disability and a social model.[5] In general, the medical model frames disability as a deficit within individuals that needs to be cured and/or managed through medical intervention so that the disabled individual may lead a more "normal" life. In contrast, a social model of disability differentiates impairments (an individual attribute) from disability (a social process of disempowerment). In this formulation, society disables individuals through institutionalized forms of oppression. While Murphy and Falchuk's freak discourse fails to address underlying systemic issues of ableism, which I address in the next subsection, the show does include some elements of this social model in its casting and narrative.

By featuring a cast of actors with disabilities, the show provides visibility of non-normative bodies and showcases the talents of impaired actors. The opportunity to work on a popular mainstream television show is rare for actors with disabilities, and *Freak Show* provides them with an income and public recognition. Having a space wherein these actors may perform helps to show disability as a variation rather than an inherent deficit. Furthermore, having both actors with and without disabilities in an ensemble cast could be read as showing "freakishness" to be a social construction. Instead of having the disabled actors perform as "freaks" on display for the able-bodied, both sets of actors embody "freakishness," thereby demonstrating how the characteristic may be performed by anyone. Such a reading of the casting aligns with the show's "wir sind alle freaks" discourse that emphasizes universal sameness.

In terms of the show's narrative, *Freak Show* can be read as aligning with a social model of disability because the plot consistently demonstrates how society disables the "freaks." At the beginning of the season, Jessica Lange's character, Elsa, owner of the titular freak show, "rescues" disabled individuals from various oppressive situations and makes them part of her performance troupe. The space of the freak show initially provides a safe haven for the performers, wherein they form a community and develop a positive collective identity. When the able-bodied Penny falls in love with freak show performer Paul the "Illustrated Seal," her father rejects their relationship and ultimately disfigures Penny in order to disown her. After this incident, Paul and the freak show performers welcome Penny into their community, and some of the performers even help her enact retribution against her father. The freak show provides a subcultural space for the heterosexual couple of Penny and Paul to thrive.[6] In contrast, the "freaks" experience harassment when they enter able-bodied spaces, such as when they go into town to eat at a diner ("Massacres and Matinees"). The patrons gawk at the performers with disgust, tell the "freaks" that their mere presence upsets a child, and ultimately ask them to leave for not conforming to able-bodied norms. Through these examples, *AHS*'s freak discourse could be read as showcasing ableism as an oppressive institution that disables the performers, who merely desire open access and agency in their lives.[7]

Whereas traditionally in freak discourse the non-normative body represents the "inhuman," *American Horror Story*'s narrative reverses the binary and frames monstrosity as a characteristic of the able-bodied. The villainous characters are largely "typical" individuals in social positions of power, such as police officers, townspeople who harass the performers, and a rich sociopath, Dandy, who fetishizes and murders the "freaks."[8] One of the main villains, Denis O'Hare's character Stanley, seeks to kill and/or dismember the disabled performers in order to sell their bodies to the curator of the "American Morbidity Museum," who then displays the deceased as oddities for able-bodied consumption. By contrast, the "freaks" do not set out to harass or murder the "typical" townspeople. When they commit murder, the "freaks" generally do so out of self-defense or for retribution, such as when Evan Peters's Jimmy murders a police officer to protect Sarah Paulson's Dot and Bette, when Elsa murders Kathy Bates's Ethel to protect herself from being charged with murder, and when Angela Bassett's Desiree murders the curator of the American Morbidity Museum to avenge her deceased comrades. Setting up the season's protagonists and antagonists in this way disrupts the traditional equation of "freaks" with monstrosity, providing a more nuanced characterization of people with disabilities.

Exploitation of the Disabled Cast

Despite these potentially progressive elements of the show's narrative and casting, the show's contemporary freak discourse ultimately relies upon a superficial celebration of difference that fails to account for how ableism operates on an institutional level. This oversight occurs in part because able-bodied individuals are the ones primarily espousing the "wir sind alle freaks" rhetoric. *Freak Show*'s official poster, which contains the season's tagline, features the names of only the "typical" cast members and the image of only one cast member with a disability (West). The main cast fills the poster's center, while extras who are not actors on the show fill in the background. The poster features more than enough space to include the actors with disabilities, so their exclusion is a deliberate decision. Because of this lack of representation, the phrase's "wir" ("we") refers primarily to the able-bodied show runners who create the tagline and the main cast who appear on the advertisement. The declaration "we are all freaks," then, positions normative bodies as claiming the identity of "freak" without having experienced the marginalization and complex history that accompanies such an identity.

Able-bodied individuals do not have the same stakes in claiming the term "freak" as disabled individuals do in reclaiming the term as a positive identity. For example, actor Mat Fraser, who plays Paul, has researched the history of freak shows, has performed in the Coney Island freak show, and has chosen to identity as a "freak actor playing a freak" ("*American Horror Story* FX," "Mat Fraser"). When he performs as a freak with Coney Island, Fraser has the ability to create his own characterization and to espouse a narrative of his own choosing. Fraser reclaims the term "freak" in order to destigmatize the identity, to challenge "typical" audiences' perceptions of his ability, and to affirm his own agency. This reclamation and celebration of the identity "freak" serves a political purpose because of Fraser's history and identity as a disabled performer. In contrast, the political purpose of *American Horror Story*'s "wir sind alle freaks" discourse is to recognize the shared humanity between typical and atypical bodies. This rhetoric is flawed because the inherent humanity of disabled individuals is not something for the wealthy, white, able-bodied male series co-creators to bestow. Such freak discourse could lead audiences to feel paternalistic sympathy or pity for the disabled because the show's rhetoric does not come from the voices of disabled individuals, who have a more nuanced understanding of what it means to claim the identity "freak."

While excluded from the show's poster, the actors with disabilities do receive their own promotional videos on the franchise's official YouTube channel. These videos provide the actors with a voice in the show's representation; however, the videos received between approximately 43, 500 to 110, 000 views compared to *Freak Show*'s first episode, which received 6.13 million views (Kondolojy). In the individual YouTube videos that range from approximately two-to-five minutes, actors Jyoti Amge, Erika Ervin, Mat Fraser, Rose Siggins, and Ben Woolf introduce themselves to the viewing audience. The narrative for each video follows a similar structure, with the cast members naming their "disabilities" and discussing their characters. Most of the actors challenge the concept of normality, such as when Ben Woolf deconstructs the identity of "freak" by saying: "we're all freaks in our own way. If there were no freaks then everyone would be normal" ("*American Horror Story* FX," "Ben Woolf"). Ben's logic aligns with the "wir sind alle freaks" rhetoric; however, he also includes in his video an indictment of contemporary forms of ableism. Discussing his experience living in Los Angeles, Ben says: "you think that [LA residents would] be more accepting of people who are different, and it's kind of not. Kind of the opposite actually. Sometimes a lot of people don't … realize that I am an adult and don't give me the value that I deserve." Because Ben's discourse comes from a person with a disability, his insight is more layered than *American Horror Story*'s freak discourse. Whereas *Freak Show* takes place in 1952 and frames oppression against disabled people as a past phenomenon, Ben's video foregrounds how people with disabilities face contemporary systemic inequality.[9] Therefore, while Ben does align his rhetoric with elements of the "wir sind alle freaks" discourse, he speaks to larger dynamics of power that Murphy and Falchuk's rhetoric ignores.

Through its casting, *Freak Show* gives the able-bodied actors more agency and voice within the narrative than the actors with disabilities. The show's main cast consists entirely of "typical" individuals who perform the spectacle of disability using makeup, prosthetics, and special effects. The show's wealthy, successful main cast members who perform disability for a television show do not share the same lived experiences as the show's impaired actors or impaired audiences who face the realities of ableist prejudice and marginalization daily. For the primary cast, visible disability is neither a lived experience nor a political identity but a characteristic that may be taken on and off at will.[10] After filming ends, the main cast retains their able-bodied privilege and class status. Furthermore, performing a spectacle of disability can easily turn into an offensive caricature. Actors Naomi Grossman and Christopher Neiman play "pinheads" Pepper and Salty, respectively, and to portray the characters, they perform erratic movements and speak mostly gibberish. This situation puts a burden on at least one of the actors with disabilities, as Fraser finds it difficult to work with able-bodied actors who portray characters with learning disabilities (Walters). While Fraser does not label Grossman and Neiman's performances as outright offensive, his discomfort with witnessing such performances speaks to a systemic issue of nondisabled actors turning disability into a spectacle.

Though the show does feature actors with disabilities, these performers are mostly relegated to the background. Of these actors, only Mat Fraser has a significant amount of dialogue and character development throughout the season. In responding to the question of what has been the most challenging thing about working on *Freak Show*, Fraser says:

> To basically be a subsidiary character in the portrayal of my own cultural heritage as a disabled performer—moreover, one whose presence lends an authenticity to the production that it would not otherwise enjoy.... To be the one person on set who has for a lifetime lived and breathed the experience of being a physical outsider, and has actually both acted and been a performing freak professionally.... That has made it hard to be asked to stand, sit and be in the background to so many scenes where a non-disabled actor delivers passionate speeches about being different, being a freak in this cruel world et cetera et cetera et fucking cetera. It's had me very upset privately many times [Walters].

Fraser's quotation reveals how the *AHS* creative team exploits the actors whom Murphy hopes to empower. Instead of having their own voices within the show, the actors with disabilities authenticate the voices of the able-bodied writers, producers, and co-creators, by virtue of their barely more than visual inclusion in the show. Of significant note is the fact that Fraser specifically says he was upset "privately," which suggests that he feels neither comfortable nor able to air his grievances in a more public manner on the set or with show runners. This situation raises the question of how much consent Fraser ultimately has in his character's representation, given the power imbalance between actors and showrunners. Furthermore, Fraser's individual YouTube promo, directed by Ryan Murphy, features none of the critiques he presents in this interview—once again, Fraser's voice is absent from the show's official media ("*American Horror Story* FX," "Mat Fraser"). While *Freak Show* preaches a superficial equality, the show fails to address its own underlying power imbalances that silence and marginalize the actors with disabilities.

One of these imbalances involves the show's narrative, which often requires the impaired actors to perform practices that they normally critique. For instance, in an interview about her role in *Freak Show*, Jyoti Amge, who plays Ma Petite, criticizes how society infantilizes her on a regular basis. Amge says, "When people see me on TV, they become very happy because they don't have to interact with me. When they start interacting with me they ask me questions like I'm a baby or treat me like I'm a baby and hold me like I'm a baby, and that's what they do wrong, really" ("*American Horror Story*'s Ma Petite"). While Jyoti critiques such infantilizing behaviors from nondisabled individuals, she is forced to perform these behaviors on screen because her character is depicted as an adorable child whom the other actors constantly pick up without asking her permission. Elsa often refers to Ma Petite as "my cuddle" or "my darling" and holds her in a type of baby bjorn as Ma Petite clings to Elsa in loving adoration. When Elsa receives presents for her birthday, Ma Petite appears wrapped inside a giant box like a commodity for Elsa's enjoyment ("Bullseye"). Even Ma Petite's backstory infantilizes her: sensing that the "pinhead" Pepper desires a baby, Elsa "purchases" Ma Petite from the "Maharaja of Kapurthala" ("Orphans"). This Orientalist scene frames the Maharaja as an "uncivilized" Other who holds Ma Petite by a leash attached to her neck and refers to her as his "favorite pet." After Elsa gives him three cases of Dr. Pepper, the Maharaja decides to sell his "pet." In addition to infantilizing and dehumanizing Ma Petite, this exchange perpetuates the stereotype of non–Western people of color as ignorant cultural Others who are so "savage" as to exchange humans for trivial Western products. Even in Amge's video featured on the *AHS* YouTube channel, images of Ma Petite being held intersperse with Amge telling the audience she does not like being carried like a baby ("*American Horror Story* FX," "Jyoti Amge"). By presenting these paternalistic, Orientalist images and relegating Amge's critique to a secondary YouTube video, *Freak Show* risks presenting this infantilization as unproblematic to its audience who, in turn, may treat Amge in this same manner.

Mat Fraser faces a similar situation when he has to recite dialogue that directly contradicts his own politics and lived experience. Fraser has multiple tattoos covering his body, and *Freak Show*'s creators originally intend his character to have a tattooed face. Fraser protested this decision because he did not want to be unrecognizable for the biggest break in his career (Walters). In the show's narrative, Fraser's character describes why he decides to tattoo his body but not his face:

> PAUL: The world hated me, but no more than I hated myself. They wanted a monster? I decided to give them one. I could never make the world love me. Maybe I could make it fear me.
> EDWARD MORDRAKE: Why not the face?
> PAUL: I thought about it, but at the last minute I chickened out.
> EDWARD MORDRAKE: Why?
> PAUL: 'Cause I have a handsome face. I have the face of a pretty lad. Can you imagine this mug on a normal body? I could've ruled the world ["Edward Mordrake, Pt. 2"].

On the one hand, this exchange accurately reflects how disabled individuals often develop self-hatred from internalizing ableist norms. Because society shames Paul into hating his body, he wants to become the "monster" that society believes him to be by visibly "Othering" his body. However, having the character maintain a tattoo-less face upholds a normative understanding of ability that frames the character's "pretty" face as desirable and his tattooed, "disabled" limbs and neck as freakish. The show perpetuates the connection of tattooing and disability with abnormality by including this dialogue as the character's backstory. The original plan to have the character tattoo his face reinforces this understanding by further overemphasizing Paul's "freakishness" through supposed corporeal abnormality. Saying these lines and referring to his own tattoos in this manner contradicts Fraser's own beliefs. Reflecting on the dialogue about his character's appearance, Fraser says:

> I think that line was my punishment for not letting them tattoo my face! [...] Everyone thinks that is me talking—it's not! It's written by non-disabled writers who have bought into the vision of disability that mainstream culture gives them, including the classic clichéd able-bodied notion, squeezed through a mangle of modern body culture, that the normal part of me is the best bit, and that I would have preferred to have long arms. Both untrue! [...] I do the lines on the page because it's my job! I would have written something more layered and dimensional [Walters].

As this quotation demonstrates, Fraser has little-to-no voice in his own representation within the show. His "disabled" body serves as a mouthpiece for the show's writers who have less of an understanding of what it means to live as a disabled person, both in the 1950s U.S. and as a contemporary actor on a mainstream hit television show. Forcing Fraser to say these lines and assume this characterization despite his own belief system dismisses his agency.

Because Fraser lacks the same amount of power in this situation as his bosses, he must conform to their desires. Sarcasm aside, that Fraser believes he is "punished" for refusing to tattoo his face speaks to how these differences of power operate on *Freak Show*.

Erasing How Ableism Operates Intersectionally

In developing the season's narrative, the writers of *AHS* fail to account for how intersectionality influences the lives and histories of disabled people. Intersectionality refers to a way of conceptualizing discrimination and politics that understands identity as multi-layered rather than structured around singular issues (Crenshaw 167). Deployments of ableism necessarily differ according to how other forms of discrimination operate along the lines of the disabled subject's multiple identities. In other words, the experiences and histories of a disabled heterosexual white woman necessarily differ from those of a disabled queer woman of color. This nuanced understanding of how disability operates does not translate into *American Horror Story*'s representation of freak show history. While the show does include Born Freaks, Made Freaks, Novelty Acts, and Gaffed Freaks in its typology, the characters are overwhelmingly white.[11] Of the four groups historically enfreaked, no nondisabled people of color from the U.S. appear on the show. Despite the importance of eugenicist logic and common practices of enslavement to this history, *AHS* depicts only ableism as an organizing logic of freak shows. The show's writers erase all constructions of nonwhite bodies as "Natives" and "Exotics from the Wild." Because the show fails to include any examples of U.S. domestic racism, *Freak Show* perpetuates an ahistorical "postracial" narrative that removes the nuances of how freak discourse Others nondisabled people of color differently than white bodies. This whitewashed history ignores the significance of U.S. racist ideologies and legal policies in 1950s Southern freak show history. Furthermore, this omission is particularly egregious because Murphy references the Civil Rights movement as a point of inspiration for the season; in essence, he appropriates a Civil Rights narrative and erases black lives and histories from it.

By ignoring the intersectional identities of the show's characters and cast, *American Horror Story*'s writers present an inaccurate version of freak show history that perpetuates racist stereotypes, whitewashes the experiences of people of color, and excludes the histories of trans women. To demonstrate these points, I analyze the writer's treatments of the characters played by Angela Bassett, Sarah Paulson, and Erika Ervin. My purpose is not to offer a comprehensive analysis of these examples, for each one could be a separate article in-and-of itself. Rather, I make connections among these examples in order to demonstrate how *Freak Show*'s writers ultimately take more care in constructing the white gay male character's story than the stories of trans women and people of color.

In telling the story of the show's one disabled black female character, Angela Bassett's Desiree, *Freak Show*'s writers fail to explore how racism organizes the logics of her enfreakment. Bassett plays an "intersex" character with three breasts whose "disability" and storyline revolve around her being a self-identified "full-blown hermaphrodite" ("Massacres and Matinees").[12] *Freak Show*'s creative team requires Bassett to wear a prosthetic third breast that oversexualizes her and obliges her to display her body for the show's predominantly white television audience.[13] By making Desiree's "disability" her exoticized body, the show's writers reproduce a legacy of violence against black women in freak shows. Desiree's characterization evokes the history of Sarah Baartman, the Khoekhoe woman from southern Africa exhibited for white European audiences.[14] Historically, Baartman serves as a sign of racial difference that these audiences use to justify white supremacy and colonialism. Baartman's treatment helps to create modern stereotypes about black women's sexuality, including the trope of the hypersexualized jezebel (Collins, *Black Sexual Politics* 28). Similar to Baartman, Desiree's enfreakment revolves around her Othered body and genitalia. Desiree functions as an oversexualized jezebel whose sexual agency centers on her ability to please white men. Desiree marries Dell, a closeted white gay man, and early in the season sleeps with white gay men as a favor in order to "turn" them straight ("Massacres and Matinees"). Because of her "non-normative" genitalia and "lascivious" sexuality, Desiree serves as a conduit for white gay men to claim a heterosexual identity. *Freak Show*'s writers fail to address how representing Desiree as sexually available to white men is part of the jezebel trope that historically justifies white male sexual assault and ownership of black women (Collins, *Black Feminist Thought* 89). By failing to critique these tropes, *Freak Show*'s writers end up perpetuating them.

Unlike Sarah Baartman, Desiree has control over her act and does not undergo any invasive medical procedures that enfreaked black women historically face.[15] Indeed, within the show's narrative, the ableism Desiree faces differs little from the ableism the white characters face. The show's writers frame Desiree's blackness as a "nonissue" in her enfreakment, thereby erasing the ways in which disabled black women face marginalization differently than disabled white individuals. Rather than exploring how racism and ableism operate together to oppress Desiree, the show's writers fail to acknowledge her intersectional identity. The show's narrative ignores the role of racism in Desiree's enfreakment, but at the same time, the show's writers enfreak Desiree and Angela Bassett according to the racist logics of Baartman's display. In characterizing Desiree, *Freak Show*'s writers reproduce the tropes of the jezebel and fail to present an historically accurate portrayal of how racism operates in freak shows.

The show's writers similarly ignore the significance of U.S. imperialism and domestic racism in their depiction of Sarah Paulson's characters. Paulson plays conjoined twins Bette and Dot Tattler, who directly reference real conjoined twins Chang and Eng Bunker. Born in the kingdom of Siam (contemporary Thailand) in the early nineteenth century, Chang and Eng were taken to the United States in 1829 after being "discovered" in their village by Scottish merchant Robert Hunter. When they first arrived in the United States, Chang and Eng were forced to work under Abel Coffin, a business associate of the mariner who met them during his travels in Siam. After initially being forced into this position of indentured servitude, Chang and Eng eventually became the owners of their own act, gained a measure of financial affluence, became naturalized as U.S. citizens at a time when naturalization was available only to free white persons, married two white women before the repeal of antimiscegenation laws, and became slave-owners. Chang and Eng's class mobility and absorption into white America were unprecedented at this time. As one of, if not the most, popular pairs of conjoined twins in history, Chang and Eng toured extensively throughout North America, Europe, and parts of Latin America. They became so well known as public figures and so ubiquitous as conjoined twins that the term "Siamese twins" eventually came to describe all such twins (Wu 2).

By applying Orientalist labels used to describe Chang and Eng to Paulson's characters, *Freak Show*'s writers whitewash this history and the disabled bodies of Chang and Eng. Instead of modeling Bette and Dot after white conjoined twins such as Daisy and Violet Hilton, the showrunners inextricably tie the white characters to Chang and Eng. *Freak Show*'s creative team clearly knows Chang and Eng's story: when Stanley visits the American Morbidity Museum and inquires about an object on the shelf, the museum's curator informs him that the jar contains the liver of Chang and Eng ("Edward Mordrake, Pt. 1"). Through *Freak Show*'s advertising and narrative, the creative team applies Orientalist phrases to the whitewashed bodies of Bette and Dot. The show's official advertising labels Paulson's character "the Siamese Twins," and within the show's narrative, the twins are billed as "Siamese Sisters" (The-Complex). When Michael Chiklis's Dell introduces the twins to a crowded audience, he says: "Ladies and gentlemen, from the exotic land of Siam, the Spectacular Siamese Sisters" ("Massacres and Matinees"). The label "Siamese twins" develops because of Western audiences' Orientalist responses to Chang and Eng. White audiences imagine "Siam" to be a mythical location in "the East," and the display of Chang and Eng's racialized, disabled, immigrant bodies reinforces white people's notions of "the East" as exotic and uncivilized. Conjoined white twins would not face the same labeling because they do not face the same Orientalist processes of Othering that Chang and Eng undergo. By casting Paulson in this role while continuing to describe her characters in this way, the show applies racist speech to a whitewashed body, thereby appropriating the history but erasing the bodies of Chang and Eng. This whitewashing ignores the interlocking systems of racism, ableism, and U.S. imperialism that inform both Chang and Eng's story and the deployments of this language. This historical erasure frames race and nationality as nonissues within the history of freak shows, and Murphy and Falchuck's resulting freak discourse produces a neoliberal "post-racial" narrative that further marginalizes the histories and experiences of disabled people of color.

In their treatment of Erika Ervin's Amazon Eve, *Freak Show*'s writers similarly erase her intersectional identity from her character's representation. In her promotional video for *American Horror Story*'s official YouTube channel, Ervin discusses how her experience as a transgender woman informs both her identity and her experience on *AHS*. Whereas the other promotional videos feature the actors discussing their disabilities at length, Ervin mentions in passing that she is a "giantess" ("*American Horror Story* FX," "Erika Ervin"). Her video focuses on her experience as a transgender woman, detailing how she grew up feeling "different" because of her gender identity and how her family disowned her when she came out as transgender in 2004. When she auditioned for the role of Amazon Eve, which was initially intended for a male actor, Ervin closeted her trans identity and performed in male drag with slicked-back hair, no makeup, a flannel shirt, bound breasts, and a lowered voice. After earning the role, Ervin contended with how her identity as a transgender woman translates into the show. As she says in the video:

> [The season's] story itself is taking me on my own personal journey and seeing where I personally fit into the paradigm called "*Freak Show*"... I think the transgender movement could actually learn from the freak narrative—the narrative of extraordinary bodies, differences, celebrating our differences. It's a place for people who are different to come together and find a sense of community. It's more than just a freak show. There's a family here.

For Ervin, her transgender identity is inextricable from her experience both as a "disabled" individual and as an actress on the show. Her quotation explores intersections between trans and disabled identities, as well as how narratives of these lived experiences could mutually benefit one another.[16] Even though *American Horror Story*'s creators alter her character specifically for Ervin, they fail to incorporate Ervin's trans identity into the show. Amazon Eve becomes a cisgender woman whose defining characteristic is her identity as a "giantess." The show's narrative erases Ervin's multilayered identity in favor of defining her solely by her "disability." *Freak Show*'s writers have the opportunity to explore how a white transgender individual with a "disability" navigates the 1950s, which would provide a unique opportunity to make visible aspects of transgender histories that frequently go unrepresented. Exploring this history could also provide an opportunity to include narratives from trans women of color and explorations of how disability, gender identity, and race operate together. This story would align with Murphy's plan to give voice to those whom society marginalizes, particularly in this contemporary moment when transgender women of color face violence, suicide, and homicide at rates far higher than most individuals. While the show does provide insight into what life was like for a white gay man in the 1950s, *AHS* fails to give the same consideration to trans women.

Emphasizing the Oppression of White Gay Men

While the *American Horror Story* creative team fails to present historically accurate representations of racism and U.S. imperialism in freak shows, they take more care in depicting how homophobia operates in the 1950s United States. During this time period, the American Psychiatric Association categorized homosexuality as a mental disorder, and U.S. domestic policies largely criminalized same-sex behaviors. The show's two significant white gay male characters, Dell and Stanley, understand their sexualities according to these conditions. Dell hides his sexuality in shame, does not "come out" to anyone in the freak show, and has no love scenes with men. In contrast, Stanley feels no shame in his homosexuality, conceals his identity only out of a need to protect his well-being, is open about his gayness with Emma Roberts's character, Maggie, and sleeps with multiple male partners. Dell's depiction emphasizes the negative aspects of the severely closeted time period, and his decision not to "come out" corresponds with pre-gay liberation politics that do not yet emphasize a coming out narrative as integral to claiming a sexual identity. Stanley's representation demonstrates how some white gay men could live more openly in the 1950s U.S. without developing shame from internalized homophobia. These two contrasting characters provide a view into different ways that white gay men navigate the closet and understand their sexual identities. Additionally, the show accurately depicts some of the living conditions that white gay men must navigate because of homophobia. The local gay bar owner pays off the police so that his customers avoid harassment, and Dell's love interest Andy works as a hustler to survive ("Pink Cupcakes"). After seeing Dell at the gay bar, Stanley (one of the show's primary villains) blackmails Dell and threatens to reveal his sexuality to the "freaks" ("Test of Strength"). These storylines showcase how white gay men survive during this era of homosexual criminalization, as well as how they face potential extortion if someone discovers their sexuality. In these ways, Dell's and Stanley's characterizations and storylines offer a sincere depiction of certain aspects of homosexual subcultures in the 1950s U.S. (D'Emilio 49).

However, a problem arises with *Freak Show*'s comparison of gayness to "freakishness." Homosexuality and Disability do share similar aspects and histories: in their pathologization and medicalization, how they both involve gawking from straight and "typical" individuals, and how they intertwine with shame and isolation (Clare, *Exile and Pride* 112). However, comparing the two identities risks creates artificial binaries that unintentionally hierarchize different forms of marginalization (Samuels, "My Body, My Closet" 317). Instead of exploring the intersectional nuances of how disability and sexuality operate in 1950s Florida, *Freak Show* generates a hierarchy of oppression that places white gay men at the top. This hierarchy is apparent in a scene when Maggie notices gay erotica that falls out of Stanley's suitcase. She warns Stanley to be more careful in hiding his sexuality because: "The only thing people in Jupiter hate more than freaks are poofs" ("Pink Cupcakes"). This dialogue both distinguishes "freaks" from "poofs" and creates a spectrum of oppression that situates homosexuals above the show's disabled characters. *Freak Show*'s oppression hierarchy is further evidenced through Ryan Murphy's reaction to the murder of Andy, Dell's lover. Dell daydreams about running away with Andy, but this fantasy never comes to fruition, after the sociopath Dandy murders and dismembers Andy during what the latter thinks will be a gay hookup. Murphy calls this event "one of the most disturbing things we've ever done and a true horror scene" (Weinstein). While Andy's fate is horrific, the fact that Murphy thinks his murder is one of the most horrific scenes in the show's history (a history that includes the massacre of black women, dismemberment of children, and multiple scenes of rape and violence against women), says a lot about how Murphy understands violence against white gay men in comparison to violence against other marginalized groups.

Through the characterization of Dell and his relationship to disability, *Freak Show* suggests that the psychic turmoil of living a closeted life is a more difficult lived experience than having a physical disability.[17] Within the show's narrative, Dell has a complex relationship with disability because he can "pass" as able-bodied. The former husband of Ethel the "Bearded Lady," father to Jimmy the "Lobster Boy," and current husband to Desiree, Dell appears to be a Novelty Act in the freak show who lacks any visible impairments. However, Dell's father and brothers have ectrodactyly (also known as split hands), and they ostracize Dell for being the one family member without the impairment ("Magical Thinking"). In Dell's family, he "[becomes] a freak for being normal" ("Magical Thinking"). Despite Dell's seeming "normality," he retains this disability as part of his heritage/bloodline, and he passes the variation onto his son Jimmy. Because he does not inherit ectrodactyly, Dell remains visibly able-bodied and benefits from his privileged ability to "pass" as someone without a disability. Because he appears as a hypermasculine, able-bodied white man, Dell has more access to social spaces than the other "freaks" and faces no harassment when he walks through the town of Jupiter and visits local bars ("Massacres and Matinees"; "Test of Strength"). Stanley has no interest in selling Dell's body to the American Morbidity Museum, so Dell does not face the same risks of being murdered and/or dismembered as the other "freaks."

Despite these various privileges, Dell appears in the narrative as one of the most tormented characters because of his closeted sexuality. Dell's homosexuality is not initially visible because his hypermasculinity masks his gayness through stereotypical gender presentation, and *Freak Show*'s audience does not learn of Dell's sexuality until the season's fifth episode (three episodes after the character's introduction). Before revealing Dell's secret to the audience, the show frames the character as violent for no reason and a threat to the "freaks." In his first three episodes, Dell appears to be one of the season's main villains without any moral ambiguity. Once Dell enters the safe space of the gay bar his characterization shifts significantly. Dell expresses his sexuality openly only at the bar where he spends time with his lover Andy. After seeing Dell at the gay bar, Stanley blackmails him into murdering Ma Petite in order to prevent Dell's outing ("Test of Strength"). The resulting guilt Dell experiences from the murder, combined with feelings of shame and abandonment after being told that Andy has left town, drive Dell to attempt suicide. During the scene where Dell attempts to hang himself, he has a conversation with a vision of his dead ex-wife, Ethel, which explicitly conflates Dell's sexuality with disability:

DELL: I am a coward. I just can't take the shame of it no more, being what I am.
ETHEL: A freak.
DELL: As it turns out, yeah. I swear to Christ Ethel, I don't know how you and the others manage it.
ETHEL: We manage it because we have to. We wear our shame on the outside. There's no hiding it. It's just who we are. Now, you carry your shame on the inside. You keep it trapped in there. It eats away at you, feeding on you like a living thing 'til there's nothing left but the rot.
DELL: I've been fighting it for so long. I just don't have any fight left in me ["Tupperware Party Massacre"].

While this exchange between Ethel and Dell does accurately depict how internalized homophobia and self-hate can produce an emotional "rot," the dialogue unnecessarily compares a homosexual's experience to the experiences of visibly disabled individuals. The scene suggests that being a closeted gay man is somehow more oppressive because the situation results in psychic turmoil. Whereas visibly disabled individuals learn how to manage their "shame,"

Dell lacks the same luxury because he must keep his homosexuality hidden. This dialogue fails to account for the various privileges Dell enjoys because of his ability to "pass," including not being murdered by Stanley. Instead, Dell's psychological torment takes precedence as his defining characteristic.

Part of Dell's internal struggle results from his inability to be "out" in the freak show. Because individuals with nonvisible disabilities face marginalization within disability communities and the dominant culture, Dell faces potential discrimination from both society as a whole and the freak show (Samuels, "My Body, My Closet" 324). Dell's sexuality isolates him from everyone outside the confines of the gay bar, including the other "freaks." Whereas the heterosexual couple of Penny and Paul find solace and a sense of community with the "freaks," Dell seemingly lacks the same ability. The "freaks" do not discuss homosexuality openly, so the show gives no indication whether or not the environment would be welcoming to Dell. The freak show appears not to accept homosexuality because the show never raises the prospect of Dell living openly with the "freaks." Within the subcultural world of "freaks," homosexuality remains on the margins, an unspoken and unrecognized identity. Therefore, despite the show's "wir sind alle freaks" rhetoric, Dell remains too "freakish" even for the freaks and, ultimately, the most marginalized individual in the show.

Conclusion

In framing *Freak Show* as an exploration of oppression against "freaks," Ryan Murphy gives this season of *American Horror Story* an overtly political aim: to give underrepresented people with disabilities a voice that they otherwise would not have. This season's casting does provide visibility and an income to impaired actors, and the narrative does include some potentially progressive elements of a social model of disability. However, in creating this fictionalized history of freak shows, *American Horror Story* presents an historically inaccurate representation that over-rides the voices of disabled actors and elevates the oppression of white gay men at the expense of the impaired actors and the histories of disabled people of color and trans women. *Freak Show*'s portrayal of disability matters because so few positive representations of disabled lives and employment opportunities for impaired actors on mainstream U.S. shows currently exist. Despite its positive attributes, the show is ultimately a missed opportunity for exploring how ableism operates alongside other forms of oppression.

NOTES

1. I refer to the supporting cast members as actors with disabilities because the cast self-identify as individuals with disabilities, as evidenced by their videos on *American Horror Story*'s official YouTube channel (*American Horror Story* FX). To vary my language usage, I

also refer to them at times as actors with impairments. I use both "disabilities" and "impairments" in aligning with a social model of disability that understands this terminology as referring to individual variations rather than deficits.

2. For a more comprehensive history of U.S. freak shows, see Robert Bogdan's *Freak Show: Presenting Human Oddities for Amusement and Profit* (Chicago: University of Chicago Press, 1988).

3. In her analysis of freak discourse in Western culture, Rosemarie Garland Thomson focuses specifically on the shift in representation from "the ancient to the modern era" (2). She argues that the genealogy of freak discourse is characterized by a movement from a narrative of disability as marvelous to deviant. Although Garland Thomson focuses on this specific time period, she recognizes that deployments of freak discourse vary in each sociohistorical context.

4. Ableism refers generally to a form of discrimination and/or social prejudice against people with disabilities.

5. For more information on these contemporary conversations, see Lennard Davis's (Ed.) *Disability Studies Reader*, 4th ed. (New York: Routledge, 2013).

6. Mat Fraser's character in particular represents the complexity of *American Horror Story*'s freak discourse because Paul is superficially progressive but ultimately perpetuates offensive tropes. The progressive element of Paul's characterization revolves around his being one of the show's leading love interests. In most representations of disability, the disabled character is rarely shown to be a desiring subject or an object of desire (Mollow and McRuer 1). When disabled characters are sexualized, these portrayals generally frame their sexual identities as tragically deficient or freakishly excessive (1). *Freak Show* disrupts this pattern by representing Paul as a sexual being with agency who is neither pitiable nor shameful. Paul is initially in two relationships: a sexual relationship with Jessica Lange's Elsa Mars and a romantic relationship with the able-bodied Penny. Penny and Paul have, arguably, the most functional relationship in the show, and the progression of their coupling over the course of the season demonstrates how disability is not anathema to sexuality and intimacy. However, reading the relationship in this manner requires ignoring the pair's initial characterization. During the season's first episode, Paul partakes in a drug-fueled, videotaped orgy with the able-bodied Penny and other "freaks." Penny has no recollection of the encounter, and as she views the film with Elsa, Penny clearly understands herself to be the victim of sexual assault. This scene shows the "freaks" to be sexual deviants who take advantage of an able-bodied woman. After this initial episode, *Freak Show* drops the rape plotline entirely, and the next time Penny appears in the narrative she is in an intimate relationship with Paul. Poor writing and plot development aside, the dismissal of this assault normalizes the supposed deviancy of disabled sexuality: only by drugging a woman are the "freaks" able to sleep with a "normal" person. Despite the later positive elements of the Penny/Paul relationship, this initial characterization perpetuates offensive stereotypes of the disabled sexual deviant that contradict the show's supposedly progressive freak discourse.

7. Other instances of society oppressing the "freaks" include Pepper's sister and brother-in-law framing her for the murder of their child, and conjoined twins Bette and Dot's mother hiding them in the house for fear of what the "typical" neighbors will think if the twins are seen.

8. Another main villain, the murderous clown Twisty, presents no threat to the disabled performers. Although he plays a significant role in the season's first four episodes, Twisty ultimately does not harm the "freaks."

9. Ben Woolf's critique is particularly poignant because he passed away on February 23, 2015, after being hit by an SUV's mirror while he was crossing the street.

10. I do not claim that the show's main cast members lack any disabilities because they may identify as having an impairment. However, because the main cast members are visibly able-bodied, I distinguish them from the show's supporting actors with disabilities. In addition to having visibly able-bodied privilege, the main cast retains an amount of class privilege and power that the supporting cast cannot attain.

11. The show's "Born Freaks" include Jyoti Amge's Ma Petite, Angela Bassett's Desiree, Erika Ervin's Amazon Eve, Mat Fraser's Paul, Naomi Grossman's Pepper, Christopher

Neiman's Salty, Sarah Paulson's Bette and Dot, Evan Peters's Jimmy, Drew Rin Varick's Toulouse, Rose Siggins's Legless Suzi, and Ben Woolf's Meep. The "Made Freaks" include Kathy Bates's Ethel and Jessica Lange's Elsa. The "Novelty Act" includes Neil Patrick Harris's Chester, and the "Gaffed Freak" includes Emma Roberts's Maggie. As I demonstrate later in the essay, Michael Chiklis's Dell initially appears to be a "Novelty Act," but the show complicates this characterization as the narrative progresses.

12. Later in the season, after bleeding from a sexual encounter with another white man, Desiree goes to a doctor and discovers that she has an enlarged clitoris rather than a penis. I put her "intersex" identity in quotations because the character's progression challenges this initial representation.

13. By making this argument, I do not intend to frame Bassett as solely exploited by the show because doing so would deny her own agency. Rather, as with the disabled actors, Basset engages in *Freak Show*'s complex process of exploitation and remuneration: she benefits financially from appearing on the show but lacks the same power as *Freak Show*'s creative team in defining her character.

14. For more information on Sarah Baartman, see Deborah Willis's edited collection *Black Venus 2010: They Called Her "Hottentot"* (Philadelphia: Temple University Press, 2010) and, Natasha Gordon-Chipembere's *Representation and Black Womanhood: The Legacy of Sarah Baartman* (New York: Palgrave Macmillan, 2011).

15. For more information on the types of invasive medical procedures that disabled people of color face, see Ellen Samuels's "Examining Millie and Christine McCoy: Where Enslavement and Enfreakment Meet," *Signs* 37.1 (2011): 53–81.

16. For additional consideration of the intersections between trans and disabled identities, see Eli Clare's "Body Shame, Body Pride: Lessons From the Disability Rights Movement," *The Transgender Studies Reader*, 2nd ed, Eds. Susan Stryker and Aren Z. Aizura (New York: Routledge, 2013), 316–332.

17. Because Stanley is not part of the freak show, his character provides a less interesting reading than Dell's in terms of how the characters' "disabilities" intersect with their sexualities. Stanley's "disability" revolves around having an abnormally large penis, and the character functions as a stereotype of the hypersexual, hypermasculine villainous gay man. In contrast, Dell has a much more significant role in the freak show.

Works Cited

"*American Horror Story* FX." "*American Horror Story: Freak Show* Extra Ordinary Artists— Ben Woolf." Online video clip. *YouTube*. YouTube, 10 October 2014. Web. 20 February 2015.

"*American Horror Story* FX." "*American Horror Story: Freak Show* Extra Ordinary Artists— Erika Ervin." Online video clip. *YouTube*. YouTube, 6 October 2014. Web. 20 February 2015.

"*American Horror Story* FX." "*American Horror Story: Freak Show* Extra Ordinary Artists— Jyoti Amge." Online video clip. *YouTube*. YouTube, 7 October 2014. Web. 20 February 2015.

"*American Horror Story* FX." "*American Horror Story: Freak Show* Extra Ordinary Artists— Mat Fraser." Online video clip. *YouTube*. YouTube, 3 October 2014. Web. 20 February 2015.

"*American Horror Story*'s Ma Petite: Don't Treat Me Like a Baby." *ETOnline*. Entertainment Tonight, 25 November 2014. Web. 20 February 2015.

Bogdan, Robert. *Freak Show: Presenting Human Oddities for Amusement and Profit*. Chicago: University of Chicago Press, 1988. Print.

_____. "The Social Construction of Freaks." *Freakery: Cultural Spectacles of the Extraordinary Body*. Ed. Rosemarie Garland Thomson. New York: New York University Press, 1996. 23–37. Print.

"Bullseye." *American Horror Story: Freak Show*. *The Complete Fourth Season*. Writ. John J. Gray. Dir. Howard Deutch. Twentieth Century Fox, 2015. DVD.

Clare, Eli. "Body Shame, Body Pride: Lessons From the Disability Rights Movement." *The*

Transgender Studies Reader. 2nd ed. Eds. Susan Stryker and Aren Z. Aizura. New York: Routledge, 2013: 261–265. Print.

_____. *Exile and Pride: Disability, Queerness and Liberation.* 1999. Cambridge: South End Press, 2009. Print.

Collins, Patricia Hill. *Black Feminist Thought: Knowledge, Consciousness, and the Politics of Empowerment.* New York: Routledge, 2000. Print.

_____. *Black Sexual Politics: African Americans, Gender, and the New Racism.* New York: Routledge, 2005. Print.

Crenshaw, Kimberle. "Demarginalizing the Intersection of Race and Sex: A Black Feminist Critique of Antidiscrimination Doctrine, Feminist Theory and Antiracist Politics." *University of Chicago Legal Forum* 8.1 (1989): 139–167. Print.

Davis, Lennard, ed. *The Disability Studies Reader.* 4th ed. New York: Routledge, 2013. Print.

D'Emilio, John. *Sexual Politics, Sexual Communities: The Making of a Homosexual Minority in the United States, 1940–1970.* 2nd ed. Chicago: University of Chicago Press, 1998. Print.

Dos Santos, Kristin. "The World's Smallest Woman Is 'the biggest diva!' Get to Know (and Love) *American Horror Story*'s Unique New Stars." *EOnline.* E Entertainment Television, 6 October 2014. Web. 20 February 2015.

"Edward Mordrake, Pt. 1." *American Horror Story: Freak Show. The Complete Fourth Season.* Writ. James Wong. Dir. Michael Uppendahl. Twentieth Century Fox, 2015. DVD.

"Edward Mordrake, Pt. 2." *American Horror Story: Freak Show. The Complete Fourth Season.* Writ. Jennifer Salt. Dir. Howard Deutch. Twentieth Century Fox, 2015. DVD.

Garland Thomson, Rosemarie. "Introduction: From Wonder to Error—A Genealogy of Freak Discourse in Modernity." *Freakery: Cultural Spectacles of the Extraordinary Body.* Ed. Rosemarie Garland Thomson. New York: New York University Press, 1996. 1–19. Print.

Gerber, David A. "The 'Careers' of People Exhibited in Freak Shows: The Problem of Volition and Valorization." *Freakery: Cultural Spectacles of the Extraordinary Body.* Ed. Rosemarie Garland Thomson. New York: New York University Press, 1996. 38–54. Print.

Gordon-Chipembere, Natasha, ed. *Representation and Black Womanhood: The Legacy of Sarah Baartman.* New York: Palgrave Macmillan, 2011. Print.

Hevey, David. *The Creatures Time Forgot: Photography and Disability Imagery.* New York: Routledge, 1992. Print.

Kondolojy, Amanda. "Wednesday Cable Ratings: *American Horror Story* Tops Night + *South Park, Teen Mom II, The Daily Show, Key & Peele* & More." *TV By The Numbers.* Tribune Digital Ventures, 9 October 2014. Web. 20 February 2015.

"Magical Thinking." *American Horror Story: Freak Show. The Complete Fourth Season.* Writ. Jennifer Salt. Dir. Michael Goi. Twentieth Century Fox, 2015. DVD.

"Massacres and Matinees." *American Horror Story: Freak Show. The Complete Fourth Season.* Writ. Tim Minear. Dir. Alfonso Gómez-Rejón. Twentieth Century Fox, 2015. DVD.

Mollow, Anna, and Robert McRuer. "Introduction." *Sex and Disability.* Eds. Robert McRuer and Anna Mollow. Durham: Duke University Press, 2012. 1–36. Print.

"Monsters Among Us." *American Horror Story: Freak Show. The Complete Fourth Season.* Writ. Ryan Murphy and Brad Falchuck. Dir. Ryan Murphy. Twentieth Century Fox, 2015. DVD.

"Orphans." *American Horror Story: Freak Show. The Complete Fourth Season.* Writ. James Wong. Dir. Bradley Buecker. Twentieth Century Fox, 2015. DVD.

"Pink Cupcakes." *American Horror Story: Freak Show. The Complete Fourth Season.* Writ. Jessica Sharzer. Dir. Michael Uppendahl. Twentieth Century Fox, 2015. DVD.

Reiss, Benjamin. *The Showman and the Slave: Race, Death, and Memory in Barnum's America.* Cambridge: Harvard University Press, 2001. Print.

Samuels, Ellen. "Examining Millie and Christine McCoy: Where Enslavement and Enfreakment Meet." *Signs* 37.1 (2011): 53–81. Electronic.

_____. "My Body, My Closet: Invisible Disability and the Limits of Coming Out." *The Disability Studies Reader.* 4th ed. Ed. Lennard Davis. New York: Routledge, 2013. 316–332. Print.

Stack, Tim. "Ryan Murphy on *AHS: Freak Show*: 'This season, once you die, you're dead.'"

Entertainment Weekly. Entertainment Weekly, 15 September 2014. Web. 20 February 2015.

"Test of Strength." *American Horror Story: Freak Show. The Complete Fourth Season.* Writ. Crystal Liu. Dir. Anthony Hemingway. Twentieth Century Fox, 2015. DVD.

TheComplex. "New *AHS: Freak Show* Character/Plot Details Revealed + First Extended Teaser." *Sinuous Magazine.* Sinuous Magazine, 11 September 2014. Web. 20 February 2015.

"Tupperware Party Massacre." *American Horror Story: Freak Show. The Complete Fourth Season.* Writ. Brad Falchuk. Dir. Loni Peristere. Twentieth Century Fox, 2015. DVD.

Walters, Ben. "*AHS: Freak Show*'s Paul—aka Mat Fraser—on Being a Sex Object, Bradley Cooper and 'crip confidence.'" *NotTelevision.* NotTelevision, 12 November 2014. Web. 20 February 2015.

Weinstein, Shelli. "Ryan Murphy Previews the 'Dastardly' and 'Disturbing' Scares Ahead in *AHS: Freak Show*." *Variety.* Variety Media, 8 October 2014. Web. 20 February 2015.

West, Kelly. "American Horror Story Freak Show: Let's Take a Closer Look at This Poster." *CinemaBlend.* CinemaBlend, n.d. Web. 13 August 2014.

Willis, Deborah, ed. *Black Venus 2010: They Called Her "Hottentot."* Philadelphia: Temple University Press, 2010. Print.

Wu, Cynthia. *Chang and Eng Reconnected: The Original Siamese Twins in American Culture.* Philadelphia: Temple University Press, 2012. Print.

PART THREE

Genre Tropes
and the Horror of History

"There's a power in it.
A power we can use"
Perpetuating the Past in Murder House

Rebecca Janicker

Following the immediate appeal of series co-creators Ryan Murphy and Brad Falchuk's new television horror drama, what was to become Season One became known as *American Horror Story: Murder House*. This new title, in laying bare the underlying remit of the original show (the telling of a haunted house tale), also indexes the hold that narratives of death and violence—especially those tied to a domestic context—continue to exert over the American popular imagination. This essay examines ways in which *Murder House* epitomizes what I call the *haunted house motif*. As explored in my book on haunted house literature,[1] this concept is concerned with how a text's protagonists and consumers engage with the experience of haunting. Enacted within the confines of a troubled space, haunted house tales demonstrate the lingering hold of the past while highlighting the complexities of the culture from which they arise. As the first installment of an ongoing horror story made especially for television, *Murder House* helps further an understanding of what the small screen has to offer to the horror genre and is here considered in light of the narrative and formal concerns pertaining to the medium.

This essay examines ways in which haunting facilitates an encounter with forces beyond the remit of everyday existence. The events of *Murder House* are set in motion when the Harmon family seeks a new home. Through the liminal power of haunting, these characters are obliged to contend with ghostly presences that pose a challenge to their former way of life and throw their established mindsets into question. In particular, I focus on how father Ben's time in this haunted house forces him to confront his own behavior and to reassess his values. With its inherently domestic setting and increas-

128

ingly sophisticated visual repertoire, television has come to offer a particularly compelling mode of engagement with tales of haunting. After outlining the nature and function of the haunted house motif, I consider how this motif plays out within the context of television, drawing on examples from *Murder House* to show that haunting is an intrinsically liminal experience in which historical events and processes work to impact upon the present.

The Haunted House Motif

As Eino Railo investigates in his seminal study of the same name, the iconic *Haunted Castle* (1927) originated in both literal and literary form with the eighteenth-century English writer Horace Walpole, whose Thames-side home of Strawberry Hill was transformed into a vision of antiquarianism through such embellishments as towers, stained glass and assorted weaponry (1–3).[2] Walpole's *The Castle of Otranto* (1764)—widely considered to be the first Gothic novel—imbues the eponymous structure with a disquieting atmosphere that was crucial to the book's success and later deemed essential to the Gothic genre. The novel relates a series of violent incidents, ultimately attributed to the castle's past usurpation, and utilizes the supernatural throughout to signal a grim heritage. This link between a place and its history, forged time and again in Gothic fictions, is integral to the haunted house motif.

In her study of the haunted house as cultural icon, Sylvia Grider discerns the implications that America's lack of medieval architecture has had for its literature (180). With the shift to the New World, and over the centuries since, the intimidating medieval fortress that loomed so large in eighteenth-century European Gothic transmuted into the rather more commonplace domestic setting of American Gothic and thus became a *house* rather than a *castle*. Developing from the initial idea of the haunted castle, the later notion of the haunted house soon came to have wider resonance. For Stephen King, haunted house tales hold a significant place in the domain of Gothic fictions and in *Danse Macabre* (1981) he argues that: "The archetype of the Ghost is, after all, the Mississippi of supernatural fiction" (66). As both consumer and creator of fictional works of horror, King suggests that such places invoke deeply-held superstitions, aptly reducing them to their simplest state with his observation that "we might call this particular archetype the Bad Place" (296). It is patently clear that the evocatively named Murder House is a dwelling that perpetuates this dark legacy of secrecy and dread.

Contemporary fiction about haunting clearly exhibits themes and func-tions that are no longer tied to the historically-prescribed set of circumstances symbolized by the original Gothic castle. For instance, there no longer seems to be any particular necessity for such tales to hark back to an archaic setting or to an imagined past. Yet the literary impetus to turn to the Gothic as a means of contending with history persists. Recognizing how this key Gothic trope has evolved, I employ the term haunted house motif in my explorations of those tales that deal with haunting and haunted spaces.[3] To speak of the haunted house in this sense—as a *motif* and not purely as a *building*—is to refer to a set of literary themes and conventions that appears throughout the sub-genre of haunted fiction. Moreover this motif, in combining physical setting with the Gothic trope of haunting, creates a special kind of narrative space in which fictional characters—and those who share their experiences—can engage with the events portrayed in these narratives.

The quality of liminality is of central importance to the haunted house motif. With its roots in social anthropology, this term derives from research into the temporarily "in between" positioning of those undergoing a change in status within social groups, for example individuals participating in tribal initiations (Turner, *The Forest of Symbols* 93). Such experiences typically involve immersion in temporal and spatial zones distinct from those of normal daily life. In this way, the novitiate, or liminar, is given the time and opportunity to absorb the kind of knowledge considered essential to their anticipated progress (Van Gennep 105–106). Building on Arnold van Gennep's work on initiation practices, Victor Turner explains that the liminar can be described in the following way: "ambiguous, neither here nor there, betwixt and between all fixed points of classification" (*Dramas, Fields, and Metaphors* 232). Freed from mundane concerns to contemplate the wider mysteries of life and confined to a space shrouded in mystery for those who do not share it, the liminar undergoes a time of trial and confrontation for the purpose of progression.

The concept of liminality has also been extended to literature and Manuel Aguirre, Roberta Quance and Philip Sutton stress that those texts and genres that are designated as liminal are characterized by: "a crossover, a transgression or an entry into the Other" (9). Liminality is thus associated with borderland territory and with the potential for boundary-crossing. Ideas about "in betweenness" are readily applicable to the Gothic since it is a genre that routinely transgresses accepted boundaries, e.g., between fundamentally discrete states like past and present, life and death. Further, given that haunted fiction is necessarily concerned with ghostly presences and historical events, it can be seen that haunting is intrinsically liminal. The haunted house motif combines the properties of the Gothic genre and the power of liminality, placing them within a troubled space. In doing so, it creates a distinctive narrative arena that affords an engagement with the histories it evokes and perhaps demands a confrontation with those ideological forces found within. The intimacy and familiarity of television lends itself to depicting tales of domestic terror, as well as affording opportunities for protagonists to develop as these tales unfold.

TV Horror

Courtesy of both literary adaptations and original productions, horror has been a compelling presence right from the earliest years of cinema. Likewise, in *TV Horror: Investigating the Dark Side of the Small Screen* (2013) Lorna Jowett and Stacey Abbott discern that "television is, and has always been, a significant location for horror" (*xiv*). Helen Wheatley's *Gothic Television* (2006) also affirms that "television is the ideal medium for the Gothic" and that Gothic TV can specifically be understood as "a domestic form of a genre which is deeply concerned with the domestic" (1). Horror and the Gothic have always held a certain appeal and it seems that the viewing context for these genres has taken an increasingly homely turn in recent years. From investigative dramas such as *Dexter* (2006–2014), *True Detective* (2014–) and *Hannibal* (2013–2015) to supernatural offerings like *The Walking Dead* (2010–), *Sleepy Hollow* (2013–) and *Outcast* (2016–), television horror has flourished over the last decade and viewers' appetites for mystery, violence and—to a greater or lesser degree—blood and gore seems undiminished.

One important development that must be borne in mind is the fact that television has undergone something of an industrial and technological revolution over the last twenty five years or so. First Wheatley, then Jowett and Abbott, indicate the increased possibilities for both making and showing TV horror from the 1990s onwards. The likes of *Twin Peaks* (1990–1991) and *American Gothic* (1995–1996), which exhibited a new kind of "highly complex visual style" (Wheatley 175), appeared at a time when increased competition from cable channels necessitated an emphatic creative and fiscal response from established TV networks like ABC, NBC and CBS (173). Further, Jowett and Abbott describe the impact wrought by technical changes:

> Increasing advances in technology and effects and more focus on TV aesthetics also enhances TV horror as spectacle (*Masters of Horror, The Walking Dead, Pushing Daisies*). Comments about the visual "limitations" of the small screen … now seem largely unfounded given advances in widescreen, HD and 3D … constant innovation [e.g. in CGI, animatronics and prosthetics] is seen by producers of TV horror as essential because they know audiences are savvy about effects, in television as well as in cinema [13–14].

Such innovations served to pave the way for a show like *American Horror Story*—replete with allusions to other genre texts and resplendent with an abundance of special effects, *AHS* stands as testament to the rich horror tradition of which it now forms a significant part.

However, the evolution of the small screen can be seen to extend beyond mere claims to technological advancement. Arguably, the very nature of TV drama itself has benefitted from a renaissance in the last few years. In *Complex TV: The Poetics of Contemporary Television Storytelling* (2015), Jason Mittell takes stock of such shifts in claiming that the medium has progressed over the last two decades to achieve what he sees as a new kind of storytelling (17). Mittell asserts that: "Television's narrative complexity is predicated on specific facets of storytelling that seem uniquely suited to the television series structure apart from film and literature and that distinguish it from conventional modes of episodic and serial forms" (18). According to this view, TV is not only comparable to other modes of storytelling, but may well have claims to superiority. In a televisual era dominated by acclaimed shows such as *The Sopranos* (1999–2007) and *The Wire* (2002–2008), Mittell discerns that audiences have become more and more accustomed to—and thus desirous of—heightened levels of narrative intricacy and new depths of characterization. Given this context, it is no surprise that TV horror has followed suit with convoluted storylines and complicated characters of its own.

So what does television bring to horror and the Gothic? One striking advantage that TV boasts over cinema—and a feature that seems part and parcel of its quotidian nature—is its inherent seriality. This property affects the very construction of the text. Drawing on remarks from Mick Garris, director of two Stephen King mini-series adaptations—*The Stand* (1994) and *The Shining* (1997)—Jowett and Abbott explain that the dispersal of television storylines over numerous instalments helps generate horror, concluding that "the creator of a horror mini-series paces the narrative to ensure that unease intensifies with each episode, gradually building to a horrific climax" (37). Audiences tune in week after week, inviting the same beleaguered (or beleaguering) characters into their homes time and again. This sizeable investment of time and intensifying outlay of emotional energy increases suspense, while anxiety about the fate of protagonists becomes heightened by simple virtue of their familiarity.

However, the seriality of television, whether in the case of a mini-series or something more prolonged, means more than just viewer anticipation about the latest plot twist. Mittell insists on "the vital role of character in serialized complex television" (118), pointing to Walter White in *Breaking Bad* (2008–2013) as a case study of how TV can foster sustained audience engagement with, and sympathy for, even the most morally dubious of characters (163). Discussing horror, Jowett and Abbott too maintain that: "Character is also embedded in narrative serialization" (53). Clearly, the device of the charismatic protagonist with the power to drive a storyline and inspire loyalty has found resonance with contemporary television audiences. And, as with characters in other types of drama, "horror" characters like Dexter

Morgan and Will Graham, Rick Grimes and Kyle Barnes harbor hidden pasts and psychological complexities to be revealed, only gradually, by the luxury of time that this medium permits.

In the age of "quality television"—marked out by an abundance of polished media products lauded by critics and sought after by sophisticated audiences—horror and the Gothic have gone from strength to strength. Enjoying the creative attentions of established TV horror auteurs like Chris Carter, creator of *The X-Files* (1993–2002; 2016–), Eric Kripke, creator of *Supernatural* (2005–) and Kim Manners, producer and director on both these programs, TV has exploited fresh technical possibilities and unveiled complex characters to tell engaging new tales of horror. Ryan Murphy and Brad Falchuk have followed in their footsteps in creating their own *American Horror Story* and the ways in which *Murder House* plays to its televisual strengths is explored in the next part of this essay.

Inside the Murder House

In true Gothic—and televisual—fashion, the initial *American Horror Story* is an overtly domestic narrative. In 2011, the troubled Harmon family needs a fresh start once Vivien's miscarriage, and husband Ben's subsequent infidelity, threaten to destroy their life together. Along with teenage daughter Violet and dog Hallie, they move across the country and take up residence in a "classic LA Victorian" mansion ("Pilot"). However, the family's relocation from Boston to Los Angeles does not result in the closure that they seek. For, unbeknownst to them, their new home is the infamous "Murder House," backdrop to many a violent and fatal incident throughout the twentieth century and beyond. Steeped in history and since enshrined in folklore—Vivien learns of the original inhabitants, a surgeon who performed illegal abortions in the basement and his unhappy wife, on the "Eternal Darkness" sightseeing tour that incorporates their home as a ghoulish highlight—this house is a twenty-first-century incarnation of the haunted house archetype so long embedded in the American Gothic tradition.

An *Entertainment Weekly* piece from 2014 emphasizes the centrality of space to *AHS* in remarking that: "Each cycle, we witness the same cast (Jessica Lange, Sarah Paulson, Evan Peters, etc.) get the bejesus scared out of them as new characters in new terrifying situations (haunted house, mental institution, coven, traveling sideshow)" (Stack 16). Practical constraints of industry aside—the development of a new, self-contained set will be required for each new season on the grounds of both economy and expediency—this feature of the show also highlights how Gothic repeatedly draws on place to serve its narrative and thematic purposes. Indeed, the Harmons' new home, haunted by a panoply of ghosts whose ranks they themselves are destined to swell, epitomizes the haunted house motif. This imposing and gloomy old abode, acting as a repository for all the dark deeds committed within its walls, provides a physical setting in which the past constantly comes back to disturb the present. Caught between past and present, life and death, in this intrinsically liminal place—and increasingly isolated from normal existence—the Harmons not only encounter the sweep of history contained within this edifice but are also forced to confront the secrets, past and present, that beset their own family unit. The remainder of this essay thus focuses on how Ben Harmon interacts with the ghostly forces he encounters and then learns from these experiences in order to progress.

Reflecting on the subject of characterization in serial TV drama, Mittell suggests a number of ways in which a character could be said to undergo change. He proposes that one such "frequent character arc might be considered *character education*, in which a mature adult learns a key life lesson over the course of a series and ends up a changed person [original emphases]" (138). As discussed above, characters have become integral to television drama and *American Horror Story* is no exception. The narrative courses of many such serialized TV dramas, with their recurrent stress on character development, can be likened to the process of liminality. Ben, as one of the main protagonists of *Murder House*, effectively takes on the role of a liminar. Dylan McDermott, who plays Ben, says of his character that: "Ben is an interesting guy because he's a psychiatrist himself, but I think that he probably needs more therapy than anybody else in the house" ("Behind the Fright"). Through the liminality of haunting, Ben is indeed poised to learn much about himself and his bond with his family.

Focusing heavily on the need for progress from the outset, Ben seeks to lay a firm foundation for his future role as a devoted husband and father by announcing to Marcy, the realtor who shows the Harmons around their new home, that: "I'm planning on seeing patients here so I can spend more time with the family" ("Pilot"). His later insistence that "We're gonna be happy here" quickly underscores his primary goal of reconciling with his wife and daughter and furnishing them all with a secure home, safely removed from their former life and seemingly untarnished by past tragedies and transgressions. Yet, as soon becomes apparent, their new home has other plans in store for them. The show commences with a scene set in 1978, in which twin boys gleefully rampage through the abandoned house until meeting a mysterious and violent end in the basement. Another portent of the violence within the house is Marcy's disclosure to the Harmons of the murder-suicide of the previous home-owners. Once the family moves in, other signs that all is not as idyllic as it seems quickly begin to emerge. Haunted by the ghosts of people whose deaths are well known and of those whose deaths are still to be discovered—all of whom have their own preoccupations and agendas—this house is a liminal space that forces Ben to face the past he left behind before he can find the domestic harmony for which he so longs.

Tate

David Peterson del Mar remarks that "Men tend to link fathering with marriage, to view being a husband, father, breadwinner, and home owner as a 'package deal'" (126). Having procured a promising new home for the family, Ben is eager to develop his professional role by starting up his business. Thus working hard to cultivate the various components of this "package deal" for himself, his thoughts soon turn to parenthood. True to his word, Ben begins to see patients in his home office and the first person he meets in this capacity is troubled teen Tate Langdon. Tate is thus established as a major character early on in the show and the relationship he has with Ben, coupled with the intense romantic connection he comes to share with Violet, both prove to be crucial aspects of the Harmons' experience of haunting. Mindful of the strain placed on the family in recent months, Ben is determined to address his own shortcomings as a family member. His encounter with Tate, who is only gradually made known to the Harmons as a ghost, is central in this regard. The time Ben spends with Tate, both during and beyond the counseling sessions, compels Ben to confront his issues about parenting. A core aspect of Ben's identity is his responsibility as a father to Violet and his relationship with the ghostly Tate is key to his liminal experience.

Given that he is a ghost, Tate's physical appearance is noteworthy. Portraying the "unrepresentable" has long been a challenge for Gothic television, particularly in the case of the ghost story (Wheatley 26). Here, the audience is given an immediate clue as to Tate's true nature, with a glimpse of a sombre-looking Tate, his face dripping with blood, standing behind Ben at the same time as Tate is shown seated opposite Ben on the patients' couch. However, the teen does not appear to be a ghost as far as the family is concerned. Janani Subramanian says that the ghosts of *Murder House* contrast with traditional ghosts which are "ethereal and intangible" (115) and Dawn Keetley concurs in observing that they are "indistinguishable from the non-dead, tangibly embodied" (91). On a technical level, these ghosts avoid the problem of showing the unshowable because they resemble the living. Yet the fact that they are undetectable creates a new problem at a phenomenological level. Their fundamental ambiguity makes these ghosts all the more compelling and contributes strongly to a mood of suspense, as judgments about characters have to be continually revised in light of new information. Tate's plausible physical presence is a distinctive feature of the show and one that works well to enhance Ben's experience of haunting. In a departure from more conventional depictions of ghosts as essentially unsettling or outright repugnant, Tate is sufficiently lifelike to develop a relationship with the human residents of the Murder House. Unfolding week after week, his story steadily gains traction both with his fellow characters and with the audience allowing his agenda to be revealed.

A soul trapped in torment in the liminal Murder House, Tate is forever mired in his resentment towards his family. As discussed above, haunting is bound up with the impetus to address a troubled past (Briggs 15). If haunting must serve a purpose, in Tate's case one clear purpose is surely to keep this bitterness alive. Tate feels that his upbringing has been severely lacking and he uses his sessions with Ben to air his grievances. He is quick to divulge that his mother was having an affair with the man next door and that his father—towards whom Tate also harbors antipathy—left and thus abandoned him, Tate, as a result. These accusations of parental neglect, coupled with the teen's disclosure about his recurring "fantasies" in which he kills his classmates at high school ("Pilot"), indicate a considerable degree of emotional turmoil. Tate's character seems to index anxieties about American family life. On the subject of parental separation and familial breakdown, del Mar notes that:

> The impact of divorce on children has been a contentious field of academic and popular study for decades. But a rough consensus has emerged. Children of divorced parents are more likely than those in more stable homes to exhibit a wide range of social and personal problems, from suicide to low achievement in school [124].

Tate responds to Ben as a father substitute from the first. Early on, having befriended Violet, he advises her of Ben that: "He's a great dad. He really cares. You're lucky like that" ("Murder House"). As time goes on, Tate articulates his pain more openly in declaring that: "You know, I really like talking to you, Dr. Harmon. You've helped me a lot. I wish you were my father. My life would have been a lot different" ("Open House"). Ben's own anxiety about family breakdown has been apparent from the first episode, when he confesses to Vivien: "in all my life the only thing I've been truly scared of is losing you, losing this family" ("Pilot"). His time with the ghostly Tate seems to reinforce the notion that having a stable family life is of paramount importance.

Tate's predicament takes on greater meaning with the eventual revelation that he died in the early 1990s. Underscoring the cost that "family fragmentation" exacts from children, del Mar points to Kurt Cobain, lead singer of Nineties rock band Nirvana, as a high-profile example of such social problems. He observes that the reported "trauma and anger" felt by nine-year-old Cobain when his parents divorced led to a "'Nevermind' zeitgeist [that] articulated a generation's disgust with the pieties, artificialities, and hypocrisies of the 'Morning in America' Reagan years" (130). Tate Langdon, with his unkempt blond hair, grunge attire and pessimistic mindset, here makes the spirit of Cobain manifest. Though he is ten years younger than Cobain, Tate conducts the killing spree (initially presented to Ben as a mere fantasy) that culminates in his own fatal shooting by police in 1994, the year that Cobain committed suicide, and he even cites Cobain as a role model during his frank discussion with Violet about his disenchantment with life in general and high school in particular. In their very first meeting, Tate conveys his bleak world-view to Ben: "The world is a filthy place. It's a filthy, goddamn, horror show. There's so much pain, you know?" ("Pilot").

As a therapist and as a father figure, Ben is initially keen to help Tate. When he decides to keep the teen at a distance because of his unwelcome intimacy with Violet, Ben offers to see him away from the house. Since it is Halloween, a time when ghosts are free to roam beyond the confines of their customary haunts, Tate is able to meet him at a local pumpkin patch. Drawn to Tate because the teen reminds him of his younger self, Ben falls into an emotional state of reminiscence about past Halloween celebrations with Vivien and Violet, marveling at the "amazing gift of family" ("Halloween, Pt. 1") that life has given him. After the move, Vivien becomes pregnant and this sharpens Ben's focus on family even further. The liminal power of haunting, specifically here in the form of his time with the perennially angst-ridden Tate, obliges him to look back over his time as a parent until he comes to grasp the value of his relationship with his daughter. Looking to repair his damaged bond with Violet, he eventually confronts his recent inadequacies. In a heartfelt exchange, Violet tells Ben that she knows he tries to be a good father and he reflects that her feelings have been overlooked, admitting to her that: "I've been a lousy father lately" ("Smoldering Children"). Though Tate ultimately proves to be beyond redemption, as a ghost he functions to foreground long-standing fissures within Ben's own family dynamic which the latter clearly recognizes and is finally able to address.

Moira, Hayden and Elizabeth

Having established that Tate draws out Ben's paternal side, we now turn our attention to the effects of other ghostly interactions instigated by the Murder House. Another matter that has come to plague the Harmons is the affair that Ben had with one of his students back in Boston. The fact of his having been unfaithful to Vivien, and with a far younger woman, raises issues about Ben's attitudes towards women and sexuality. Larry Harvey, the former resident of the house with whom Tate's mother had her own extramarital affair, alerts Ben to the manipulative power of the place in the second episode: "Whatever's tearing you apart, the house knows about it. It'll use it against you" he cautions ("Home Invasion"). This prophecy certainly holds true. Mobilizing an array of female ghosts representative of various stages of its history, the Murder House continually targets Ben's resolve to be a caring and loyal husband to Vivien. Here, the liminal power of haunting works to stage a prolonged confrontation with issues thrown up by mistakes Ben has made within his marriage.

A key figure in charting Ben's progress in the house is Moira O'Hara, the ghostly housekeeper. Like Tate, Moira looks as if she is a normal, living human being and the Harmons consequently accept her as such. Nevertheless, also like Tate, Moira's physical appearance raises immediate questions for the TV audience. She is unique amongst the ghosts of the house because she repeatedly presents herself in one of two diverse ways. Played in turn by Alexandra Breckenridge and Frances Conroy, Moira is either depicted as young and blatantly seductive, or as much older and rather more reserved. Somewhat akin to the literary trope of the unreliable narrator, through which a reader gradually comes to question his or her reading of a tale on realizing that information has been withheld or distorted, Moira's ambiguity renders her an elusive figure. This feature of her ghostly nature is well-suited to television as it is relatively straightforward to convey in an audiovisual medium. It rapidly becomes clear to the viewer that Ben always sees the younger Moira even as Vivien—along with other female characters—always sees the older, truer Moira. Although this device does become routinized, as Moira is a major character, her sudden switches can still be used to destabilizing effect, especially when she is shown with more than one member of the Harmon family at the same time. With their fixed physical manifestations, the other ghosts retain the appearance that they bore at their times of death. The implication is that, in contrast to these other spirits, Moira has actually continued to mature as a person even in death and that her appearance connotes this growth. Highly attuned to male perceptions of females, she does much to provoke Ben into reassessing his treatment of women and ultimately into reaching new levels of maturity himself.

Moira uses her ability to test Ben from the outset and it is evident that he finds her excessively sexualized demeanor perpetually disconcerting. In the first episode he expresses to Vivien his surprise that she would want to employ Moira, which Vivien deems puzzling. Moving on from this, he discovers Moira to be relentless in her efforts to seduce him, for example by unbuttoning the bodice of her skimpy, fetishized maid's outfit (which contrasts sharply with older Moira's modest attire) and adopting provocative poses. When she fails to elicit a response, she makes explicit requests for Ben's attention: "Am I distracting you?" she demands, "Why don't you touch me a little?" ("Pilot"). As time passes, flashbacks inform us that Moira was a victim of the unhappy Langdon marriage. Back in 1983, in a moment of weakness, she sleeps with Tate's father, Hugo, while working as their maid in the Murder House. When Tate's mother, Constance, finds Hugo trying to force himself on an unwilling Moira at a later date, she shoots the pair dead. It seems that Moira perceives the adulterous Ben Harmon as a latter-day version of Hugo Langdon. Refusing to accept that Ben might be capable of change, she accuses him of having a "diseased mind" several months after their first meeting ("Spooky Little Girl"). Moira is therefore determined to use her wiles to entrap Ben and to prove to Vivien that he is unworthy of a second chance.

By way of her dual appearance, Moira problematizes entrenched social views on women. Although she has strong sexual allure, amplified by her availability, Younger Moira is brazen and seemingly insatiable. A sexually aggressive female who both attracts and repels, she makes ambivalent male attitudes towards female sexuality, detected by the likes of Barbara Creed (5), incarnate. Older Moira is ever ready to verbalize these debates. Ben proves to be much more resistant to Moira's charms than she anticipates and, when she pushes him too far, he tells her that she is fired. Ben angrily denounces Moira's flirtatious conduct and clothing to a bewildered Vivien, who literally cannot see the fraught sexual dynamic that repeatedly plays out between the pair. Older Moira gives voice to her dismissal of Ben's seemingly-ludicrous claims, declaring that: "I'm not naive to the ways of men—their need to objectify, conquer. They see what they want to see" ("Murder House"). Her tirade chimes with notions of the problematic history of women being regarded in sexual terms. Ben recognizes this tendency within himself, and the viewers, on account of Moira's ghostly power, can observe this directly. Yet, as with his goal of being a better father, Ben is trying hard to be a better husband. Desperate to be honest with his wife, he tells Vivien that he has been rejecting Moira: "I have rebuffed every advance, and believe me there have been many, but she just won't stop" ("Murder House").

Crucially, Ben is the only member of the Harmon family that sees both versions of Moira and this detail provides insights into the extent of his liminal journey. By the end of the series, his efforts to treat his wife with greater consideration do begin to bear fruit and it is Moira who helps to make this change so visible. Returning to earlier discussions about character change in TV drama, Mittell argues that "There are many ways to assess changed interiority on the basis of exterior markers," such as dialogue, costume and appearance (134). For instance, a character might be dressed differently in order to signify a personality change. In *Murder House*, exterior markers pertaining to Moira's character actually offer clues as to growth in Ben's character rather than to growth in her own. For instance, when Ben grasps that he should have placed greater trust in his wife and tells Moira so, the latter at last shows him her true self: "Congratulations, Dr. Harmon," Younger Moira says, morphing into Older Moira before informing him that "You're finally beginning to see things as they are" ("Spooky Little Girl"). It is the liminality of haunting that makes this moment possible. Further, this links back to notions of seriality, as the protracted nature of episodic viewing ensures that this feels like a hard-earned life lesson and offers real evidence of progression for Ben's character.

Another ghostly character vital to Ben's liminal experience is Hayden McClaine, the student with whom he had an affair. Hayden is especially interesting because she starts the show as a living human, but is made into a ghost by the end of the third episode ("Murder House"). Commenting on the typical sense of certainty about the fate of important characters that underpins serial television, Mittell remarks that "we all assume that main characters are bound to stay on their programs and highly unlikely to die or depart the story, unless motivated by off-screen factors" (123). In this program, at least in Season One, death is no barrier to participation. Most notably amongst all the series of *AHS*, *Murder House* frequently plays around with this deeply-held convention by not only bringing dead characters back to join the living, but by doing so in a manner that seems to belie the fact of those deaths in the first place. In a similar vein to Moira, Hayden denotes Ben's shifting attitudes towards women and her death contributes further to his liminal experience.

Hayden embodies the Gothic trope of the return of the repressed (Clemens 3–4) in more ways than one. Her affair with Ben is one reason for the family's relocation and he is set on leaving that part of his life behind in Boston. When Hayden contacts him to reveal that she is pregnant, Ben tells Vivien that he has to return to Boston for business. In reality, this is a ruse enabling him to accompany Hayden when she has an abortion. Subsequently, in Episode Three, Hayden appears on the Murder House doorstep and declares to Ben that she will be keeping the baby. This marks the first unwelcome return of that which was thought to be repressed, as Hayden—refusing to comply with Ben's wishes—intrudes upon the new family home. The second return is even more perturbing. Larry Harvey kills Hayden and he and an agitated Ben bury her body in the garden, with Ben building a gazebo over the site soon afterwards. Hayden then stuns Ben by reappearing, apparently alive and well, since anyone who dies on the Murder House property will return in ghostly form. Later, Hayden confronts Ben about his callous disposal of her: "Is that what you think of women, Ben? That they're just some disposable nothings that you can sit on top of as you casually drink iced tea?" ("Halloween, Pt. 2"). With Tate and Moira, Ben has already had to contend with past ghosts but this place even has the power to make ghosts of the newly departed. The combined efforts of all these haunting powers demand that Ben urgently examine his continued poor treatment of the women in his life.

Eventually, Ben arrives at an understanding about his relationship with Hayden. Shortly before he learns the truth about Moira, he has a candid conversation with his former lover about their shared past. While she still views their time together in a romanticized light, Ben now feels very differently and admits that it was a professional and a moral failure on his part. Accordingly he acknowledges a difficult truth: "My marriage was a mess when we met. We're not meant to be together. I don't love you, Hayden. I'm sorry. I never did" ("Spooky Little Girl"). Despite Ben's commitment to be a model husband with the move to LA, throughout *Murder House* he compromises his promise by deceiving Vivien, dismissing Hayden and disregarding Vivien's claims that she has been attacked in the house. As was the case with Moira, this exchange seems to signal that Ben's time with Hayden has provided him with a valuable lesson in his flaws as a husband.

The third female ghost who impacts Ben's liminal experience is a far older apparition. As a haunted house tale, *Murder House* is concerned with the display of the past, and, as a serial television drama, it is driven (in part) by the need to create suspense. The narrative advances by planting seeds of intrigue and building to regular cliffhangers, all the while slowly unraveling mysteries and fleshing out character back-stories, thus incrementally establishing the full story of the Murder House (at least to date) by the season's close. Integral to this process are visions of the house in bygone eras, including the re-enactment of traumatic past events. Episode Nine ("Spooky Little Girl") starts with one such flashback to 1947, in which Elizabeth Short, immortalized as the "Black Dahlia" (see Glossary), visits the Murder House to receive dental treatment from Dr. David Curan. He anesthetizes Elizabeth in order to rape her, inadvertently killing her in the process. The original homeowner, surgeon Dr. Charles Montgomery, then appears and butchers her body prior to its disposal elsewhere. Shown as a glamorous star-in-the-making, exploited for her beauty before being literally cast aside, this fictionalized version of Short dramatizes the deep-rooted cultural view that the value of females lies chiefly in their youth and physical attractiveness.

As previously mentioned, Moira's haunting power literalizes Ben's predisposition to view women in sexual terms. However, due to his focus on getting his life and his family in order, this susceptibility seems to be on the wane. Elizabeth's ghost resurrects the matter. Back in 2011, increasingly convinced of his wife's instability and refusing to give her claims of an attack any credence, by this point in the narrative Ben has had Vivien hospitalized. Trying to maintain a routine, he welcomes in Elizabeth, believing her to be a patient. After making initial reference to her anxiety issues, she goes on to divulge that: "I do things with men. Things I shouldn't" ("Spooky Little Girl"). In a Gothic repetition of the scene with Curan that leads to her demise, Elizabeth says that she cannot afford to pay Ben and insinuates that she will offer him sexual favors in return for his help with her compulsive behavior. Fighting to keep things professional and calling attention to the irony of the situation, Ben tells her that this is inappropriate and says: "You never need to do that with me." A few scenes later, in a last attempt to ensnare him, Moira persuades Elizabeth to join her in a steamy embrace in order to seduce Ben. In a hazy, haunting sequence, the befuddled Ben imagines himself in a sexual scenario with the women until he manages to rouse himself and orders them to leave. Coming shortly before the moment when he sees Moira as her true self, this confrontation represents a clear moment of progress for Ben as a liminar.

Ben's time in the Murder House obliges him to tackle problems that have plagued him and undermined his relationship with his family for many months. In the final episodes, the haunting reaches ever greater heights, as many of the ghosts from the house's long and violent history congregate around Vivien as she goes into labor. To Ben's great distress, Vivien dies in childbirth and thus joins Violet—who, we have learned, was successful in her suicide attempt some time ago—in haunting the house. Though Vivien and Violet hope that Ben will leave and start his life anew elsewhere, the vengeful Hayden thwarts this plan by killing him and ensuring that he remains. United in death with his wife and daughter, as well as with their baby son who survived only momentarily after birth, Ben finally attains the peace that eluded him in life. As the Harmon family unit gathers around a bedecked and twinkling Christmas tree in a potent vision of domestic harmony, he affirms his new-found contentment in declaring: "I didn't think it was possible for me, Vivien. But I'm happy" ("Afterbirth").

Conclusion

Making use of critical work on the Gothic, as well as of recent scholarship pertaining to the nature of contemporary television drama, this essay demonstrates that the haunted house motif is a persistent and inter-medial form that serves to illuminate and comment upon long-standing issues embedded deep within American culture. The Gothic trope of haunting, implanted within the forbidding setting of an old house with a tragic history, gives rise to a liminal environment with the capacity to challenge and transform those who linger in its sphere of influence. Although the haunted house tale stems from literature, in both the European and American variants of Gothic fiction, it has long found expression in other media formats such as cinema, theatre, radio and television.

In paying particular attention to one of the chief protagonists of this haunted house tale, Dr. Ben Harmon, my analysis shows that the haunted house motif can and does transplant most effectively to the small screen. Retaining the fundamental properties of a sinister location, a cast of ghostly characters and a succession of taxing scenarios that cast doubt on previously accepted truths, the first *American Horror Story* offers an intriguing new, televisual development for the tradition of the ghost story. Recalling ways in which scholars have distinguished television Gothic from other types of horror texts, it can be seen that the episodic nature of *Murder House* augments the haunting events it portrays. Further, the ghostly characters so essential to the narrative—principally, I argue here, Tate Langdon, Moira O'Hara, Hayden McClaine and Elizabeth Short—offer Ben, like a true liminar, the opportunity to learn from his experiences in this troubling, haunting version of domesticity, but only with the fullness of time that TV permits.

Haunting has the potential to bring about change. Sometime after her murder, Hayden, as one of the Murder House's newest ghostly occupants, has an illuminating exchange with Nora Montgomery, wife of Charles and one of the original ghosts responsible for the grim legacy of the place. Hayden enlightens the eternally forlorn Nora by informing her that they are both ghosts, reflecting as she does that their undead status is not without its advantages: "There's a power in it. A power we can use. We can make ourselves unknown … and when we really need it, we can make ourselves known [original ellipsis]" ("Rubber Man"). There is certainly a special kind of power at play when these ghostly individuals choose to interact with the still-living members of the household. Overall, examining the ghosts that befriend and bewilder the human inhabitants of the liminal Murder House reveals the power of TV horror to tell tales that critique culture and engage the audience.

NOTES

1. See Rebecca Janicker, *The Literary Haunted House: Lovecraft, Matheson, King and the Horror in Between* (Jefferson, NC: McFarland, 2015).

2. Despite the relative artificiality of Walpole's renovations, Strawberry Hill soon came to embody a real life version of the literary Gothic castle.

3. For an analysis of the haunted house formula—concentrating on conventions of setting, characters, plot and themes—in a range of American haunted house fictions, see Dale Bailey's *American Nightmares: The Haunted House Formula in American Popular Fiction* (Bowling Green, OH: Bowling Green State University Popular Press, 1999).

WORKS CITED

"Afterbirth." *American Horror Story: The Complete First Season*. Writ. Jessica Sharzer. Dir. Bradley Buecker. Twentieth Century Fox, 2012. DVD.

Aguirre, Manuel, Roberta Quance, and Philip Sutton. "Introduction: The Concept of Liminality." *Margins and Thresholds: An Enquiry into the Concept of Liminality in Text Studies, Studies in Liminality and Literature 1*. Eds. Manuel Aguirre, Roberta Quance and Philip Sutton. Madrid: Gateway Press, 2000. 1–10. Print.

Bailey, Dale. *American Nightmares: The Haunted House Formula in American Popular Fiction*. Bowling Green, OH: Bowling Green State University Popular Press, 1999. Print.

"Behind the Fright: The Making of *American Horror Story*." *American Horror Story: The Complete First Season*. Twentieth Century Fox, 2012. DVD.

Briggs, Julia. *Night Visitors: The Rise and Fall of the English Ghost Story*. London: Faber and Faber, 1977. Print.

Clemens, Valdine. *The Return of the Repressed: Gothic Horror from "The Castle of Otranto" to "Alien."* Albany: State University of New York Press, 1999. Print.

Creed, Barbara. *The Monstrous-Feminine: Film, Feminism, Psychoanalysis.* London: Routledge, 1993. Print.

Del Mar, David Peterson. *The American Family: From Obligation to Freedom.* New York: Palgrave Macmillan, 2011. Print.

Grider, Sylvia. "The Haunted House in Literature, Popular Culture, and Tradition: A Consistent Image." *Contemporary Legend* 2 (1999): 174–204. Print.

"Halloween, Pt. 1." *American Horror Story: The Complete First Season.* Writ. James Wong. Dir. David Semel. Twentieth Century Fox, 2012. DVD.

"Halloween, Pt. 2." *American Horror Story: The Complete First Season.* Writ. Tim Minear. Dir. David Semel. Twentieth Century Fox, 2012. DVD.

"Home Invasion." *American Horror Story: The Complete First Season.* Writ. Ryan Murphy and Brad Falchuk. Dir. Alfonso Gomez-Rejon. Twentieth Century Fox, 2012. DVD.

Janicker, Rebecca. *The Literary Haunted House: Lovecraft, Matheson, King and the Horror in Between.* Jefferson, NC: McFarland, 2015. Print.

Jowett, Lorna, and Stacey Abbott. *TV Horror: Investigating the Dark Side of the Small Screen.* London: I.B. Tauris, 2013. Print.

Keetley, Dawn. "Stillborn: The Entropic Gothic of *American Horror Story.*" *Gothic Studies* 15.2 (2013): 89–107. Print.

King, Stephen. *Danse Macabre.* 1981. London: Warner Books, 1993. Print.

Mittell, Jason. *Complex TV: The Poetics of Contemporary Television Storytelling.* New York: New York University Press, 2015. Print.

"Murder House." *American Horror Story: The Complete First Season.* Writ. Jennifer Salt. Dir. Bradley Buecker. Twentieth Century Fox, 2012. DVD.

"Open House." *American Horror Story: The Complete First Season.* Writ. Brad Falchuk. Dir. Tim Hunter. Twentieth Century Fox, 2012. DVD.

"Pilot." *American Horror Story: The Complete First Season.* Writ. Ryan Murphy and Brad Falchuk. Dir. Ryan Murphy. Twentieth Century Fox, 2012. DVD.

Railo, Eino. *The Haunted Castle: A Study of the Elements of English Romanticism.* London: Routledge, 1927. Print.

"Rubber Man." *American Horror Story: The Complete First Season.* Writ. Ryan Murphy. Dir. Miguel Arteta. Twentieth Century Fox, 2012. DVD.

"Smoldering Children." *American Horror Story: The Complete First Season.* Writ. James Wong. Dir. Michael Lehmann. Twentieth Century Fox, 2012. DVD.

"Spooky Little Girl." *American Horror Story: The Complete First Season.* Writ. Jennifer Salt. Dir. John Scott. Twentieth Century Fox, 2012. DVD.

Stack, Tim. "*American Horror Story*'s Worlds Collide." *Entertainment Weekly.* Entertainment Weekly, Special Reunions Double 2014. Web. 16 March 2015.

Subramanian, Janani. "The Monstrous Makeover: *American Horror Story*, Femininity and Special Effects." *Critical Studies in Television* 8.3 (2013): 108–123. Print.

Turner, Victor. *Dramas, Fields, and Metaphors: Symbolic Action in Human Society.* Ithaca, NY: Cornell University Press, 1974. Print.

_____. *The Forest of Symbols: Aspects of Ndembu Ritual.* Ithaca, NY: Cornell University Press, 1967. Print.

Van Gennep, Arnold. *The Rites of Passage.* Trans. Monika B. Vizedom and Gabrielle L. Caffee. London: Routledge and Kegan Paul, 1960. Print.

Wheatley, Helen. *Gothic Television.* Manchester: Manchester University Press, 2006. Print.

"They were monsters"

The Alien Abduction Plotline and Race, Sexuality and Social Unrest in Asylum

PHILIP L. SIMPSON

Progressive and retrograde ideologies clash violently throughout the duration of *American Horror Story: Asylum*, appropriately enough given the show's primary temporal setting in the tumultuous decade of the American 1960s when traditional and countercultural values clashed for dominance. Sister Jude, representing the repressive force of institutionalized religion, and Dr. Arthur Arden, representing the dehumanizing extremes of patriarchal science, jointly brutalize the hapless inmates of Briarcliff Asylum, each of whom as quintessential "Others" represents various deviances from the social order. The show's primary avatar of progressivism, Kit Walker, is one such "deviant," a lower-class white male, previously the subject of community suspicion because of his interracial marriage to an African American woman, unjustly committed to Briarcliff for the murder of his wife and two other women. Believed by almost all to be the "Bloody Face" serial killer, Kit insists not only on his innocence, but that his wife, Alma, was abducted by extraterrestrials.

The "alien abduction" subplot in the second season of *American Horror Story* was greeted by many fans and critics alike with varying degrees of disbelief, puzzlement, and even anger. Trent Moore may fairly be said to speaking for all of these folks when he writes, "So what the heck was up with the aliens?" (Moore). Lily Hoagland calls the alien angle "the most useless storyline about aliens to have ever been put to screen" (Hoagland). Others found the season to be an overly busy mash-up of disparate genres, such as Jess Cagle, who says archly that "You know a show has a lot going on when the occasional appearance of extraterrestrials is no more surprising than spotting a Prius on *Modern Family*," (Cagle) or Verne Gay, who calls the second season a "messy, overstuffed cartoon.... *Asylum* ... is bloated with elements from half a dozen horror genres, including splatter films, alien abductions, pulp, sci-fi and so called 'body horror,' which concerns itself with mutations" (Gay).

By contrast, Alicia Lutes is one of the few "first responders" to Season Two who calls the storyline "brilliant." She elaborates that "the alien storyline is a direct foil to the religious control that runs through the entire series. Ryan Murphy is making a commentary on religion through ... little green ... men.... Religion and aliens, both outside of this earth's literal sphere, explain things that are out of grasp" (Lutes). Keeping Lutes's insights about control and otherness in mind, the aliens' presence in the storyline hinging on Kit and his marriage to Alma makes thematic sense. Kit's biracial marriage, transgressive for his time and place in history, is an appropriate magnet for the alien abductors and in fact is partially inspired by the alleged alien abduction of married interracial couple Barney and Betty Hill in 1961. Alien abduction narratives often include a range of phenomena, including uncomfortable or painful medical procedures that can result in the creation of alien/human hybrid babies.[1] Betty Hill, for example, claimed that during her abduction she was subjected to a "pregnancy test" with a long needle. The "typical" abduction narrative's morbid focus on human reproductive agency, and the violation or rape of the helpless human abductee whether male or female, renders this subplot more relevant than it may first seem. The second season of *American Horror Story* returns cyclically to the themes of dominance as manifested in rape, murder, torture, inhumane treatment of inmates, and involuntary committals intended to silence those who threaten the power structure. The aliens who return to Kit again and again, simultaneously protecting him from his Briarcliff tormentors (Dr. Arden in particular) but also wreaking unwelcome havoc on his life, are one more manifestation of the violators who populate the show's narrative landscape but also stand in for God in a season heavily focused on questions of religious faith.

A Brief Cultural History of the Alien Abduction Narrative

Alien abduction narratives have been a recognizable, if marginalized, feature of American cultural life since the latter half of the twentieth century. Not coincidentally, the rise to notoriety of the alien abduction narrative accompanied the escalation in world tensions between the nuclear super powers during the Cold War as well as a generalized apprehension about the promises and peril, the seductions and uncertainties, of a technological future. To this point, Jodi Dean contends that "...alien abduction narratives highlight with particular effect concern about the future of the species ... [and] provide a program for organizing suspicions about contemporary life" (156–157). The alien abduction narrative as metaphor evolved into a versatile tool for confronting, however obliquely, the terrors of the nuclear age, environmental destruction, future shock, and social inequities and injustices. In this sense, alien abductions are an extension of the "visionary rumours," or psychic manifestations, that C.G. Jung concludes are rooted in a collective psychological need to look "for help from extra-terrestrial sources since it cannot be found on earth" (17) when confronted with existential threats. However, the alien abduction narrative is the shadow side of this yearning for outside intervention. When some people look toward the cosmos, they see not hope but only more fear, in the form of alien abductors whose motives are inscrutable and methods are as terrifying as they are transformative. These accounts also filter out into the culture, which in turn draws upon them to create media representations of alien abduction.

Several high-profile books, purporting to be based on actual experiences, popularized the alien abduction narrative beginning in the late 1960s. The most influential of these included journalist John G. Fuller's *The Interrupted Journey* (1966), artist Budd Hopkins's *Missing Time* (1981), novelist Whitley Strieber's autobiographical *Communion* (1987), historian David Michael Jacob's *Secret Life* (1992), and Pulitzer-Prize winning Harvard psychiatrist John E. Mack's *Abduction: Human Encounters with Aliens* (1994). Additionally, visual media were quick to follow suit. A television movie adaptation of Fuller's book about the abduction of Barney and Betty Hill, *The UFO Incident*, aired on the NBC network in 1975, starring noted actor James Earl Jones as Barney Hill. As Curtis Peebles notes, the movie went to great lengths to present the incident as a metaphor for the tensions of the Hills's interracial marriage in the 1960s: "The film was an examination of two people trying to cope with a difficult situation—very little of which had to do with the UFO sighting" (272–273). Additionally, the movie's depiction of the aliens as short, hairless, and gray humanoids with slanted dark eyes, while not unprecedented in visual media, would come to dominate iconography of aliens in the years to come, leading to the ubiquitous presence of the "Alien Gray" in contemporary American culture (273).

Regarding the popularity of the extraterrestrial/abduction trope in media, two examples will suffice. One of the most famous UFO movies of all time, *Close Encounters of the Third Kind*, premiered in 1977, directed by rising *wunderkind* Steven Spielberg. This film too depicts alien abductions, ranging from that of the disappearance of naval aviators during World War II off the Florida coast (a real-life case that achieved renewed notoriety in the 1970s with a spate of popular books and movies about mysterious, possibly other-worldly phenomena allegedly responsible for scores of such disappearances in the so-called "Devil's Triangle") to that of a little boy literally grabbed from his mother's arms, albeit to be returned safely by the film's climax. This film also portrays the aliens as short, bulbous-headed, dark-eyed humanoids whose motives in abducting people are ostensibly more benign than that of the "Grays" as depicted in other media but who do not care at all for disrupting human lives, as illustrated in the torment suffered by protagonists Roy Neary and Jillian Guiler as they are plagued by persistent visions (subconsciously planted in their minds by the extraterrestrials) drawing them inexorably toward the alien landing site at Devil's Tower in Wyoming. From *Close Encounters*, one can easily enough trace a cultural through line to the "missing time"–era abductee reports of the 1980s and 1990s.

Perhaps the cultural high-water mark of the alien abduction narrative found its distillation in the enormously popular television series *The X-Files*, which aired on the Fox network from 1993 to 2002 and was then revived for a limited six-episode run in 2016 (Harrison). Following the weekly paranormal investigations of FBI agents Fox Mulder and Dana Scully, the show is structured through its run by the so-called "mythology" arc, in which for selected episodes of each season the two intrepid agents must battle a far-reaching conspiracy between the traitorous "shadow" U.S. government and invading extraterrestrials (portrayed as the now-expected "Grays" in appearance) designed to facilitate a global alien takeover by the then-far off year of 2012. Mulder's motivation for his quixotic career chasing aliens (as well as the stand-alone "monsters of the week" in other episodes) in the FBI stems from what he believes to have been the alien abduction of his sister Samantha (still missing during the timeframe of the series) during childhood.

All of these multi-media representations based on a shared cultural knowledge of high-profile "close encounters" cases not only lent credence to the notion that alien abductions were a real phenomenon, but established the template for the alien abduction narrative in fiction, cinema, and television, that persists through today. The creative team behind *American Horror Story* looked toward alien abduction as the structuring metaphor for a season which interrogated the abuses of power inflicted upon society's most helpless by corrupt individuals within corrupting systems: the Catholic Church and the medical profession. In that individuals who have reported alien abductions usually have trouble finding the words to describe what is a dream-like or visionary experience, because of memory erasure or the incomprehensibility of what is experienced or both, its very ineffability suits the season's project of investigating the fraught relationship between flawed human beings and their conceptions of the divine, which for the believers can only be accessed in this world through faith and visions.

The Alien Abduction Storyline in Asylum

The second season of *American Horror Story* is focused on the high-concept idea of various bloody goings-on in and around a former tuberculosis ward turned Catholic sanitarium located in rural Massachusetts but that would not be out of place in Gothic melodrama. The season is populated with more plots and subplots (corrupt church officials, a Nazi doctor, a serial killer psychiatrist, a serial killer son of said psychiatrist, mutated cannibals, a murderous Santa Claus cosplayer, and even a musical/dance number) than there are inmates in Briarcliff, the titular asylum. However, the alien abduction of Alma Walker in 1964 as depicted in the first scenes after the opening credits of the premiere episode, "Welcome to Briarcliff," is actually the catalyst that sets the season's plot into motion, introduces the signature social themes of the season, and unites all the seemingly disparate storylines by the end of the season.[2]

AHS producer Ryan Murphy spells it out for those skeptical of the aliens' inclusion in an already stuffed season: "For me, [aliens] were always an obvious metaphor for God. It fit very easily into the world of a Catholic sanitarium asylum" (Li). Co-producer Tim Minear further acknowledges the indirect inspiration of the Betty and Barney Hill abduction case in creating the season's unifying metaphor: "The Betty and Barney Hill story of the fifties, sixties, was one of the first abduction stories. It was an interracial couple, we weren't taking from that specifically, but it was in the water, in our experience, the stories that we all knew." He concludes by acknowledging how the alien storyline divided fans but still defending the creative choice: "If you think about it, those aliens are the closest things to angels, on our show about sort of religion versus science, there was nothing incongruous to me about any of that stuff" (Li). The alien-as-God metaphor, complementing the show's running commentary on the American social environment of the 1960s—including the deliberate neglect of the nation's practically non-existent mental health care system and the country's Civil Rights era confrontation with its own deeply ingrained history of both individual and institutionalized racism—provides the lens through which the season comes into sharpest focus.

Tellingly, the abduction scene in "Welcome to Briarcliff" is immediately preceded by a tense encounter between Kit and a trio of local racists led by Billy Marshall at the gas station where Kit works alone on the night shift. In this scene, Billy has taken Kit's gun from its storage cabinet without Kit's knowledge or permission and "jokingly" points it at Kit. He says he wants to use it to frighten "a nigger (who) tried to mess with Rainey's little sister," but his real intent seems twofold: to let Kit know he knows the truth about the sexual relationship (if not the secret marriage) between Kit and Alma and to threaten him with the prospect of violent reprisal for it. Billy reveals his agenda when he says in a leering, insinuating manner, "Hear you got yourself a maid. That's what I hear, anyway." Then he suggestively places a square of chocolate in his mouth and says, "Mmmm, chocolate," signaling to Kit that his secretive sexual relations with a "chocolate" woman are nonetheless known in the outer white racist community. The scene ends without overt violence and the boys leave without Kit's gun, but Kit is clearly apprehensive as he returns home to Alma. After they greet each other warmly, he speaks long-ingly of the desire to tell everyone about their marriage because, after all, "we didn't commit a crime." Alma, who knows much better than Billy the kind of community in which they live, tells him the world will change, imply-ing that to live openly in interracial marriage right now is premature at best. He replies, clearly referring to Billy and his ilk, that "the world is wrong" and that living in the shadows like this "makes me feel like I can't protect my own family." Kit doesn't know how right he is, of course. He believes he can protect Alma from Billy, but what he doesn't know is that aliens have targeted the couple, and against this kind of otherworldly power he finds himself to be quite helpless.

The confrontation scene between these local boys at the gas station also foreshadows the abduction sequence in that the interior and exterior lights at the gas station flicker and dim and cows begin lowing in the distance, sug-gesting some mysterious intruder or intruders are the cause. Kit, investigating the strange occurrence, is startled by the sudden appearance of Billy and his cronies, although whether they (or the aliens, tracking Kit from above) dis-rupted the station's electricity is left ambiguous. Later, at Kit's house, the radio (playing Frank FaFara's "Lovemaker, Lovebreaker," whose lyric "Please don't take her out of my life" sets the stage for Alma's abduction) flares into unex-pected static just before all hell breaks loose. In Episode Three, "Nor'easter," Dr. Arden's desk radio also foreshadows an alien appearance in that it is relay-ing news reports of strange lights seen in the sky before static interrupts the newscast. Given that UFO sightings have long been associated with electro-magnetic disturbances that wreak havoc on manmade technology, the mys-terious disruptions to the lighting and radio broadcasts could certainly indicate the aliens' first subtle intrusion upon Kit's world as well as forge a thematic connection between the voyeuristic racism represented by Billy and the interest by the aliens in the sexuality between Kit and Alma.

After Alma and Kit make love that same night, the sanctity of their house is besieged by what Kit first assumes to be Billy and his gang, come to either terrorize or harm Alma and himself for their transgression. An intense white light blazes through their bedroom window, prompting Kit, yelling Billy's name, to run into the yard with a shotgun. Instead, Kit is pummeled by a fierce, leaf-blowing cyclone generated by an unseen, blinding white craft above him. (The leaf vortex buffeting the astounded contactee appears to be a reprise of a similar scene in the first episode of the first season of *The X-Files*, thus paying homage to that show's alien mythology.) The post-coital timing of the alien contact is surely not coincidental; the alien preoccupation with human sexuality in abduction narrative has been noted earlier. It is repeated here in this story but within a racial context that suggests the "hybrid" marriage of Kit and Alma provides the appropriate "seed" of a eugenics program designed to alter human genetic destiny.

Though exaggerated for maximum visual impact, the standard features of UFO/alien abduction lore are accounted for in this sequence as if on a checklist so that the audience will know immediately what is happening, even if Kit and Alma do not. The familiar, safe domestic space shared by Kit and Alma transforms into a place of bizarre nocturnal nightmare. An electrical storm ionizes the air. A sonic blast hurls Kit to the floor as he rushes back into the house. Laws of Newtonian physics are suspended as household items float as if in zero gravity and Kit is violently thrust up to the ceiling, accompanied by another deafening blast of sound, and held there helpless until dropped. He has a brief hallucinatory glimpse of a humanoid but unmistakably alien being, barely discernible through the sensory assault of the bright white light, reaching out to him with ambiguous intent. Alma herself disappears during the sequence, taken by the aliens, while Kit is left behind to try to make sense of what just happened.

As is typical of many "experiencers," Kit's memory of the event is fragmented at best, as one may dimly recall parts of a nightmare in the logical light of day. He has flash memories of being taken aboard the blazing white interior of the alien craft himself and tortured in various hideously painful ways. This extraterrestrial disruption is a rip in the fabric of causal reality itself as a formerly sedate, orderly world becomes wildly chaotic and unhinged, as if this moment so soon after the assassination of President John F. Kennedy in November 1963 (which is alluded to by Monsignor Timothy Howard to Sister Jude later this same episode) prefigures the social disruptions to come of the mid-to-late-1960s, such as the assassination in 1968 of Martin Luther King, Jr. King's murder is referenced in a television broadcast watched by Sister Jude in Episode Twelve, "Continuum." The hallucinatory nature of the alien episode, as well as Kit's fairly comprehensive memory loss as a result, is more than a little suggestive of a "bad trip," soon to become a familiar rite-of-passage in the hallucinogen-fueled drug counterculture of the 1960s and about as apt a description of the great disillusionment of the bloody late 1960s as any.

Kit's bad trip continues when he is accused of murdering his wife and two other women. Because of the extreme nature of the gruesome murders, he is committed to Briarcliff for evaluation to determine whether he is sane and thus capable of standing trial for the "Bloody Face" murders. Though despised and feared by almost all, he maintains his innocence and upon his intake in "Welcome to Briarcliff" objects to Sister Jude calling his tormentors "little green men": "They weren't human. They were monsters." She dismisses his story by saying, prematurely, "All monsters are human. You're a monster." In Episode Two, "Tricks and Treats," Dr. Oliver Thredson, his court-appointed psychiatric evaluator, also refers to the aliens as "the men from outer space," suggesting the majority scientific establishment's dismissive attitude toward such outlandish claims.

Kit's incarceration in the asylum mirrors in several significant ways the alien abduction, which conflates the monstrosity of the alien and the human into one coherent narrative arc. Held against his will, his limbs bound by a straightjacket, his life completely shattered, he is quite helpless. Worse, he attracts the scientific interest of Dr. Arden, the asylum's medical unit director, who also is a psychosexual sadist/fetishist with a bald head (giving him a more-than-passing resemblance to the aliens) and a former Nazi to boot. True to his SS origins, Dr. Arden as a kind of bush-league Mengele (see Glossary) considers the asylum's patients to be his own experimental subjects, whom he thinks nothing of operating upon, subjecting to electroshocks, and otherwise medically torturing, far beyond the pale of any acceptable scientific protocols or conduct. Intrigued by the "Bloody Face" murderer's methodology of skinning his victims, Dr. Arden decides he will replicate this methodology upon Kit.

As Dr. Arden enters Kit's solitary cell to take him to surgery, white light floods in, recalling how the alien abduction was signaled by a similar blinding light. From Kit's subjective point of view, a brief flash of an alien's hairless head is superimposed upon Dr. Arden's bald head, cementing the equivalence between the two just as Dr. Arden sedates him. From Kit's cell, Kit is taken to Dr. Arden's private operating theater, where Kit awakens to nightmare, just as he did in the alien craft. He is strapped to the surgical table, his head restrained and his eyelids held mercilessly open by a device similar to that employed upon Alex DeLarge in Stanley Kubrick's film *A Clockwork Orange* (1971). As Dr. Arden explains to Kit what his clinical interest in him is as the supposed "Bloody Face" killer, Kit experiences traumatic flashbacks of being similarly bound to a table aboard the alien craft: a hideously organic alien probe apparently probing his penis or anus, a long needle penetrating his open eye.

Before Dr. Arden can commence what will likely be Kit's flaying, however, he is distracted by a hard lump on the left side of Kit's neck. Taking his scalpel, he slices Kit's neck open and extracts what appears to be a circuit board of some sort. Though the words "alien implant" are never uttered, the *X-Files* savvy viewer knows immediately what this peculiar instrumentality is. In case there is any doubt about the device's extraterrestrial origin, it immediately grows spidery legs from each side and then scampers away into the darkness of the asylum. In the next episode, "Nor' easter," Dr. Arden has recaptured the implant and segmented it, but when the radio reports UFO activity in the vicinity during the storm, the pieces reassemble into one while Dr. Arden watches. Now knowing there is more to Kit than meets the eye, Dr. Arden continues his experiments upon Kit, just as the aliens do.

Many times, the alien abduction is visually and verbally referenced in Kit's ongoing ordeal on Dr. Arden's table. A glaring white spotlight washes out Kit's face and body while he is bound and prone beneath Dr. Arden's scalpel. Dr. Arden threatens to violate his bodily orifices in search for implants. The entire set of experiences, from extraction from Kit's cell to his return to it, parallels what happened to Kit that night at his home. It also draws an equivalence between the motives of the alien abductors and Dr. Arden's pathologically sadistic need to control everyone around him through violation guised in professionalism. A list of Dr. Arden's other atrocities includes his turning of select inmates through injections and surgeries into cannibalistic "Raspers" whom he sets loose in the forest outside the asylum as a kind of living perimeter fence to prevent inmate escapes; electroshock torture of involuntarily committed journalist Lana Winters to erase her memories; a transorbital lobotomy performed on a woman suffering from postpartum depression who believes herself to be Anne Frank as part of a psychological escape from the media-reinforced conformist role of new mother and housewife, only to have this emergent identity stolen from her by Dr. Arden's surgical violation; and his punishment of the sexually liberated Shelley for what he calls her "whorish" or "slutty ways" by first amputating her legs and then injecting her repeatedly in the eyeball (again, paralleling what the aliens do their abductees) with the mixture of tuberculosis and syphilis that begins torturously transforming her into a Rasper.

Dr. Arden's motivations, sadistic though they may be, are not solely to satiate his fetishes. He claims a higher purpose, making him a visionary psychopath or "mad scientist," an instantly recognizable stock character in horror. Through his unethical end-justifies-the-means search for occult knowledge, he represents the Faustus, "evil alchemist" type of mad scientist as classified by Roslynn D. Haynes. Note how closely Haynes's description of the typology matches Dr. Arden: "Driven to pursue an arcane intellectual goal that carries suggestions of ideological evil, this figure has been reincarnated recently as the sinister biologist producing new (and hence allegedly unlawful) species through the quasi-magical processes of genetic engineering" (3). Haunted by his past, Dr. Arden further exemplifies what Christopher Frayling identifies as the mad scientist whose "career choice was due to a personal trauma buried deep in his past" (128). In keeping with his Nazi youth, Dr. Arden strives to place his own imprimatur upon human biology to create his version of a master race, using the inmates as damaged raw material. He reveals this motivation to Monsignor Howard in Episode Six, "The Origins of Monstrosity": "My aim was to give these wasted lives purpose, meaning, and I've succeeded beyond my wildest imagination…. When they arrived here, these patients were less than men. Now, because of me, they're more than human." He further proclaims: "I'm not a monster. I'm a visionary." Through the megalomaniacal eugenics project of Dr. Arden and the power-hungry corruption of Sister Jude (though she is later redeemed through Kit's Christ-like forgiveness) and Monsignor Howard as he aspires toward the papacy, a larger sociocultural indictment is handed down upon the retrograde treatment practices for the mentally ill available in the early 1960s. These were dependent upon an unholy alliance between unethical medical procedures and tyrannical religious control, leading to violation of human subjects without regard for individual agency, consent, or liberty. The aliens' motivations are equally visionary and as rooted in eugenics as Dr. Arden's, in that they are using Kit as genetic stock to produce an alien/human hybrid who will, to put it in messianic terms, transform humanity.

Kit spends the first four episodes proclaiming his innocence and repeating his abduction story, regardless of how outrageous it may sound to others, without variation. He even does so under Dr. Arden's infliction of further surgical torture in "Nor'easter," when Arden dismisses his story about aliens, in spite of the evidence of the implant, and accuses him of being a spy for foreign governments or perhaps even a branch of the American government, populated by what Dr. Arden calls with disdain "Jews and fellow travelers." The "Jews" remark foreshadows the revelation of his Nazi past as Dr. Hans Gruper in Episode Four, "I Am Anne Frank, Pt. 1," and "fellow travelers" harkens back to the communist "witch hunts" of the 1950s McCarthy era in the United States, neatly suturing together the history of Nazi Germany and the United States as reflections or parasitic twins of the other. Uttered during the performance of a painful procedure upon Kit, the statement is associated in the audience's mind with Dr. Arden's methodology, which involves drug sedation and surgical mutilation. This procedure carried out upon an unwilling subject corresponds not only to those carried out in the past by then-SS Dr. Gruper, but also the "Bloody Face" murders and the methodology of the aliens themselves. The statement suggests that Dr. Arden's story is one of not only fanatical belief but participation in the worst cultural crime of recent history, which he re-enacts in microcosm on his operating theater table. By contrast, Kit's story speaks to his status as saintly sufferer of inflicted evil, first losing his wife, then his liberty and reputation, and perhaps even his life if Dr. Thredson determines him to be sane enough to face trial for capital murder. The alien abduction story that Kit clings to paradoxically grounds him in the midst of Briarcliff's insanity. In this same "Anne Frank" episode, he affirms to his new friend and future lover, Grace, that "your story is who you are" while asking her to share with him her story of how she ended up at Briarcliff. Though the aliens have destroyed his life as he knew it, the story still provides him with an identity as an innocent, unjustly imprisoned man in an environment constructed to break his integrity and strip away the last of his besieged psychological stability.

The first real shock to Kit's unusually solid sense of self and identity occurs in Episode Four, "I Am Anne Frank, Pt. 1." Dr. Thredson has been suggesting to Kit since his first evaluation interview with the inmate in Episode Two, "Tricks and Treats," that Kit has constructed this elaborate story of alien abduction as a screen or shield to protect himself against the bitter memory of what really happened: he murdered Alma as a result of repressed guilt and shame over an illicit marriage, with a reaction-formation of growing rage that finally exploded the night that Billy and his friends confronted Kit, over what his society considers "an illicit coupling," in Dr. Thredson's terminology. At first Kit, his incarceration still a novel experience, is immune to the seductive simplicity of this counter narrative to his alien abduction story. However, following the stress of his prolonged surgical sessions with Dr. Arden and his discovery that Grace's claim of innocence in the axe murder of her father and stepmother is a false narrative, he begins to wonder if Dr. Thredson is right when the latter insists again that this "elaborate fantasy about alien abduction [is] to absolve you of your guilt." Dr. Thredson proposes not only that Kit is the murderer of two other women but also provides a compelling and more realistic scenario of what happened to Alma: that Billy and his friends came to the house that night, not aliens, and hiding from them made something snap in Kit that led to him beating his wife to death. Kit still has no memory of killing anyone, but Dr. Thredson has sown enough doubt in him to compel him to confess to Sister Jude that "those creatures really can't exist" and that he *must* have murdered two women and his wife.

Of course, while Dr. Thredson at this early point in the season's arc still appears to be a mostly sympathetic character, largely on the basis of his expressed professional dismay regarding Sister Jude's cruel methods and his championship of the wrongly incarcerated and betrayed Lana, cracks appear in his façade, hinting at his true nature. His dubious imposition of aversion/conversion therapy upon Lana, who is so desperate to get out of the asylum she will try anything to "cure" her of her lesbianism, is one more instance of what the audience of the 2000s would recognize as a dangerously misguided medical practice within the malpractice committed daily in Briarcliff upon its much wronged wards. But it is also a dark hint that Dr. Thredson shares something of Dr. Arden's repressed sexual deviance manifesting as voyeuristic sadism. It lays the groundwork for Thredson's later unmasking as the "Bloody Face" killer in Episode Five, "I Am Anne Frank, Pt. 2." In retrospect, then, Dr. Thredson's real purpose in shaking Kit's faith in his own story is clear: Thredson wants to cover his tracks by getting an innocent man to confess to crimes he did not commit. Like the aliens, Dr. Thredson manipulates Kit for his own inscrutable (to Kit, anyway, and most of the audience at this early point) reasons.

Season Two's men of science and medicine, Dr. Thredson and Dr. Arden, one a court-appointed psychiatrist who is also a serial killer of women, and the other a sadistic SS doctor brought to the United States under the auspices of the infamous "Operation Paperclip" project to provide new identities to Nazis valuable to national security/scientific advancement,[3] serve as an indictment of government sanctioned science, or at least of the unethical kind practiced by such cruel men upon helpless captives, as an instrument of dehumanization. They represent the worst anti-human aspects of science. They find their apotheosis in the aliens, who are literally inhuman (or "monsters," Kit calls them) and also subject terrified captives to painful, intrusive medical procedures for their own reasons. The aliens are particularly focused on female reproductive organs, but not in any medically helpful way. The aliens want them only as breeding vessels for Kit's "sperm." They harvest women special to Kit without thought or regard for their suffering, leaving Alma suffering from encroaching madness and Grace bleeding from her invaded womb. This violent exploitation of women likens them to Dr. Thredson and Dr. Arden in another way, as symbols of a brutalizing patriarchal science intent on plundering the regenerative organs of women for lofty but ultimately sexually psychotic aims.

Dr. Thredson's methodology, like Dr. Arden's, is associated with the alien abduction method and imagery on multiple occasions. In addition to his endeavor to frame Kit for his own murders, he "breaks out" Lana from the asylum to supposedly shelter her in his house for the night before going to the police in the morning to reveal all about Briarcliff's horrors. In reality, however, he has engineered a kidnapping of Lana and takes her to his house to hold her prisoner chained in the basement, where he reveals his alter ego identity as "Bloody Face." Suffering from pathological maternal abandonment issues, Dr. Thredson believes from his long observation of Lana that she, finally, is "the One" who can become his surrogate mother after he found so many other women lacking and killed them for it. Another maternally fixated sexual psychopath and serial killer in an already crowded field of them in the horror genre, bearing more than a little and certainly intentional resemblance to Norman Bates, Dr. Thredson rapes Lana, whose stuporous, drug-addled reaction to this violation mirrors that of Kit during his abduction and subsequent sessions on Dr. Arden's surgical table.

Dr. Thredson's pathology is further linked to Dr. Arden's through the former's construction of human-skin lampshades, a free-floating signifier in the popular imagination of Nazi atrocities because of the apocryphal stories of same found in the Buchenwald concentration camp. Additionally, both

Thredson and Arden share deeply repressed sexualities, both manifesting in different directions and executed through differing practice but toward the same end: the domination of women who represent both idealistic purity and love but whose very unattainability produces a rage ending in murder. Dr. Arden gravitates toward the purity of Sister Mary Eunice (before her demonic possession) but is repulsed by women he considers to be "sluts," such as Shelley; nevertheless, his repressed sexual attraction toward the promiscuous Shelley enrages him to the point where he attempts to rape her. Her laughing at his small penis during the failed attempt has the predictable result, ending in her torture and death. Dr. Thredson, looking for the unconditional love of a mother who left him as a child to grow up in an orphanage, attempts to build replacements by skinning and decapitating women (beginning with already dead women, easily accessible to him as a medical student) who in some way remind him of his idealized image of his mother. However, this longing for the absent maternal is also inextricably bound to a sexualized desire to punish and kill women. The corpses of women he didn't kill ultimately fail to satisfy his desire, so he "graduates" to living women. Lana's captivity inevitably ends up with her rape by Thredson, an act which impregnates her and will ultimately lead to the next generation's "Bloody Face," their son Johnny. Incapable of normal sexual relations, Dr. Arden and Dr. Thredson enact violations upon women similar to what the aliens do to female abductees and, in Thredson's instance, toward the same end: breeding.

As the Angel of Death (Shachath) and the Devil who has come to Briarcliff through possession of the formerly pure Sister Mary Eunice have their respective ways with the spiritually embattled inmates and staff, the aliens hover—godlike and indifferent to the machinations of God, the Devil, and man—somewhere above the sanitarium. However, like God watching over his Chosen People, the aliens are only interested in Briarcliff because Kit, their Chosen One, is incarcerated there. On the "dark and stormy night" of the nor'easter when Kit, Grace, and Lana try to escape but are forced back into the asylum to escape the Raspers, Sister Jude encounters one of the aliens in the dark corridors of Briarcliff. Why they are tracking Kit this closely becomes clearer when Kit becomes sexually involved with Grace. Shortly after they have sex and are facing a threatened (but ultimately never imposed) sentence of involuntary sterilization for it, the aliens abduct Grace. As she is held captive in the null white space that has visually come to represent the alien realm in the show, she sees a naked and pregnant Alma, foreshadowing Grace's later pregnancy. When Grace is returned, she is bleeding vaginally, presumably from the forced sterilization but really from what the aliens have done to her through their reproductive bioengineering.

When Grace is fatally shot by a guard gunning for Kit, her unexpected death compels the aliens to intercede again in the dark affairs of Briarcliff on behalf of their test subject. As Dr. Arden attempts to dispose of her body by taking it out to feed the Raspers, the aliens appear amid their signature electrical storm, sonic blasts, and blinding lights to take her body. Finally convinced by the evidence of the implant combined with the abduction of Grace's corpse that Kit's aliens are real, in Episode Nine, "The Coat Hanger," Dr. Arden articulates a hypothesis to Kit (and the audience) as to the extraterrestrials' true motives, basing it on the aliens' focus on Kit's sexual partners: "They're experimenting. Probably refining some kind of eugenics.... They're studying you, Mr. Walker. You're obviously valuable to them. And a good scientist always protects his subject. For example, if your life were threatened, they would have to act to protect their specimen." Arden tests his hypothesis by chemically bringing Kit to the brink of death. The aliens not only return at this moment of danger to Kit but they bring an unexpected surprise: Grace, not only alive but visibly pregnant. They have also worked another miracle by repairing the microcephalic Pepper's neurological functions and placing her with Grace as her protector. As Grace has seen, Alma is also alive and pregnant. The aliens' reproductively focused experiment with Kit is bearing fruit.

Grace explains to Kit why the aliens took her and Alma: "Our only link is you.... You're special, Kit. Our baby is special. People will listen to him. He's going to change the way people think." This messianic theme, reminiscent of the religiously tinged UFO contactee tales of the 1950s, is one more manifestation of Season Two's disquisition on hyper religiosity. On the face of it, Grace's interpretation of her miraculous experience as a religious one seems to be presented unironically enough. However, layers of ambiguity surround even Grace's relatively uncompromised, sincere expressions of faith. For one thing, she chooses to name her and Kit's seemingly anointed baby "Thomas," a Biblically significant name in that Thomas is the apostle who both embodies doubt (by questioning Jesus's resurrection) and belief (by later accepting it). For another, Kit never really accepts that the aliens are benign in intent, though he later comes to forgive them (and others who have wronged him, such as Sister Jude). He calls them "terrifying," "monsters." Grace, while more favorably inclined toward them, acknowledges their ambiguous nature in Episode Eleven, "Spilt Milk": "They're not like us. They're not cruel ... [but] they're not perfect. They make mistakes."

While it is true the aliens protect Kit, they also blast apart (with light and sound and electromagnetic storm) his life, and the lives of the two women dearest to him, without invitation. Like Job, Kit is arbitrarily punished by a divine force in league with the devil, or in this case, a simulacrum of God; like Job, he must make peace with it. For a heartbreakingly brief period, it seems as if Kit has found his happy ending. He, Grace, and Alma form a makeshift family in Episodes Eleven and Twelve, practicing a polygamous relationship analogous to the experiments in communal living popping up across the American landscape during the 1960s. (Timothy Miller, for example, writes that "In the mid–1960s communitarian idealism erupted in what was to be by far its largest manifestation ever, when hundreds of thousands, perhaps even a million, of mostly young Americans sought to rebuild from the ground up what they perceived as a decadent, rotten society" [327].) Episode Twelve, "Continuum," is one of the most self-consciously "1960s" episodes in the season. Now free to explore the world, Kit becomes part of the countercultural revolution, dressing in the colorful garb of youthful progressives (or "hippies," if you will) and bringing his non-traditional family to Civil Rights marches to mingle with what he calls "like-minded people."

Of course, the transgressive goings-on in the Walker house do not escape the baleful notice of the retrograde locals, such as Billy. A group of men, likely led by Billy, carries out a nocturnal attack, one that initially makes Alma believe the aliens have returned for her and the children, on the house. The act of terror sends a clear message to Kit that the community is determined to punish him and his family for undermining traditional family values. The point is brought home when the responding police officer refuses to investigate the crime and instead warns Kit that polygamy is illegal. Beset by troubles from the outside, life inside the Walker house is not turning out to be so idyllic either. In spite of both women agreeing to sharing Kit emotionally and sexually, it becomes clear from Alma's discontent in overhearing Grace and Kit having sex one night that the course of their polygamy does not always run smoothly. In addition to sexual jealousy, Alma also suffers from a kind of post-traumatic stress disorder, or PTSD, related to the abduction. She does not share Grace's belief in the aliens' benevolence. She tells Kit the aliens treat humanity as if they are pulling the wings off an insect. She would prefer to forget everything about them and live in the past when she and Kit were untroubled and happy. By contrast, Grace looks toward the future promised by the alien/human hybrid race. She views what happened to her as a blessing. In the episode "Continuum," she sketches the aliens' faces to show the children so that they will, as she tells Kit, "know where they came from." Her last words to Kit are "the future is coming … no matter what." Alma, increasingly tormented by her memories of her abduction and her anger that Grace views the experience as a religious one, kills Grace with an axe and is committed to Briarcliff. Kit, stricken with pancreatic cancer, is taken by the aliens again, this time never to return. By now, the answer to the question, "Are the aliens protecting or harming Kit?" is clear. They do both.

Conclusion

Undeniably, the aliens keep Kit relatively safe from the horrors of Briarcliff, in that they don't let him die. But the asylum is a place he would never have been if the aliens had not taken Alma away and left Kit to take the blame for her murder. It is indisputable, regardless of whatever temporary happiness Kit, Grace, and Alma cobble together with their two children after the aliens are seemingly done with them, that human welfare is not really a concern for the aliens. Placed into a cosmic experiment he did not ask for in the service of a grand design he will never see fulfilled, Kit is the noblest character in the season. His first name means in Greek "carrier of Christ" (Lutes) and, amongst his other selfless acts, Kit trusts Lana after her betrayal of him during the first escape attempt and offers to take the full brunt of Sister Jude's caning upon himself to protect Grace. He later forgives Sister Jude by taking her into his house to live out her days in peace. But he also suffers torture at the hands of man and alien alike.

If the aliens represent metaphorically some of the worst traits of humanity depicted in the season—sexual psychopathy, genocidal megalomania, scientific dehumanization, hyper religiosity at the expense of compassion—Kit, Grace, and Alma are their most innocent victims. Alma is driven mad and Grace is killed with an axe just as she killed her sexually abusive father and lying stepmother in the same way years before. This fate would surely have never been theirs had the aliens left Kit out of their eugenics experiment. Like the absent Christ so dogmatically but meaninglessly invoked by the nuns of Briarcliff, Kit undergoes his own kind of passion play for the sins of others while scorned and tormented by those same others. At the end, his mission of helping Lana Winters shut down Briarcliff done and his miraculously-conceived children presumably destined to change the world, Kit is borne into the heavens beyond human reach. All of this has been done to him without any regard for his own wishes as to how to live his life, while his lovers died terrible deaths during the experiment. As the show's creators say, the aliens stand in for God in the symbolic structure of the second season, working miracles on behalf of humanity in an age where science and religion vie for control over the masses. At the same time, this is a flawed God of terrifying power, callous disregard for individual human life in the service of some greater cosmic mission, and opaque intentions. While Kit says he no longer believes in a God "who would create the things I saw," the beings that do transform his life are, for all practical purposes from a limited earthbound perspective, God. It is no wonder that Kit calls this God "monster."

NOTES

1. For a detailed description of the "typical" abduction experience, please refer to John E. Mack's *Abduction: Human Encounters with Aliens* (New York: Charles Scribner's Sons, 1994).

2. Now that *American Horror Story* has concluded its fifth season, *Hotel*, it has become increasingly apparent that, in spite of its anthology approach, the show carries over from season to season more than just many of the same actors, such as Evan Peters. The sprawling

storylines create a "shared universe" in which many characters and themes repeat. The work that needs to be done to mine the commonalities of the *AHS* universe goes beyond the scope of this essay, but suffice it to say, one of those unifying themes throughout each season is how the domestic space, such as that co-habited by Kit and Alma, is threatened by tensions within and terrors without. Dawn Keetley cites *AHS* as "an important addition to a specifically televisual Gothic … raising recognizably real early twenty-first century anxieties about homes and families" (91).

   3. For a recent, comprehensive book-length overview of "Operation Paperclip," please refer to Annie Jacobsen's *Operation Paperclip: The Secret Intelligence Program That Brought Nazi Scientists to America* (New York: Little, Brown and Company, 2014).

WORKS CITED

Cagle, Jess. "This Was the Year That … TV Went Insane: *American Horror Story: Asylum* Captured and Terrified the Minds of Audiences in 2012." *Entertainment Weekly*. Entertainment Weekly, 21 December 2012. Web. 9 January 2016.

"The Coat Hanger." *American Horror Story: Asylum*. Writ. Jennifer Salt. Dir. Jeremy Podeswa. FX Network. 12 December 2012. Television.

"Continuum." *American Horror Story: Asylum*. Writ. Ryan Murphy. Dir. Craig Zisk. FX Network. 16 January 2013. Television.

Dean, Jodi. *Aliens in America*. Ithaca, NY: Cornell University Press, 1998. Print.

Frayling, Christopher. *Mad, Bad and Dangerous: The Scientist and the Cinema*. London: Reaktion Books, 2005. Print.

Gay, Verne. "'*American Horror Story: Asylum* Not Much of a Story." *Newsday*. October 2012. Web. 9 January 2016.

Harrison, Andrew. "Can *The X-Files* Exist in a Post–9/11 World?" *New Statesman*. New Statesman, 29 December 2015. Web. 9 January 2016.

Haynes, Roslynn D. *From Faust to Strangelove: Representations of the Scientist in Western Literature*. Baltimore: Johns Hopkins University Press, 1994. Print.

Hoagland, Lily. "*American Horror Story* Recap: What Were Those Aliens There for, Again?" *Vanity Fair Hollywood*. Vanity Fair, 4 January 2013. Web. 9 January 2016.

"I Am Anne Frank, Pt. 1." *American Horror Story: Asylum*. Writ. Jessica Sharzer. Dir. Michael Uppendahl. FX Network. 7 November 2012. Television.

"I Am Anne Frank, Pt. 2." *American Horror Story: Asylum*. Writ. Brad Falchuk. Dir. Alfonso Gomez-Rejon. FX Network. 14 November 2012. Television.

Jacobsen, Annie. *Operation Paperclip: The Secret Intelligence Program That Brought Nazi Scientists to America*. New York: Little, Brown and Company, 2014. Print.

Jung, C.G. *Flying Saucers: A Modern Myth of Things Seen in the Skies*. Trans. R.F.C. Hull. Princeton: Princeton University Press, 1978. Print.

Keetley, Dawn. "Stillborn: The Entropic Gothic of *American Horror Story*." *Gothic Studies* 15.2 (2013): 89–107. Print.

Li, Shirley. "*American Horror Story*: Creators Reveal Secrets of 'Asylum.'" *Entertainment Weekly*. 2 Oct. 2013. Web. 7 March 2016.

Lutes, Alicia. "*American Horror Story: Asylum*: Ryan Murphy's Aliens Are Secretly Brilliant." Hollywoodwww. 23 January 2013. Web. 9 January 2016.

Mack, John E. *Abduction: Human Encounters with Aliens*. New York: Charles Scribner's Sons, 1994. Print.

Miller, Timothy. "The Sixties-Era Communes." *Imagine Nation: The American Counterculture of the 1960s and '70s*. Eds. Peter Braunstein and Michael William Doyle. New York: Routledge, 2002. 327–352. Print.

Moore, Trent. "*American Horror Story* Producers Finally Explain What Was Up with the Aliens." *blastr*. 3 October 2013. Web. 9 January 2016.

"Nor'easter." *American Horror Story: Asylum*. Writ. Jennifer Salt. Dir. Michael Uppendahl. FX Network. 31 October 2012. Television.

"The Origins of Monstrosity." *American Horror Story: Asylum*. Writ. Ryan Murphy. Dir. David Semel. FX Network. 21 November 2012. Television.

Peebles, Curtis. *Watch the Skies: A Chronicle of the Flying Saucer Myth*. Washington, D.C.: Smithsonian Institute Press, 1995. Print.

Randle, Kevin D., Russ Estes, and William P. Cone. *The Abduction Enigma: The Truth Behind the Mass Alien Abductions of the Late Twentieth Century*. 1999. New York: Forge, 2000. Print.

"Spilt Milk." *American Horror Story: Asylum*. Writ. Brad Falchuk. Dir. Alfonso Gomez-Rejon. FX Network. 9 January 2013. Television.

"Tricks and Treats." *American Horror Story: Asylum*. Writ. James Wong. Dir. Bradley Buecker. FX Network. 24 October 2012. Television.

"Welcome to Briarcliff." *American Horror Story: Asylum*. Writ. Tim Minear. Dir. Bradley Buecker. FX Network. 17 October 2012. Television.

Piecing It Together
Genre Frameworks *in* American Horror Story

EMMA AUSTIN

The critical reception of each new season of *American Horror Story* (*AHS*) has been marked by reviews that highlight the supposedly piecemeal approach to narrative, structure and intent: what Gary Hoppenstand refers to as a "disturbing mish-mash of horror conventions and graphic images" for *AHS: Murder House* (1). E. A Hanks agrees that "the show leans on classic horror tropes to act as foundation" but its main concern is "invested in a theatricality." Interestingly, the review continues that this is focused on "big impact visuals," part of a generic and stylistic relationship between horror and camp. This perception is echoed by J. Bryan Lowder in his review that "Camp, not horror, is the soul and motivating force of *AHS*." These dialogues indicate we should interrogate what generic structures *AHS* is following to determine if we can position it purely within the horror genre, or as a newer evocation of changing generic tastes. As Phillip Maciak's incisive 2012 review notes: "The success of this series forces us to ask where precisely it fits, what exactly it even is, when placed in a line-up with a gallery of television shows that look nothing like it," noting that Ryan Murphy's previous work *Glee* (2009–2015) links to a camp aesthetic and spectacle that in *AHS* are offered as "grotesque inversions of themselves." (Maciak). The willingness of *AHS* to combine and distort key structural signifiers, and this "knowingness" of genre templates is the keynote of this exploration: what genre frameworks does *AHS* choose to emphasize, and to what generic purpose?

We could begin by classifying these mutated signifiers as part of postmodern horror, which Isabel Cristina Pinedo argues is characterized by transgressions of previous generic rules, but also references them to make its translation clear. She continues: "the postmodern horror film draws upon other generic codes and structures … to concoct hybrids" (14). In particular, "the genre audience acquires a taste for the destructuring tendency of the contemporary horror film, and a willingness not to resist it. Consequently, the genre audience greets a new horror film with the expectation of being surprised by a clever overturning of convention." Eddie Robson refines these ideas in relation to Gothic television: "In an environment such as American TV where genres are very clearly defined, generic hybrids are easier to create and this suits Gothic well" (245). Generic identity may be particularly linked to the context of modern American TV broadcasting, part of the strategy of "narrowcasting: targeting programming to smaller, demographically defined market segments, as opposed to a broad, mass audience of everyone from everywhere" (Bottomley 483). *AHS* in particular seems predicated on displaying extremes of eroticism and horror though the channel FX, aimed at a "defined" adult audience. But the way the program is constructed structurally and serially, and indeed in terms of its textual components, seems a patchwork of aims and concerns. To quote Maciak: "might American Horror Story be an aesthetic rather than a narrative project?" To address these ideas of televisual constructs, generic referentiality and deconstruction in *AHS*, this essay begins by outlining concepts surrounding seriality and repetition in the series construction and narrative arcs, to identify what repetitions *AHS* situates in its overall construction. Through this we can identify intersections of narrative and aesthetic choices to see whether generic or aesthetic considerations are key: is *AHS* knowingly constructed as excessive, transgressive and progressive, moving beyond established televisual genre boundaries?

Seriality and Stories: Positioning Genre Television

It is useful to discuss the length of each *AHS* series, as this situates the key factors of repetition and seriality—these two terms link both the history of TV horror presentation and *AHS* as a text focused on drawing attention to its generic construction. The length of each series of is currently from 12–13 episodes per series, it is broadcast weekly and each new series is normally premiered in October in the U.S. *AHS* initially positioned itself as a self-contained series: as Ryan Murphy phrased it: "it's a beginning, middle, and end" (Martin). This has led to a multiplicity of descriptions applied to *AHS*: several commentators have positioned the television program as an anthology series (Heuring, 2012; Guthrie, 2013; Neel, 2013; Nussbaum, 2014) or a mini-series, including in the nominations for industry awards (Stack, 2012; Martin 2012).

However, if we take as our starting point Lorna Jowett and Stacey Abbott's definition of an anthology series as "an episodic format generally broadcast weekly, but each episode stands alone much like short stories" (33) we can see immediate issues with applying this notion to any series of *AHS*, where the focus of each episode may be different, or offer a completed plot line, but always ties in with previous or later episodes. This is exampled in the episodes "I Am Anne Frank" (Pts. 1 and 2) in *AHS: Asylum*, where suburban housewife Charlotte Brown (Franka Potente) is convinced she is Anne Frank, and that Dr. Arden (James Cromwell) is an escaped Nazi extermination camp doctor. The first episode features Charlotte admitted to Briarcliff Manor and the second her lobotomy by Arden. However this is alongside other plots featuring main characters, and acts as a spur to Sister Jude's (Jessica Lange) growing suspicions about Dr. Arden and her catastrophic struggles for power within the asylum, followed over the next episodes.

A more fluid definition may be to consider *AHS* as an amalgamation of the anthology series and the "serialized format (or soap opera)" (Jowett and Abbott 34) over a shorter time frame than extended horror series such as *Dark Shadows* (1966–1971), *Twin Peaks* (1990–1991) and *American Gothic* (1995–1996). These bear obvious resemblances to *AHS* through their "melodramatic, serialized narrative arcs that focused on home families and communities besieged by the supernatural" (Subramanian 112). We should also note that the two most recent series, *AHS: Freak Show* and *AHS: Hotel* also explicitly link to characters and events in other series, providing a longer narrative arc of influence and backstory than originally offered in Seasons One to Three. Therefore we may wish to consider each series of *AHS* as a conscious and continual reformatting of televisual and filmic formats: as Hoppenstand notes, the show is a "deliberate send-up of the traditional TV soap opera" (2).

Jowett and Abbott outline several theorists who have argued for modern horror television construction as an amalgamation of previous formats: they quote Sergio Angelini and Miles Booy's discussion of how contemporary TV drama embraces seriality through "both repetitive, episodic horror and ongoing character development" (50) and Glen Creeber's argument on how "intimacy and continuity are reserved for soaps" (50) but that modern television can rely on a conflation of these factors and the notion of "epicness" in miniseries (50). In particular, we can point to the symbolic importance of the use of the word "Story" in the series title. This not only emphasizes the fiction of the ensuing program, but links to "watching my stories" as a synonym for watching soap opera in America. As Michael Moon notes, "*Story* is also a term that has circulated widely in the twentieth century for screenplay, soap opera, and other extended nonnovel narrative forms. It is the long-arc serial narrative—as it has informed a number of genres across several media" (696). Moon particularly notes the intersections between melodrama and comedy plots in the early twentieth century, where "situation, suspense, and sudden reversal and revelation were the chief means by which their effects were achieved" (700). This positions soap opera as part of a long tradition of adapting the melodramatic format for conflict, interest and sensationalism in differing genres and media platforms: "With its emphasis on amplified emotions, charged personal relations, the eventual vindication of personal steadfastness, and the exposure of secret wrongdoing, soap operas close kinship with melodrama has always been clear" (700). This offers us an interesting pathway to interrogate the construction of *AHS* as both melodrama and horror, specifically through ideas surrounding the Gothic.

Melodrama, Sensationalism and Repetition: Structure in American Horror Story

Links between melodrama, Gothic and sensation are worth delineating to see if *AHS* is part of a longer continuum of generic attributes. To begin, we can look to Lisa Schmidt's argument surrounding the historical linkage of Gothic and melodrama. In particular, she notes the textual construction of "sensation novels," melodrama and the Gothic. They "tend to feature female protagonists … terrible, ostensibly 'actiony' plot activities are placed alongside story elements which emphasize emotions, relationships, the familial and domestic" (163). This is not to argue that these texts resemble film melodrama, often wrongly seen as a female genre. Schmidt refers to Ben Singer's discussions that "melodrama as understood by the Victorians was nothing like the 'woman's film'; it was a gory, action-packed spectacle" (163), similar to the early Gothic novels which were "perverse and uncompromising" (161). Indeed, following Steve Neale's construction of melodrama as: "improbable, often crime related or fantastical plots hinging on coincidence and accident, clearly drawn from the sensation drama" (163), Schmidt offers a trajectory for later horror representations stemming from sensational melodramatic texts. She argues that with their "emphasis on fantastical plots, mortal danger and the visual presentation of the extreme and the shocking, these narrative forms closely resemble what was to be the horror genre of the twentieth century" (164).

We should briefly discuss the importance of seriality as a method of narrative construction, as it draws attention to defining features of melodrama and horror. Schmidt notes that the release of some sensationalist and melodramatic fiction was through instalments (166), delaying the gratification of narrative resolution and initiating an episodic format. "Cliffhangers" and moments of action were juxtaposed with dialogues and character development leading to the notion that "action and melodrama are by no means mutually exclusive" (168). Schmidt argues that this construction also creates intricate complexities of narrative and characterization: "Seriality means that the story is built upon connections between episodes, that characters have a memory and a history, and that single episodes, while providing limited resolution in some instances, most often invite and demand viewing of the next, and the next" (166). This "absence of episodic closure" (165) in turn allows the series "astonishing levels of emotional crisis and catharsis because they have time on their side" (166). This is a keynote of *AHS*, in that the complexities of characters and development are set against increasingly horrific scenarios and events, and moments of catharsis are short lived, against escalating levels of crisis. The overall narrative and thematic arc of each series of *AHS* can be understood as entrapment and escape (both physical and mental), with each episode offering a gradual development of situation and characters to develop empathy or disgust as we recognize their layered pasts and connections with other characters, especially through the recognition of potential threats. As in Schmidt's conclusions surrounding other horror TV series, in each series of *AHS* the horror *enables* the melodrama; "the supernatural elements of the story elevate or exacerbate the situations of the characters" (169).

In terms of the episodic structure of each series, it is clear that there are spectacular peaks of tension or gore against a continual backdrop of visual pleasure in sets and costumes and horrific imagery and events. The Halloween episodes of *Murder House*, *Coven*, and *Freak Show* operate as seasonal links through their broadcast dates, but also have a symbolic function: they underscore specific visual effects and foreground horrific incursions as a trigger for character development. An excellent example is the appearance of Edward Mordrake (Wes Bentley) in the episodes "Edward Mordrake, Pt. 1" and "Edward Mordrake, Pt. 2" in *Freak Show*, which explicitly foregrounds the visual effects of his demon face, juxtaposed with his courtly character and manner of address. In the same vein, the personal stories of trauma the demon face desires fill in emotive character backstories for the viewer, such as Ethel Darling's (Kathy Bates) confession over Jimmy's birth or the tragic story of Paul, the illustrated Seal (Mat Fraser), but also allow deployments of gore and body effects, notably in Elsa Mars's (Jessica Lange) horrific snuff film trauma. This also occurs in episodes in *Murder House*, discussed later in this essay. In deciphering the deployment of horror and melodrama as generic structures in *AHS* as a whole, the use of the final episode of each series is fascinating, as it is not the final escalation of gory, horrific events: this happens throughout the series, with visions of mass murder (*Coven*, *Murder House*, *Freak Show*) or images of torture and bodily decay (*Asylum*, *Hotel*) leading to specifically violent *denouements* one or two episodes *before* the end of the series. The final episode, "Afterbirth," of *Murder House* for example deals with the aftermath of Vivien Harmon's (Connie Britton) death and the births, situates the grim fate of Ben Harmon (Dylan McDermott) and then reunites the split family as ghosts.

Overall, the final episodes in *AHS* leave threats either resolved or growing "offstage," so the series resolution is on character endings or after-effects, with a focus on moral resolution and some punishment: The "evil" ghosts in *Murder House* are positioned outside looking in at the newly connected family, forever excluded. The repetitive hell of Madame Delphine LaLaurie (Kathy Bates) and Marie Laveau (Angela Bassett) sees them endlessly re-enacting their torture (see Glossary) and the rural hell/limbo of Fiona Goode (Jessica Lange) in the "The Seven Wonders" episode of *Coven* (see Glossary), destined to remain forever with the "Axeman" (Danny Huston), make it clear this is a moral, if unfair universe. The redemption/cure of Sister Jude and the final disappearance of Kit (Evan Peters) in "Madness Ends" in *Asylum* and the trials and success of Cordelia (Sarah Paulson) in "The Seven Wonders" also indicate that certain characters' experiences lead to positive resolutions. We should remind ourselves here of Moon's characterization of soaps with their "eventual vindication of personal steadfastness, and the exposure of secret wrongdoing" (700).

However, the endings also *refuse* certain closures, with emphases on influence and repetition that are hallmarks of the entire series: as Jowett and Abbott argue, the "Televisual structure of horror relies more on repetition and cycles than linear narrative" (52) and may therefore refuse certain narrative closures, in order to create suspense: Constance Langdon (Jessica Lange) mothers the demonic Michael in *Murder House*, Lana Winters (Sarah Paulson) welcomes then kills another killer seeking the maternal in *Asylum*, and may or may not be evil herself. Here we can situate the structuring of narrative resolution in *AHS* as a characteristic hallmark of fantasy: the resolution is not as important as the development, the discovery plot of pleasure and violence which form the basis for all series. It is also an ongoing trope of soap and horror texts.

Dawn Keetley argues that repetition is a key feature of the first series, in its "claustrophobic sense of enclosure in space and repetition in time" (89). We should extend her discussion to all series, especially when considering the heritage of cinematic excess in melodrama and horror that *AHS* can be seen to be drawing upon. Repetition of formulas is key in Linda Williams's discussion of melodrama: she identifies how structures in

> fantasies are not, as sometimes thought, wish fulfilling linear narratives of mastery and control leading to closure and the attainment of desire. They are marked, rather, by the prolongation of desire, and by the lack of fixed position with respect to the objects and events fantasized [10].

This would explain the ongoing cycles of characters and traumatic events: the repeated escape narratives, the enlarging of character and motivations not through linear development, but through doubling, shifting to the past and into alternative states: dreams, memories, and the prospect of limbo. In particular, the shifting between different storylines in an episode allows a continual shifting between perspectives and desires, and an emphasis on how these can fatally meet.

Repetition is constructed symbolically and temporally in *AHS*: historical periods are specified (though time can shift, it is clearly marked through the use of intertitles, as in *Murder House*[1]) and this is a repeated trope as the past lays a burden on the present. People repeat mistakes, are fixated on past traumas which construct their current identity, or are continuously returned to situations from which they try to escape. In particular, this notion of personal repetition is an important part of the construction of audience identification and pleasure in *AHS*: in re-using a core ensemble cast, Murphy compared his early work to that of Orson Welles's Mercury Theatre (Murphy in Martin).[2] This allowed the potential for recasting each actor in each series and the repeated archetypes thus set up (dominant mothers, rebellious teenagers, troubled females, weak males) allowed the pleasures of recognition for audiences in later series in noting similarities and differences. The characters played by Evan Peters as particular oppositions (between murderous Tate in *Murder House* and victimized Kit in *Asylum*) was a textual element that creator Murphy particularly noted (Murphy in Martin). The role of Jessica Lange as the dominant female character in the first four seasons was vital in establishing consistent thematic character roles: the dominance of the feminine became an integral thematic strand, linking the series not only to Lange's star persona, but also traditional conceptions of horror, melodrama and other "low" cinematic formats.

Tainted Love: Excess, Desire and Characterization

As we have seen so far, *American Horror Story* operates through a conscious repetition of structural tropes, both horrific and otherwise to draw attention to generic constructs and expectations of televisual formats. We should now focus this discussion down to specific thematic repetitions that *AHS* offers, especially the notion of emotional and visual excess. In *AHS*, this seems to be initiated, if not always sustained, through the presentation of the female. Williams's influential discussion of cinematic genre, excess and bodies in "Film Bodies: Gender, Genre and Excess" (1991) focuses on female representation, but importantly offers a framework for understanding the systems and forms of "body genres," identified as pornography, horror and melodrama. In her discussion, melodrama is system of signification that offers insights into the concerns of these apparently disparate texts:

> Consider ... these genres under the rubric of melodrama, considered as a filmic mode of stylistic and/or emotional excess that stands in contrast to more "dominant" modes of realistic, goal orientated narrative ... a ... broad range of films marked by "lapses" in realism, by "excesses of spectacle" and displays of primal, even infantile emotions, and by narratives that seem circular and repetitive [3].

The key textual elements identified here focus around excess: firstly, excessive emotions offered through repeated plots and characters, and secondly excessive representational choices, through aesthetic choices and textual construction. We should examine these in turn to see what constructions *AHS* offers us through belonging to a body genre that can negotiate between horror and melodrama. We have already touched upon the use of repetition in melodrama and *AHS*, in particular in the construction of each series and the narrative drives, but we should also note characterizations and archetypes as important factors in determining the generic choices made in each series of *AHS*. In this the notion of melodrama and horror being texts centered on emotional excess in characters is one central to understanding the construction of *AHS*.

Gender is a key construct here: as Janani Subramanian notes, "fear of femininity and its potentially overwhelming excess" (110) is a consideration surrounding Williams's characteristics of those "excessive" body genre texts. We should start with Williams's opening discussion that "sex, violence, and emotion are fundamental elements of the sensational effects of these three types of films" (3) and are therefore not gratuitous but part of a structural system: a structure of *sensation*. Indeed, their success as texts rests on our involvement with and potential manipulation of emotion (5). In *AHS* emotions and excess form the backbone of each series, as the desires and motivations of each character come into conflict with those around them. In numerical terms, in these texts females are the focus through the sheer number of female characters: men are unfaithful husbands, tormented or tormenting sons, problematic partners and objects of desire. However, the shifts in identification the audience goes through in each series means that gendered relations are never easily fixed as binary either/or situations. As Williams notes of "sensational" genres, there are a "variety of different subject positions ... a strong mixture of passivity and activity" (8) in terms of sadistic or masochistic pleasures, and this is true of the characters in *AHS*, who suffer repeated twists of fortune through their eroticized power relations. In the most overt depiction, Elsa in *Freak Show* is a dominatrix, later physically mutilated, then in turn becomes the leader of the freak show—until other dominant characters come into play. Elsa's ambition as a defining characteristic was noted in the episode "Monsters Among Us," allowing the character's power relations to shift and form around greed and trauma later on in the series, but always enacted though sexual desire and violence. As Williams continues in her discussion of body genres: "all of these genres could, for example, be said to offer highly melodramatic enactments of sexually charged, if not sexually explicit, relations" (7) and *AHS* foregrounds sexual desire as a trigger for tragedy. Fixations and excessive desire are a central part of each series, focused on fetish and taboo in its extremes (incest in *Coven*, maternal fixations in *Murder House* and *Asylum*, torture and power in *Asylum*, *Coven* and *Hotel*, deformities as desire in *Freak Show*, addiction in *Hotel*) egotism, ambition and ongoing sexual and romantic desire as a more "normal" form of fixation throughout. Here normality and extremity in desire can co-exist and develop continuously, mutating as each series progresses.

In this we return to Schmidt's discussion of seriality and construction, and in turn the engagement of the viewer, particularly her remarks on how narrative develops through fleshing out characters and forging links between episodes, thus exacting a commitment from the audience (166). The overall construction of each season structures engagement around discovering the desires, excessive or otherwise, of each character and the trajectories of conflict to which these lead. Here the characterization and narrative are focused around desire and power relations as continual triggers, echoed in repeated use of sex scenes and aestheticized desire through costume: the emphasis of color and texture in Elsa Mars's costumes (*Freak Show*) and those of the Countess (Lady Gaga in *Hotel*) explicitly link to diva-like statuses of desire and performance linked to their sexual identity, while the ominous power embodied in the Rubber Man operates as fetish, control and finally horrific signifier of a poisoned relationship and a rapist's disguise in *Murder House*. These are only some examples of where sex and desire are played out around specific interrelationships of characters, creating some brutal shifts in the notion of pleasure and consent. In this, we could argue that eroticism and therefore *AHS* is linked to the horror genre, especially through the notion of "unhealthy" sexualities, but it is also a factor in soaps and modern melodrama aimed at adult audiences.

Supporting this argument, Schmidt notes the mixed audiences of theatrical and literary examples of melodrama and horror, appealing "to those whose taste was for action and those whose taste was for emotion" (165). However, there is still an implicit assumption

> that melodrama is often assumed to deal only with stories having to do with family and relationships, topics that are associated with women's genres and presumably women's preoccupations. Meanwhile, genres like horror (and others) are defined in terms of certain kinds of narrative action: murders, chases, hauntings and so forth [168].

In *American Horror Story*, we may be able to negotiate these assumed structural differences by paying attention not only the construction of desire but to an aspect not included in Schmidt's conclusions: the visual and aesthetic choices in depicting location and violence, specifically horrific bodies. In the next part of this essay we should consider how physicality, whether in a geographical space, body effects or a very explicit discussion of masculine monstrosity is important to understanding specific horror constructs in *AHS*. We should turn to the second deployment of excessive representational choices, through aesthetics and visual constructions of the horrific and sensational, not just through narrative deployments of the melodramatic.

Bad Places and Bloody Faces: Location, Gore and Excess

Each series of *AHS* occurs in a different part of the U.S.: Los Angeles (*Murder House* and *Hotel*), Massachusetts (*Asylum*), New Orleans (*Coven*) and Florida (*Freak Show*). Alongside the regional differences in climate and landscape and historical and cultural meaning embodied by cities or states, these locations also serve to center the action in specific, mostly bounded, locales: (a home, asylum, school, freak show and hotel) with only a few movements outside of these locations. This allows a focus on symbolic repetition and constriction, a noted tenet of Gothic texts in various media formats. In particular, the repetition of events and the imprinting of psycho-geography where "areas of landscape, objects and buildings are extensions of body-psyche" (Morgan 196) then specify patterns of behavior on the inmates: a central example would be the haunted house which psychologically or actually destroys various inhabitants, as happens in *Murder House*. This bears resonances with notions of the American Gothic and its "persistence of historical memory" (Mighall 55). One example in horror television of locale and entrapment is present in Jowett and Abbott's discussion of *Dark Shadows*, where there is a sense of an "isolated community, divorced in many ways from the larger world" (47). However, in *AHS* boundaries are fluid, as outsiders frequently desire to integrate with the community/location or prompt catastrophic changes to the relationships between the characters. This is not only a factor of melodrama and soap, where environments are hothouses for relationships and conflict but also horror texts, where locations can indicate the status of characters in a symbolic sense, through the concept of liminality.

Liminality is a central concern in symbolic studies of space and place—particularly within horror—as liminality is about transition, in social meanings of status and belonging (Turner 95–97). However, this is also applicable to the locations in *AHS*. Transition is first positioned within the spaces as the pull between the past and the present: all feature locales where the past impacts on the present. The "Murder House" is part of a sensation tour due to its unsavory past, which is also the case with Briarcliff Manor/Asylum. The Murder House, Miss Robichaux's academy and the Hotel Cortez contain ghosts and monsters who impact on the present, while the freak show and asylum foster violence in the present through the histories of those inhabiting them: what Keetley characterizes for *Murder House* as "entropic gothic" (91), where the location encourages repetition and escalation, is true of all of these locales. These locations all bear the burden of being places of liminal flux, with little sense of a desired continuity: the owners of the house either leave or die, the asylum inmates wish for freedom, as do the performers in the freak show. The school is initially a hideaway for witches, due to dwindling numbers and violence against them, and is only seen as a home for those who have nowhere else to go. They are also unsafe as home spaces, open to incursions both desired and unwanted: the "home" invasions of *Murder House, Coven* and *Freak Show* indicate that these groups are vulnerable at all points of their existence. This is continued in *Hotel*—as Ryan Murphy notes: "when you check into a hotel, there are certain things beyond your control…. Other people have the keys to your room; they can come in there. You're not exactly safe, it's a very unsettling idea" (Genis).The continual shifting of movement, safety and danger trigger contests of power and ownership which inevitably spiral into violence. This then allows the next area of the horrific to be displayed, and certainly the one that seems to characterize *AHS* as horror: the deployment of visual effects depicting gore and the horrific.

All series of *AHS* refer to the visually disturbing through digital and make-up effects. In her discussion of the use of effects in *Murder House*, Subramanian notes that *AHS* works through its use of "quality television aesthetics with the narrative and visual excesses of both melodrama and horror" and what she sees as a "consistent narrative incorporation of those effects" (113). The most obvious reiteration of horror tropes is in the representation of monsters: the zombies/revenants in *Murder House* and *Coven*, the "Raspers" in *Asylum*, the melding of man in bull in the figure of Bastien (Ameer Baraka) in *Coven*, the shattered face of Twisty (John Carroll Lynch) in *Freak Show*. As Subramanian continues, horror television focuses on "disruptive and dismembered bodies" (108) and these are no exception, threatening the physical spaces of home or school.

However, while the emphasis is on the visual spectacle of their bodies, it is notable that most of the horror creatures are controlled or created, and have little volition. The zombies in *Coven* are controlled by Marie Laveau, and can be destroyed, a link both to her past and to LaLaurie, who is faced with the zombified body of her eldest daughter. The revenants in *Murder House* can be outrun, and the creation of the "Raspers" in *Asylum* is through a combination of dismemberment, disease and cruelty. This is most heartbreakingly displayed in the figure of Shelley (Chloë Sevigny), sectioned by her husband for nymphomania. Throughout the series she uses her sexuality and body to proclaim her identity, desirability and as a bartering tool. This is then contrasted with the damage done to her body by Arden, who amputates her legs and infects her, for her to become a "Rasper." Her final appearance at a school in the episode "I Am Anne Frank, Pt. 2" is presaged by screaming children running from a "monster." When their teacher investigates, the camera moves down to focus on the pitiful sight of Shelley, unrecognizable through sores and blisters, trying to drag herself up the basement steps, moaning incomprehensibly. There is a constant reiteration of bodily change through injury to position the audiences' knowledge of a change in status in the character, or the perception of the character through other protagonists, and in most cases this is a source of empathy (as with Shelley) or of discovery.

In all cases, the wounds and bodies are direct links to the past of those injured or those who have caused the injury. In the *Murder House* Halloween episodes ("Pt. 1" and "Pt. 2"), Halloween is a time for the dead to return, and many seem drawn to the Harmons' residence, including some of the victims of Tate's rampage in his school (which is not shown until the next episode, "Piggy Piggy"). The undead teenagers in *Murder House* are literally embodied testaments to Tate's psychosis. The violent nature of their deaths is their burden as ghosts: one who was shot in the face can no longer talk. The emphasis here, as with most horror monsters in modern texts is on horrality, not only telling but showing the horror, following Phillip Brophy's argument (8): the physical effects as well as the digital ones here focus on gaping wounds, blood splatter and impact trauma. As revenants chasing Tate and Violet (Taissa Farmiga) they are positioned as the external threat, but it is eventually made quite clear that they are not the monsters: the true monster is the fresh-faced Tate.

AHS uses this reversal of expectation repeatedly: injuries that appear on "whole" characters are an important indicator of changing status, either between living and dead or as precursors to memory or change. In the episode "Boy Parts" in *Coven*, Madison (Emma Roberts) emphasizes that she will select the "best" boy parts to reconstruct Kyle. Thus follows a panning shot of body parts in the morgue, a close up of uneven stitching and the final reconstruction is a pallid, wide-eyed mute. We can note the obvious visual resonances with Frankenstein's monster here, replicated in any number of horror media texts. As with Mary Shelley's creation, Kyle is a tortured soul: his reconstructed body is a site of physical and emotional scars and his mother's incest with him is revealed through her puzzlement over his "new" body in the episode "The Replacements." Similarly, in flashback we see the conscientious Kyle refusing to be tattooed with his frat brothers, as he is aware his body will proclaim his status and integrity when acting on behalf of his community: his discovery of a tattoo on his ankle therefore triggers a final violent recognition of his undead status. Finally, in a direct reference to the seminal text *Freaks* (1932) by Tod Browning, the characters and motivations of the performers are given precedence in *Freak Show* through reactions to their bodies: they can be violent, but this is normally positioned in relation to external threats to their existence, just as with the "normal" characters.

AHS continually uses recognizable figures of horror and monstrosity already established in other media texts, especially film and television. However, the threat is often positioned clearly within the actions of those represented as physically whole: we have seen this with Tate, and it is clear that this is a repeated motif of *AHS*—the notion of the psychologically scarred, but generally physically whole, serial killer. These are mostly male, with the exception of LaLaurie in *Coven*. What is interesting here is that, unlike the re-negotiations of the monstrous seen in the figures above, these characters have few if any redeeming features, and are explicitly positioned as a cause of pain in others, regardless of their emotional triggers. In all cases their actions and motivations are characterized by the physically and emotionally excessive, a key generic identifier of both melodrama and horror as we have already identified. Indeed, here may be the source of the "American Horror" in the series title: the continued cultural and symbolic potency of the American serial killer.

The first is the clown Twisty in *Freak Show* whose mutilated face is a signifier of his past trauma. He then plays this out through murder and kidnapping, a continual perversion of his role as entertainer to the young. We can make links here to the killer John Wayne Gacy (see Glossary), who was interested in clowning (Morgan 142). Twisty is shadowed and then replaced by Dandy (Finn Wittrock), a seemingly clean-cut young man who engages in matricide and mass killing, potentially replicating the character of Norman Bates, who was in turn inspired by the real killer Ed Gein. Similarly, Dr. Thredson (Zachary Quinto) in *Asylum* is revealed to be the serial killer "Bloody Face," wearing skin masks of his victims and with home décor made of human remains, again, a homage to the American killer Ed Gein and also Tobe Hooper's *The Texas Chain Saw Massacre* (1974). He is then mimicked in turn by his son as the second "Bloody Face." The episode "Home Invasion" in *Murder House* features killings by a character very similar to those of Richard Speck (see Glossary) and *Hotel* features the visits of real-life serial killers (Aileen Wuornos, Richard Ramirez, Jeffery Dahmer, John Wayne Gacy and the "Zodiac Killer") as a plot point in the episode "Devil's Night" (see Glossary). This is as well as the Ten Commandments Killer and the creator of the hotel, the sadist James Patrick March (Evan Peters), whose resemblance to H.H. Holmes is referenced in the episode "Chutes and Ladders" (see Glossary). Further, the "Axeman" killings in New Orleans are incorporated into *Coven* (see Glossary).[3] There is sense here that the creators of *AHS* have turned to specifically American contexts of mass murder and fear, based (however loosely) on the recorded actuality of lone killers in pursuit of their own desires.

Further, in general terms the repeated fears of school shootings echoed in Tate's actions in *Murder House* and the school infection and slaughter in "Room Service" in *Hotel* by Max Ellison (Anton Lee Starkman) seem to indicate repeated American traumas. The figure of the serial or mass killer seems symbolically important to *AHS*, as arguably this is where the real horror is embodied. Killing in defence, in retribution or as a mistake happens frequently, and how the individual character responds to this action and their own guilt situates their development, but those who are serial killers invade the safe spaces of the communities and demand reactions from even the "abnormal" others. What is interesting, however, is how these reactions all seem to spiral back to emotional obsessions surrounding the feminine.

We could characterize this thematic repetition broadly as a trope of horror and melodrama that emphasizes the emotional state of the female as a major concern, specifically her suffering and trauma. If we return to Williams's discussion of generic concerns in melodrama, which includes a discussion of pornography and horror, we can note the "traditional status as bodily hysteria or excess … the woman 'afflicted'" (4) as a major aspect in all three types of genre text. In *AHS*, the woman displays the results of masculine excess and is also a focus of it, as "the primary *embodiments* of pleasure, fear and pain" [original emphasis] (4). In *AHS* the female is a trigger for violence: all the lead females cause disruption through their structures of power, and the maternal in particular is singled out as a major factor: Nora Montgomery (Lily Rabe) arguably triggers all the events in *Murder House* through her greed and later her desire for a child, Constance instigates the death of her son Beau (Sam Kinsey), and cannot control Tate. In *Coven* Madame LaLaurie, Marie Laveau, Fiona Goode and Myrtle Snow (Frances Conroy) are locked in matriarchal combat for the futures of the young witches and their own power. This is similar to Sister Jude's dominance in *Asylum*, but even more pertinently in the mother fixation of Dr. Thredson, rejected by his mother and seeking a replacement through sexual desire and killing as Bloody Face. This becomes centered on Lana, especially when she becomes pregnant. The pattern of matriarchal desire is then repeated through her rejection of their son, causing in turn his mimicking of Thredson-as-Bloody Face and in his desire to return to the maternal. In *Freak Show* mothers cause anger (Bette and Dot), dependence (Ethel Darling and Jimmy), or tacitly encourage psychotic behaviors (Gloria Mott and Dandy). In *Hotel* the literal and symbolic mother is the Countess (Lady Gaga), but her actions in turn prompt maternal roles in other characters. The maternal body is the source of continual trauma in the series, it seems, but is also a precursor for change. As Ellen Bishop notes: "The opposites of death and birth are united in a dynamic relationship that has no end, no entropy" (49). Bishop is discussing the notion of opposition and mutation as key factors in the carnivalesque and grotesque: another approach to delineate where *AHS* negotiates genre constructs.

Grotesque, Excess and Genre Fluidity: Piecing American Horror Story *Together*

Bakhtinian dialogues surrounding the carnivalesque are initially applicable to *AHS* and to horror constructs generally through two main areas: the notion of the grotesque and of excess, a key factor mentioned earlier in the essay. Initially Bakhtin's concept of carnival is useful to interrogate *AHS*, through "its maskings and gay impostures, its reversals and overturnings, its transgression of all boundaries, its exuberant staging of preposterous events, carnival is not unlike dreamwork" (Hurley 143). There is a clear link here with the fantastic as a mode of display, but it is more pertinent in the repeated narrative constructs of character development and imposture, the visual transgressions though horrific effects and the heavy use of eroticism in *AHS*.

We can focus this argument one stage further, in relation to the serial/mass killers in the series. As Jack Morgan argues, in Bakhtin's argument the Medieval Carnival, and other periods: "deal with the suspension of prosaic time and the establishment of a temporal frame in which ordinary social assumptions are in abeyance" (133). In contemporary experiences however, Carnival is private, a non-social space, marked by "a vivid sense of isolation" (140) focused around more individual spaces of expression. We can see this refracted in the locations in *AHS,* where the supposedly private may become public, or where institutional controls limit the freedom of those within. In most of the series there is a breaking out into carnival (the eruptions of song and dance routines in *Coven* and *Freak Show,* for example) but the spaces themselves magnify social pressures, usually focusing on sex and desire. However these desires can be problematic: carnivals implied freedoms "can enable aberrant impulses and lead to a carnival of the perverse" (Morgan 133). Specifically, the Carnivalesque situates a complementary frame for the psychopath who himself perpetuates, to quote Simpson in Morgan, a "wanton desire to violate and affront 'notions of Propriety and civilised conduct'" (Morgan 142). This occurs time and again in the structure of *AHS*, where the thematic focus on freedom and constraint allow the figure of the serial killer a space to embody a specifically American figure of fear, occupying the "core of the 'American Dream.' … the desire to live free from restraints, free from limitation, and to lead a life that is governed by 'freedom.' … a place that refuses to be restrained" (Edwards and Graulund 76).

The lack of restraint which in extremes leads to the horrific in *AHS* is more often deployed visually, thematically and symbolically in the grotesque pleasures offered by the rest of the text. The grotesque was birthed from the notion of the carnival, focused mainly around the actions and presentations of bodies. There are various commentators who have linked this to the fantastic. Justin D. Edwards and Rune Graulund argue that "those who emphasise the terrifying quality of the grotesque often shift it toward the realm of the mysterious and uncanny" (7) due to the grotesque's continual evocation of interstitial categories. Therefore "grotesque figures can cause the dissolution of the borders separating the normal and abnormal.... One extreme flows into another. Territories will not be bounded as clear cut divisions are dissolved" (9). This is continued by Cécile Brochard who argues that Remi Astruc's concept of the grotesque is that is operates primarily through effect, embodied in "figures of emotion or sensation" who emphasize an otherness, a moral response to conditions (11). The grotesque character is both "harmless and dangerous, the innocent and the evil, the benign and serious" (11). In the grotesque, people, places and states are in a "continuous state of flux and becoming" (Hurley 139). Here we can position the central concern of all *AHS* series.

Geoffrey Harpham argues that the grotesque functions by "opening onto vertiginous new perspectives characterized by the destruction of logic and regression to the unconscious—madness, hysteria or nightmare. But this threat depends for its effectiveness on the efficacy of the everyday, the partial fulfilment of our usual expectations" (462). In *AHS* the everyday is only ever briefly evoked: indeed the series seems determined to situate otherness in character and location as soon as possible, to focus on the fantastic in narratives constructed of part spectacle, horror and character development to keep the viewer engaged with the ruptures, the pleasures and the experiences of shock. In each series, temporal fractures may be identified though on screen titles, but they reoccur to destabilize the present, where limbo, hallucination, fantasy and the possibility of other planes of existence offer "moments of disjunction and rupture which are not smoothed over" (Hurley 142). Here, sensation is all, whether in the performance of the diva (Jessica Lange, Lady Gaga) the construction of emotion and characterization, following notions of melodramatic excess, or the envisaged horrific in actions and visual effects.

Conclusion

Returning to an earlier point over the use of repetition as theme, symbolic construct and series construct as a whole, Cécile Brochard argues that "the motives that characterise the grotesque [include] hybridity, metamorphosis, repetition" (3). This essay has argued for *AHS*'s repetitious formal structures of narrative and seriality as influenced by previous TV horror texts, but more potently soaps and melodramatic genres, and this is possibly the final evocation of the grotesque. This is evidenced in the conscious repetition of generic constructs and expectations in setting, character and visualization, but in a fractured manner, through the narrative escalation towards emotional excess and violence and an emphasis on the visual style of excess.

Isabel Cristina Pinedo, with whose work we started this essay, argues that "the postmodern genre operates on the principles of disruption, transgression, undecideability, and uncertainty" (91). This is echoed by Kelley Hurley who characterizes the "Gleeful excessiveness of Gothic Horror [as] not just admixture but multiple and aggravated admixture" (142). In both discussions, horror texts actively operate through generic fluidity, selecting aspects to reuse, mimic or discard. In *AHS* this is purposefully exaggerated: the killings, torture, gore, sex, the emphasis on the diva figure, costume and set—all of this proclaims *AHS* as an inhabitant of the media grotesque. Excess is evoked through the textures of skin, makeup, fabric, and then contrasted with broken bodies, close ups on bullet holes and monsters. Grotesque characters populate the landscape, forcing change on those who are surface "normal" but may not be underneath: in all of the series "the extreme, the decadent, the excessive and the bizarre are the 'real' of the text" (Edwards and Graulund 8). This may be the definitive hallmark of *American Horror Story,* not as a fixed generic construct, but a text focused on "an indissoluble cycle of degeneration and regeneration" (Thompson 114). Perhaps it is more fruitful not to speak of genre but intent in *American Horror Story*: a postmodern evocation of horror, eroticism and melodrama consciously occupying a space which veers between grotesque and camp, but always with an eye firmly fixed on the sensational.

NOTES

1. For example, in the episode "Spooky Little Girl" the opening section commences in 1947 in the Murder House (now a dentist's residence) to "explain" the fate of the actress Elizabeth Short (Mena Suvari) later known as the "Black Dahlia" (see Glossary). The opening credits then roll to indicate a break in this narrative. She will later return throughout the episode in the present (2011) to consult Ben Harmon and be comforted by other ghosts, a victim of male desires and her own dreams of stardom. Similar temporal breaks are used throughout all the other seasons.

2. Murphy compares his composition of the cast to the pattern established by Orson Welles for radio—a trusted ensemble cast used for different projects: "You have a cast of actors that you love and believe in and you just rotate them every season..." (Murphy in Abrams 2011).

3. These events or killers are particularly notorious for the brutality of the murders or the perceived psychological issues of the individual. Ed Gein was discovered and arrested in 1957. It is unclear how many people Gein killed, but he was an escalating fetishist whose home décor using corpses marked his killings as grotesque within the popular imagination, and hence his influence on fictional depictions of killers and their homes.

Works Cited

Abrams, Natalie. "The *American Horror Story* Finale: Ryan Murphy Tells Us Who's Coming Back for Season 2." *TV Guide.* TV Guide, 22 December 2011. Web. 2 November 2015.

"Afterbirth." *American Horror Story: The Complete First Season.* Writ. Jessica Sharzer. Dir. Bradley Buecker. Twentieth Century Fox, 2012. DVD.

Bishop, Ellen. "Bakhtin, Carnival and Comedy: The New Grotesque in *Monty Python and the Holy Grail.*" *Film Criticism* 15.1 (1990): 49–64. Print.

Bottomley, Andrew J. "Quality TV and the Branding of U.S. Network Television: Marketing and Promoting *Friday Night Lights.*" *Quarterly Review of Film and Video* 32.5 (2015) 482–497. Print.

"Boy Parts." *American Horror Story: Coven. The Complete Third Season.* Writ. Tim Minear. Dir. Michael Rymer. Twentieth Century Fox, 2014. DVD.

Brochard, Cécile. "For a Literary Anthropology: The Modern Grotesque Between Ethics and Aesthetics." *Acta Fabula* 12.2 (2011): n. pag. Web. 2 August 2015.

Brophy, Phillip. "Horrality: The Textuality of the Contemporary Horror Film." *Screen* 27.1 (1986): 2–13. Print.

"Chutes and Ladders." *American Horror Story: Hotel.* Writ. Tim Minear. Dir. Bradley Buecker. FX Network. 14 October 2015. Television.

"Devil's Night." *American Horror Story: Hotel.* Writ. Jennifer Salt. Dir. Loni Peristere. FX Network. 28 October 2015. Television.

"Edward Mordrake, Pt. 1." *American Horror Story: Freak Show. The Complete Fourth Season.* Writ. James Wong. Dir. Michael Uppendahl. Twentieth Century Fox, 2015. DVD.

"Edward Mordrake, Pt. 2." *American Horror Story: Freak Show. The Complete Fourth Season.* Writ. Jennifer Salt. Dir. Howard Deutch . Twentieth Century Fox, 2015. DVD.

Edwards, Justin. D, and Rune Graulund. *Grotesque.* Abingdon: Routledge, 2013. Print.

Freaks. Dir. Tod Browning. Warner Home Video, 1932. DVD.

Genis, Sadie. "Ryan Murphy Drops Major *American Horror Story: Hotel* Bombshells." *TV Guide.* TV Guide, 19 June 2015. Web. 5 September 2015.

Guthrie, Marisa. "Interview: Ryan Murphy." *Hollywood Reporter* 36 18 October 2013: 50–51. Web. 7 September 2015.

"Halloween, Pt. 1." *American Horror Story: The Complete First Season.* Writ. James Wong. Dir. David Semel. Twentieth Century Fox, 2012. DVD.

"Halloween, Pt. 2." *American Horror Story: The Complete First Season.* Writ. Tim Minear. Dir. David Semel. Twentieth Century Fox, 2012. DVD.

Hanks, E.A. "*American Horror Story* Recap: Lady Gaga Checks In." *New York Times.* New York Times, 8 October 2015. Web. 19 September 2015.

Harpham, Geoffrey. "The Grotesque: First Principles." *The Journal of Aesthetics and Art Criticism* 34.4 (1976): 461–468. Print.

Heuring, David. "Bedlam's New Address." *American Cinematographer* (2012): 76–84. Print.

"Home Invasion." *American Horror Story: The Complete First Season.* Writ. Ryan Murphy and Brad Falchuk. Dir. Alfonso Gomez-Rejon. Twentieth Century Fox, 2012. DVD.

Hoppenstand, Gary. "Editorial: The Horror of It All." *Journal of Popular Culture* 45.1 (2012): 1–2. Print.

Hurley, Kelley. "Abject and Grotesque." *The Routledge Companion to Gothic.* Eds. Catherine Spooner and Emma McEvoy. London: Routledge, 2007. 137–146. Print.

"I Am Anne Frank, Pt. 1." *American Horror Story: Asylum. The Complete Second Season.* Writ. Jessica Sharzer. Dir. Michael Uppendahl. Twentieth Century Fox, 2013. DVD.

"I Am Anne Frank, Pt. 2." *American Horror Story: Asylum. The Complete Second Season.* Writ. Brad Falchuk. Dir. Alfonso Gomez-Rejon. Twentieth Century Fox, 2013. DVD.

Jowett, Lorna, and Stacey Abbott. *TV Horror: Investigating the Dark Side of the Small Screen.* London: I.B. Tauris, 2013. Print.

Keetley, Dawn. "Stillborn: The Entropic Gothic of *American Horror Story.*" *Gothic Studies* 15.2 (2013): 89–107. Print.

Lowder, J. Bryan. "Why I'm Vibe-Watching *American Horror Story.*" *Slate.* 17 October 2012. Web. 29 August 2015

Maciak, Phillip. "Is *American Horror Story* the Future of TV?" *Salon*. 15 October 2012. Web. 29 August 2015

"Madness Ends." *American Horror Story: Asylum. The Complete Second Season*. Writ. Tim Minear. Dir. Alfonso Gomez-Rejon. Twentieth Century Fox, 2013. DVD.

Martin, Denise. "Interview: Ryan Murphy Dissects *Glee* and *American Horror Story*, Addresses Fans and Critics." *Vulture*. 22 May 2012. Web. 5 September 2015.

Mighall, Robert. "Gothic Cities." *The Routledge Companion to Gothic*. Eds. Catherine Spooner and Emma McEvoy. London: Routledge, 2007. 54–62. Print.

"Monsters Among Us." *American Horror Story: Freak Show. The Complete Fourth Season*. Writ. Ryan Murphy and Brad Falchuk. Dir. Ryan Murphy. Twentieth Century Fox, 2015. DVD.

Moon, Michael. "Medium Envy: A Response to Marcie Frank's 'At the Intersections of Mode, Genre, and Media: A Dossier of Essays on Melodrama.'" *Criticism* 55.4 (2013): 695–703. Print.

Morgan, Jack. *The Biology of Horror: Gothic Literature and Film*. Carbondale: Southern Illinois University Press, 2002. Print.

Neel, K.C. "The Fright Stuff." *Broadcasting and Cable*. Broadcasting and Cable, 21 October 2013. Web. 2 September 2015.

Nussbaum, Emily. "Review: The New Abnormal." *The New Yorker*. The New Yorker, 8 December 2014. Web. 29 August 2015.

"Piggy Piggy." *American Horror Story: The Complete First Season*. Writ. Jessica Sharzer. Dir. Michael Uppendahl. Twentieth Century Fox, 2012. DVD.

Pinedo, Isabel Cristina. *Recreational Terror: Women and the Pleasures of Horror Film Viewing*. New York: State University of New York Press, 1997. Print.

"The Replacements." *American Horror Story: Coven. The Complete Third Season*. Writ. James Wong. Dir. Alfonso Gomez-Rejon. Twentieth Century Fox, 2014. DVD.

Robson, Eddie. "Gothic Television." *The Routledge Companion to Gothic*. Eds. Catherine Spooner and Emma McEvoy. London: Routledge, 2007. 242–250. Print.

"Room Service." *American Horror Story: Hotel*. Writ. Ned Martel. Dir. Michael Goi. FX Network. 4 November 2015. Television.

Schmidt, Lisa. "Television: Horror's 'Original' Home." *Horror Studies* 4.2 (2013): 159–171. Print.

"The Seven Wonders." *American Horror Story: Coven. American Horror Story: The Complete Third Season*. Writ. Douglas Petrie. Dir. Alfonso Gomez-Rejon. Twentieth Century Fox, 2014. DVD.

"Spooky Little Girl." *American Horror Story: The Complete First Season*. Writ. Jennifer Salt. Dir. John Scott . Twentieth Century Fox, 2012. DVD.

Stack, Tim. "On the Set of *American Horror Story*." *Entertainment Weekly*. Entertainment Weekly, 31 August 2012. Web. 29 August 2015.

Subramanian, Janani. "The Monstrous Makeover: *American Horror Story*, Femininity and Special Effects." *Critical Studies in Television* 8.3 (2013): 108–123. Print.

The Texas Chain Saw Massacre. Dir. Tobe Hooper. Universal, 1974. DVD.

Thompson, Craig. "A Carnivalesque Approach to the Politics of Consumption (or) Grotesque Realism and the Analytics of the Excretory Economy." *The ANNALS of the American Academy of Political and Social Science* 611 (May 2007): 112–125. Print.

Thomson, Phillip. *The Grotesque*. London: Methuen, 1972. Print

Turner, Victor. *The Forest of Symbols: Aspects of Ndembu Ritual*. Ithaca, NY: Cornell University Press, 1967. Print

Williams, Linda. "Film Bodies: Gender, Genre and Excess." *Film Quarterly* 44.4 (1991): 2–13. Print.

Nightmares Made in America
Coven *and the Real* American Horror Story

CONNY LIPPERT

American Horror Story (2011–) is an ongoing fever-dream of Gothic delights and brazen exploitation, mixed with occasional moments of campy kitsch. It is a veritable Frankenstein's creature of horror elements, reassembled at co-creators' Ryan Murphy and Brad Falchuk's will, shambling along into its fifth (and, at the time of writing, pending sixth) season. In this essay I ask what makes *AHS* especially American. I focus on its third season, *Coven*, and the central tension established therein, namely that occurring between race and oppression, to investigate this question. I examine this nightmarish inversion of the American dream, which is often fueled by anxieties not only about the sins of the past, but also about the possibility of unwittingly repeating them.

FX's show is part of the recent revival of Gothic television series in the anthology format, including HBO's *True Detective* (2014–) and the Cohen brothers' *Fargo* (2014–) on FX. These shows seem to hark back to television classics such as *The Twilight Zone* (1959–1964; 1985–1989) and *The Outer Limits* (1963–1965; 1995–2002), which traditionally introduced an entirely new context to the viewer with each episode. The newer series, however, change their shape from season to season rather than episode to episode. Modern streaming services, which have paved the way for the consumer practice of "binge-watching," may be partially responsible for the success of this particular format. Rather than committing a substantial investment of time to a long-running show, these seasons, although collated under a cohesive brand, provide the viewer with the prospect of a finite amount of watching time to complete each individual story arc (Maurer). In *AHS*'s case actors frequently return, taking up new roles in different seasons. This has creative advantages, providing a more varied challenge to the show's actors and writers, and also saving the actors, who are often more at home in the world of film than that of the small screen, from being contract-bound for longer than a year at a time. Viewers and creators alike may therefore benefit from this format in their own way. Overarching themes, recurring faces, and occasional narrative links between the seasons further provide sufficient intertextuality to the show's stand-alone storylines to tie them all together and make *AHS* more than the sum of its grisly parts.

Rather than focusing on narrative continuity and realistic character development, *AHS* concentrates on compressing as many audio-visual and conceptual elements of the Gothic horror genre into each minute of its running time as possible. It is a conglomerate of prominent fears and tropes, often taken directly from other popular genre works and rearranged into new patterns. Many of the teaser trailers for *AHS* are illustrative examples for how well the producers understand and are able to recreate particular Gothic effects. The 15-second trailers often successfully use one or two audio-visual elements to evoke a certain feeling or reaction in the viewer. This method, perhaps more reminiscent of music videos than television narrative, is carried over into the show, attempting to evoke a particular time, place, and feeling with the broadest possible brush strokes, rather than a nuanced and substantial story. Loose ends, inconsistencies, and plot-holes tend to result from this prioritizing of atmosphere over plot, and it sometimes appears that story has been completely abandoned in favor of effect. *Slate* writer J. Bryan Lowder suggests that this need not be to the show's detriment and proposes that *AHS* lends itself to something he calls "vibe-watching" (along with such shows as *Twin Peaks* [1990–1991; 2017–] and *Six Feet Under* [2001–2005]). By this he means the enjoyment of a television show not exclusively for its plot, character development, or even its originality, but rather to gain satisfaction from the show's specific "vibe" in which the viewer may become immersed. NBC's *Hannibal* (2013–2015), especially in its third and final season, comes to mind as another prominent example for a show that may profit from being watched in this way.

While it thus seems that the show places more emphasis on the "horror" than on the "story," in this essay I focus on the "American" in *American Horror Story*. What is it, in other words, that makes *AHS* particularly American? It could feasibly be argued that the "American" in *AHS* denotes the universality of the Gothic horror elements in question. The contemporary pervasiveness of the Gothic in Western culture is, after all, married with processes of globalization and the ubiquity of Americanization seemingly inherent within it. Similar to the Gothic, one need not actively seek out Americanized culture in order to encounter it. The US's status as a world power, producing the lion's share of popular media, has led to aspects of its popular culture being admired, adapted, and consumed around the globe. This being said, I want to take *AHS* by its word and have a closer look at the show's interaction with specifically American Gothic horror as a subgenre. To do this it is helpful to keep the following question in mind: To what extent could these tropes feasibly fit into a hypothetical show called *French Horror Story*, or perhaps *Japanese Horror Story*? Focusing on Season Three, I show that *Coven*, of all the seasons aired so far, is the most firmly rooted in American soil and history, as well as the American Gothic genre, due to its dominant themes. Before honing in on this analysis of *Coven*, however, I provide a brief overview of the other seasons' relationship to their national context and to the Gothic genre.

Gothic

To outline it briefly, the Gothic in its various forms is one of the most popular contemporary media through which to address the multiple fissions and insecurities of identity, history, and place which the American people encounter within their partially self-produced and self-perpetuating myth of a nation. As Charles L. Crow observes, "Gothic seems to have become the dominant mode of American imagination" (187). A large number of America's greatest authors tend to be well-versed in the Gothic mode, and explicitly-Gothic traces can be detected in works by American writers spanning the generations and genres, as for instance Washington Irving, Nathaniel Hawthorne, Herman Melville, and Toni Morrison. There are, of course, many authors known specifically for their participation in the Gothic genre, such as Edgar Allan Poe, Shirley Jackson, or Flannery O'Connor. The Gothic is pervasive enough, however, to seep into narratives that are not overtly aligned with the genre. Other media, such as television, have also experienced a distinct increase of genre productions in the recent past, with *Buffy the Vampire Slayer* (1997–2003), *True Blood* (2008–2014), and *Penny Dreadful* (2014–2016) being just a few television-based examples.

Robert Mighall points toward history and geography as the two pillars on which the Gothic genre rests (*A Geography of Victorian Gothic Fiction* xiv). The American manifestation of the Gothic novel altered certain aspects of its Old World equivalent in adaptation to a new environment. Aristocracy, haunted castles and the Middle Ages as traditional Gothic tropes made way for the hereditary curse, haunted mansions, and the figure of the Puritan. "To understand American literature, and indeed America, one must," according to Crow, "understand the Gothic, which is, simply, the imaginative expression of the fears and forbidden desires of Americans" (1). American Gothic fiction ostensibly maps the country's fears and anxieties for the reader to address, as well as for the critic to analyze. An attempt at deciphering those sentiments expressed in the Gothic mode then opens up a new understanding of not only the wealth of anxieties festering under the surface, but also the places they inhabit in the public consciousness. The Gothic here, as always, can be interpreted in a number of ways, including the already-mentioned distillation of the genre to atmosphere and "vibe." It can be seen as a direct and immediate narrative mouthpiece for contemporary concerns and anxieties, or recognized as a dialogue with them on nuanced levels of subversion, provocation, and confession. The specific issues *AHS* aims to address are positioned on a spectrum between universal fears and specifically American anxieties.

The "Americanness of the Story"

One of the most basic and obvious elements tying *American Horror Story* to its national context is its being set in American locations. Season One takes place in Los Angeles, Season Two in Massachusetts, Season Three in New Orleans, Season Four in Florida, and Season Five, the most recent at the time of writing, has returned to Los Angeles. While the settings in *AHS* are exclusively U.S. American, not all of the main characters are, which immediately invites the viewer to think about what it means to be American and, by extension, to experience an American horror story. Does Season Four's Elsa Mars, for instance, with her ambitions to fame and riches, not speak directly to the American dream? Does her being a German immigrant add to or take away from the American Gothic context?

Many of the elements found in the respective seasons are presented to the audience as distinctly American subjects. Season One, *Murder House*, is a ghost story. It focuses on the haunted house, which, as a variation on the haunted castle, has been described as a feature of American Gothic since Hawthorne and Poe (Bailey 16). It deals with issues regarding infidelity and the resulting disintegration of the nuclear family—another trope often used in popular American narratives. Interspersed with school shootings, mediums, and evil children, it draws from the pool of disturbing elements that viewers expect from the genre. Nevertheless, the season could arguably be set in many places other than America and not lose any of its effect.

Season Two, *Asylum*, is set in a hospital for the mentally ill and criminally insane. Madness and mental fragmentation, as well as the resulting loss of autonomy, have been a core topic for the Gothic from its inception, with unreliable narrators leaving the reader or viewer with uncertainty over what is real and what is imagined. According to Fred Botting, these themes came into particular focus during the nineteenth century, when psychological disturbances, hallucinations and madness reflected wider anxieties centering on the individual and their internal world (11). While exposés such as Nellie Bly's *Ten Days in a Madhouse* (1887) made the disturbing conditions in American asylums known to the general public and brought the idea of the asylum as a Gothic location into its popular consciousness, the quintessential madhouse remains Bethlem Royal Hospital in London, better known as Bedlam, a name which has become synonymous with chaos and madness. In *Asylum,* the idea of the mental institution is combined with the looming authority of the Catholic Church, another favorite of the Gothic genre, but likewise a remnant from the Old World and not specifically American. Corrupt clergy and demonic interference have dominated the Gothic genre since the days of Matthew Lewis's *The Monk* (1796). Themes of alien abduction, escaped Nazi experimenters, and, of course, serial killers, add a veneer of American popular culture to this season. Nevertheless, neither the setting nor the themes are unequivocally American.

Season Four, *Freak Show,* in comparison seems much more deeply rooted in American soil. It focuses on a traveling carnival setting up in the fictional town of Jupiter, Florida. *Guardian* writers Kim Wall and Caterina Clerici point out that this is likely based on Gibsonton, sometimes called "Gibtown," in Florida, where many carnival artists, including the real "Lobster Boy," Grady Stiles, used to live and work. A number of them also performed in Tod Browning's famous film *Freaks* (1932), to which this season in its entirety owes a huge debt, recreating general themes as well as entire sequences from it. Wall and Clerici suggest that "exemplifying remarkable resilience and the ability to overcome obstacles, the freakshow was a direct extension of the American dream itself." Although the inspiration for *Freaks,* the short story "Spurs" (1923), was written by the American author Tod Robbins but set in France, *AHS*'s fourth season appears to be firmly tied into its American heritage and context. *Freak Show* is furthermore a valid exponent of Southern Gothic, a concept to which I return momentarily, with its depictions of grotesque bodies and minds.[1] The season does not, however, capture the same amount of fundamentally American Gothic themes as does *Coven.*

Season Five, *Hotel,* is set in Los Angeles, and plays on fears resulting from being in transit and in a place that is familiar and at the same time unfamiliar—uncanny, in other words.[2] Hotel rooms are private, yet public. They are ours, but only temporarily. They have their own history which is not immediately accessible to us, an idea strengthened by the reappearance of *Murder House*'s realtor, one of the few direct cross-overs between seasons, who sells the Hotel Cortez to its unsuspecting new owner. Stephen King's *The Shining* (1977), and especially the visual quality of Stanley Kubrick's 1980 film version, are a major influence on this season, as is the Cecil Hotel in Los

Angeles, a real-life example of a hotel wrapped in murder, mystery, and scandal. Especially the now-notorious case of Elisa Lam's mysterious death in 2013, preceded by her strange behavior captured on the security footage of one of the hotel's elevators and since gone viral, have made the Hotel Cecil famous.[3] Lam's sad fate found explicit echoes in *Hotel* and is not the only link between the hotels Cecil and Cortez. In the Halloween episode "Devil's Night" the (ghost of the) Cortez's creator, James Patrick March, hosts a party for a number of his (dead) serial killer friends, including Aileen Wuornos, John Wayne Gacy, Jeffrey Dahmer and the "Zodiac Killer," as well as Richard Ramirez, the Night Stalker, who happened to patronize the Hotel Cecil in real life (see Glossary). March's character itself is a reference to the vicious serial killer H.H. Holmes who built his own "Murder Castle" in Chicago in the late nineteenth century (see Glossary). *Hotel* thus manages to put a thick varnish of genuinely American popular culture and history onto a framework of traditional and universal Gothic tropes.

Alongside the cultural and historical references in each season, tying *AHS* to its country of origin, there are detectable undercurrents flowing through the entire series. One underlying theme common to all *AHS* seasons to date is the American dream of equality and opportunity in the form of a desire for stardom and fame, usually tied to Jessica Lange's characters. In Season One Constance Langdon's dreams of becoming a movie star have been irretrievably shattered, in Season Two Sister Jude is haunted by her past as a nightclub singer, Season Four's Elsa Mars's desperate longing to become famous is painfully tangible, and Season Five's Countess (Lady Gaga having taken over from Jessica Lange as the female lead) used to be an aspiring starlet, hoping to be immortalized on the silver screen. Season Three's witch-queen Fiona Goode retains traits of this intense longing for desirability in her violent obsession with youth and beauty. *AHS*'s continuing preoccupation with Hollywood, stardom, and conventional female beauty, as well as its portrayal of the brutality and desperation inherent therein constitute an aspect of its wider commentary on the notion of equal opportunities for success and fulfillment, and particularly its limitations.

History, Race and Power in Coven

To a degree, all seasons of *AHS* can be recognized as American horror stories in their own right, but it is only in *Coven* that we encounter a tale that could not feasibly be set anywhere but in America. The American Gothic genre's main staples are used to convey old as well as new fears, often related to oppression, and make this particular season the truest American horror story yet. While each season has featured either historical figures, characters from folklore, or at the very least hints toward them, Season Three's use of such historical figures lends it more than just verisimilitude.[4]

Coven cleverly pits two historical representatives of the tensions between its main themes against each other. By rendering the sadistic slave-mistress Delphine LaLaurie and the notorious voodoo queen Marie Laveau (see Glossary) magically immortal, Season Three bridges the gap between the past and the haunted present. It dramatizes a juxtaposition of the bleakest days of American slavery and contemporary racial attitudes with LaLaurie and Laveau's story arc as literal artefacts from a different period in time. While Laveau, whose legend really does include claims of immortality, is portrayed as having lived throughout the centuries, superficially adapting to contemporary circumstances (we see her lounging on her voodoo throne, playing solitaire on a tablet), Madame LaLaurie was cursed with life everlasting by Laveau, and then buried alive as punishment for her heinous crimes. In the end of the season's very first episode ("Bitchcraft") she is unearthed in a state of unchanged, unevolved, and unapologetic racism, which sets the stage for *Coven*'s central tension between race and oppression. Not only are LaLaurie and Laveau free to re-enact those atrocities which pitted them against one another in the past, but they also serve to showcase the fact that these crimes are not as archaic and outdated as they ought to be. In *Coven*, America is portrayed in a state of suspension between coming to terms with a nightmarish piece of its past, while struggling to avoid a repetition of the sins of its fathers.

The season revolves around the eponymous group of witches, residing in the fictional Miss Robichaux's Academy for Exceptional Young Ladies in New Orleans. This former finishing school has been repurposed to house young witches, so that they can learn to understand, hone, and control their supernatural abilities. The correlations between gender, society, and power are thus already embedded into *Coven*'s very setting, and of course the sprawling mansion itself houses its fair share of ghosts and spirits. Save for the caretaker, and the occasional appearance of headmistress Cordelia's husband Hank, this is an all-female household and it is not clear whether male witches even exist in the context of this show.[5] Most importantly, the Supreme, the most powerful witch of her generation, is always female. The viewer can discern this by studying the numerous portraits of previous Supremes on the sitting room walls. For better or for worse, *Coven* focuses on women, and while their portrayal might warrant a study of its own, it should suffice to say that questions of gender are one strand of many in the discussion of oppression and inequality therein.

The season begins with young Zoe Benson discovering that she is a descendant of the witches of Salem and being brought to the academy after she accidentally kills her boyfriend with her newfound powers. She learns that many carriers of the "Salem gene" have decided not to reproduce, treating their supernatural heritage as a genetic disorder, and thus reducing the number of living witches dramatically. Upon her arrival at Miss Robichaux's she encounters only three other students. We later learn that the dwindling number of witches is also due to the efforts of the Delphi Trust, a "sacred order" of male witch hunters, led by Hank's father, dedicated to exterminating witches. The Greek word *delphi*, etymologically related to the womb, ties the Trust to notions of reproduction and femininity and lets the viewer ponder the idea of men persecuting women for abilities they themselves do not possess or control. Together with the idea of witchcraft as a genetic fault this correlation also brings into focus notions of genetic (and racial) purity. The scene is set, then, for a narrative of victimization and hidden powers, of brotherhood, sisterhood and a rhetoric of "us versus them." Sometimes this division takes the form of gender, sometimes of race or class, and occasionally of sexuality. As is so frequently the case in contemporary popular culture, having supernatural abilities and thus being different stands in for a plethora of issues concerning power, authority, and perception.

The season's subject harks back, of course, to the archetype of witchcraft in the popular imagination: Salem (Ringel 89). According to Edward J. Ingebretsen, "Salem is an important national event because, as the Red Queen insists to Alice, memory works forward as well as reverse" (*xxvii*). Salem followed on the heels of the ferocious and numerous witch trials in early modern Europe which often had much higher death tolls (Golden 411). In 1692 the incident was not only looking back onto a history of witch crazes but also marked the lineage forward, into other kinds of mass hysterias and persecution. Arthur Miller's *The Crucible* (1953) famously uses the Salem witch trials as an allegory for contemporary McCarthyism and the "Communist witch-hunt," ensuring that Salem is forever burned into the national imagination and idiom. While the fear of witchcraft and its persecution are global phenomena, the Salem witch trials are better documented and more deeply rooted in the country's psyche than other such occurrences in any other part of the world. The dark and gloomy figure of the Puritan himself has become a staple character in American Gothic and the witch belief firmly links Puritan sensibilities to the medieval in European Gothic. Salem is a genuine staple of American Gothic fiction as a genre.

As part of its commentary on the witch trials and the brutality inherent in the concept, *Coven* frequently depicts the horrors of being burned at the stake. As Fiona suggests in "Bitchcraft," "when witches don't fight, [they] burn." And, although burn they do, all but one witch who is burned alive in *Coven* is being executed by her own kind.[6] While immolation is indeed a means of execution commonly associated with witchcraft and heresy, it should be clarified that convicted witches were not executed in this way in

America (Ingebretsen 47, Ringel 108). Mostly they were hanged, which is what British law still dictated at the time. This does not mean, however, that burning as a form of capital punishment was not used in the United States. At the time of the Salem witch trials it was chiefly slaves who were burned alive and later on, up until the nineteenth century, it was black people and civil rights activists who were the victims of lynching and immolation. This gruesome tradition has been firmly cemented in the American consciousness not least due to the popular practice of producing, buying, and sending "lynching postcards" and other macabre pictorial memorabilia.[7] Through the imagery of immolation *Coven* thus interlinks the idea of witchcraft and issues of race.

Another example of this link is the combination of witchcraft with the concept of voodoo in *Coven*. It is not clear where the distinction between witchcraft and voodoo lies, apart from the obvious difference in the color of their practitioners' skin. In the episode "Boy Parts" it is implied that white witches have learned about magic from Tituba, a slave woman from Salem who was famously implicated in the witch trials. This juxtaposition of black and white witches and the common differentiation between black and white magic moves racial connotations into focus. Queenie, as the only black witch in the otherwise white coven, provides particular insight into the issue. While she is unsure whether her place is at Miss Robichaux's or with Marie Laveau, she is the only young witch for whom choosing sides even seems to be an option. Her supernatural power is pregnant with meaning. She is a self-described "living voodoo doll" ("Bitchcraft"), which means that whatever harm she does to herself will instead be inflicted upon whomever she wishes it. The harm (or pleasure) she chooses to visit upon her own black body is magically transferred onto other parts of society. While thus representing an effigy or object to stand in for others, Queenie also happens to be one of the most sympathetic, introspective, and well-rounded characters in *Coven*. She even strikes up a grudging sort of friendship with LaLaurie, who has been made her personal "slave" by Fiona, and tries to teach her the errors of her racist ways. Not only are these interactions between the two the closest this season gets to any consistent character development, but they also provide a perfect canvas for *Coven* to discuss race-related issues openly.

The lines between white and black magic are blurred in *Coven*, and it can be read as a deliberate lacuna. The show illustrates the ways in which minorities are often not only suppressed by the majority, but, by fighting amongst themselves, do their oppressors' work for them. The ease with which the witches' chief threat in form of the Delphi Trust is eliminated once Fiona and Marie join forces against them in "Protect the Coven" serves to showcase this. Had they worked together from the beginning, the audience is invited to realize, much tragedy could have been avoided. Queenie, again, is an important figure here, being the only black witch in a situation allowing her to compete for the Supremacy by taking part in the test of "the seven wonders" in the episode of the same name. Whatever divides there may be between the show's voodoo practitioners and witches, Queenie clearly bridges them. She shifts allegiances and moves between the groups, trying to find her true "sisterhood," thus learning valuable lessons from both sides. Through her rise from fast-food-chain employee to a contender to be the Supreme, she also embodies the *deus ex machina* type of success story often found in American popular culture. Her social upward mobility is literally the result of magic.

Slavery and American attitudes toward race have often been described as the country's very own version of original sin. Leslie A. Fiedler, for instance, ranks the exploitation of dark-skinned people, along with the "rape of nature," amongst America's specific reasons for guilt (31). Racism, if not apartheid, is alive and well in present day America, however, and this "original sin" is not as far removed from the here and now as the term might suggest. Gothic vehicles for a discussion of this theme, such as possession, captivity, and loss of autonomy (bodily, mental, or otherwise) are abundant in *Coven*. This is showcased, for instance, by the slaves LaLaurie keeps in her attic, whose loss of autonomy figures not only through their status as slaves, but also through the bodily mutilations she visits upon them. Her house slave Bastien, falsely accused of raping LaLaurie's daughter, is transformed into a "minotaur" by having a severed bull's head fixed over his own ("Bitchcraft"). A Gothic blurring of boundaries between animal and human, particularly pertinent in the context of racism and slavery, as well as between natural and supernatural, occurs. LaLaurie drives the significance of this forced shift in Bastien's identity home by saying that she had always wanted a minotaur of her very own—a mythological creature of her own making and in her possession. As a slave, Bastien legally belonged to her even before his transformation, but afterwards LaLaurie feels that she has taken control of the very appearance and nature of his being. It is her absolute power over these people, along with her absolute sadism, that comprises the horror story here. One of the tortured and mutilated wretches inhabiting the nightmarish attic asks LaLaurie to justify her actions, and her answer could not be more poignant: "because I can" ("Bitchcraft"). Ignoring Louisiana's "code noir," the body of regulations defining the conditions of slavery, LaLaurie is not, in fact, within her legal rights to visit such extreme bodily harm onto her slaves. Nevertheless, she not only feels safe within her status as a white society woman, but also justified as a result of her supposed superiority over her slaves.

Slavery and the treatment of black people have often been recognized as a main staple in the American Gothic genre. Teresa A. Goddu aptly argues that one of the very first works in the American canon, J. Hector St. John de

Crèvecœur's *Letters from an American Farmer* (1782), harbors Gothic elements related intimately to race. James, the fictional author of the eponymous letters, describes encountering a slave suspended in a cage as punishment:

> I shudder when I recollect that the birds had already picked out his eyes; his cheekbones were bare; his arms had been attacked in several places; and his body seemed covered with a multitude of wounds. From the edges of the hollow sockets and from the lacerations with which he was disfigured, the blood slowly dropped and tinged the ground beneath [Goddu 19].

This image of the tortured black man's blood seeping into the soil is a pertinent one. Howard Zinn says that "there is not a country in world history in which racism has been more important, for so long a time, as the United States" (23), and race is often seen as a defining feature of the country's literary heritage. In *Playing in the Dark* (1992) Toni Morrison writes:

> Black slavery enriched the country's creative possibilities. For in that construction of blackness *and* enslavement could be found not only the not-free but also, with the dramatic polarity created by skin color, the projection of the not-me. The result was a playground for the imagination. What rose up out of collective needs to allay internal fears and to rationalize external exploitation was an American Africanism—a fabricated brew of blackness, otherness, alarm, and desire that is uniquely American [original emphasis] [38].

While engaging these notions of the "not-free" as well as the "not-me," *Coven* utilizes the Gothic register in order to imply that the "not-free" could be any of us, given the right circumstances. The very implications of slavery as a historical fact haunt the present.

Fiedler suggests that "it is, indeed, to be expected that [the country's] first eminent Southern author discover that the proper subject for American gothic is the black man, from whose shadow we have not yet emerged" (397). Associated with the earliest European settlements and therefore imbued with a sense of age and origin, Southern Gothic, represented by authors such as Flannery O'Connor or Anne Rice, along with New England Gothic, such as the works of H.P. Lovecraft and Stephen King, are the most prevalent regional varieties of the genre in American literature. Certain key elements commonly associated with these two subgenres have virtually sprung from the very quality of the land. Differences in the way that Jamestown in Virginia and Plymouth in New England, as the earliest successful European colonies, were imagined largely originated in the different methods of farming which soil and climate in the respective regions allowed. The Northern colonies were, for the most part, better suited for small, self-sufficient family farms, while the Southern colonies lent themselves to the system of large plantations for which they have become known (Honaker Herron 10). Due to the prevalence of larger plantations in the South, and the resulting reliance of the region on slave labor, the specter of slavery haunts Southern Gothic in particular. The locus of New England's Gothic fiction, on the other hand, is the farm as part of ancient small towns, as well as the surrounding wilderness. *Coven* manages to tie notions of the North and the South together in a uniquely chiastic way. The witches of New Orleans are Salem descendants, having fled "as far south as they could" to escape the trials, making New Orleans the "new Salem" ("Bitchcraft"). This is an obvious reversal of the direction slaves pursued in order to escape as far north as they could. The horrors of two kinds of oppression and persecution are thus simultaneously entwined and juxtaposed.

New Orleans is a city with a rich heritage of Gothic fiction. Lafcadio Hearn, Anne Rice, and Poppy Z. Brite are only some examples of prominent writers of New Orleans Gothic. In an interview Brad Falchuk states: "I'd never been down to New Orleans until we started shooting, and anywhere you turn the camera is sexy. Every scene has an erection. There's something going on there that is so non–American but totally American, so sexy and dark but there's hope everywhere" (Birnbaum). Mighall similarly suggests that "New Orleans is the haunted house of un–American activities, an outpost of the Old World even up until relatively recently" (*The Routledge Companion to Gothic* 58). The city is an amalgamation of distinctly European (especially French and Spanish), as well as Caribbean influences. Its exotic quality, rich culture, and colorful history make it an intriguing background, especially for Gothic stories. Crow further suggests that New Orleans could be seen as the "capital of American Gothic," and points to Louisiana's specific racial laws as one element in its being uniquely suited as a setting in Southern Gothic fiction: "While other slave-holding states had a binary racial system (a person was legally either black or white), Louisiana's laws long recognized mixed-race people as a separate category" (89). The existence of a far larger number of free people of color than in other slave-holding states made the social system and allocation of status much more complicated than elsewhere. In the show this is partially exemplified by LaLaurie's obsession with her own fading youth and beauty for fear of losing her husband to a colored mistress, which could quite possibly mean having to share property and inheritance with any potential offspring of such a liaison ("The Dead"). When New Orleans was hit by real-life horror in 2005, in the form of Hurricane Katrina, it showcased some of the very real and present shortcomings of America's attitude, particularly to its black population. In Crow's words, the destruction of the city by the hurricane has shown that it "has more past than future, that it has a strong heritage but a fragile reality, that it is a haunted place" (89).

Questions of race are thus complicated by issues of social class—an element of American Gothic that is frequently addressed in *Coven*. When the show's two supernatural leaders first meet in the second episode ("Boy Parts"), questions of affluence and social standing are quickly brought to the fore.

The setting and situation are symptomatic. True to legend, Marie Laveau is working as a hairdresser in the Ninth Ward. Fiona poses as a customer, intending to uncover Marie's secret of eternal youth. Fully aware of her identity, Marie continues to style Fiona's hair while they talk. The picture of the black woman servicing the white woman is thus established casually and underlined by their topic of conversation. Laveau notes how out of place Fiona appears, since her "manicure costs more than [Marie's] rent." Through the ensuing conversation the viewer learns about the historical relationship between the witches and the voodoo practitioners. We are given to understand that it is not only race but also class which forms the basis for their dislike of each other. Relating their current situation directly back to Salem, Fiona taunts Marie with Tituba's status as a slave who could not read or write. The picture of white privilege, she asks: "You want to tell me that some illiterate voodoo slave girl gave me my crown?"

Here, *Coven* contains another hint by omission at yet another unspoken issue of race relations in the United States. We learn that (in the show's storyline) Tituba was a descendant of the Arawak tribe and learned magic from a thousand year old line of shamans ("Boy Parts"). The figure of the American Indian once again merges with the very soil and soul of the continent, along with the African American, bleeding into its background and supplying its mythologies of origin. There is not a single American Indian character in *AHS*, but it is implied in a rough narrative sketch that the white girls in Salem learned about magic from Tituba, who in turn learned it from both the American Indian and the African influences on her life.[8] This simultaneous mythologizing and discounting of American Indian influences on U.S. development has its roots in the very beginnings of American sentiment and can be traced even in the development of the American Gothic genre.

In the preface to *The Marble Faun* (1860), Hawthorne famously postulates that the New World completely lacked ruins, or, in other words, signs of age and decay:

> No author, without a trial, can conceive of the difficulty of writing a romance about a country where there is no shadow, no antiquity, no mystery, no picturesque and gloomy wrong, nor anything but a commonplace prosperity, in broad and simple daylight, as is happily the case with my dear native land. It will be very long, I trust, before romance-writers may find congenial and easily handled themes, either in the annals of our stalwart republic, or in any characteristic and probable events of our individual lives. Romance and poetry, ivy, lichens, and wallflowers need ruin to make them grow [*vi*].

While one might be tempted to speculate that his musings in the above-quoted preface are of a somewhat facetious nature, originating, as they did, on the very eve of the American Civil War, they are also, quite plainly, wrong.[9] America, and specifically New England and the South, provided a fruitful place for the Gothic to grow from the very beginning of the nation, imbued with its own connotations of guilt, age, and secrecy. Even in the earliest stages of its colonization America was not the empty wilderness or virgin forest it was heralded to be by its "discoverers." Abandoned American Indian fields and farms, as well as graves and bones could be found in many areas, as, after having come into contact with European diseases through earlier visits and attempts at colonization, large numbers among the native population had been wiped out before the arrival of the settlers in 1620 (Pearce 19). Being surrounded by them, an immediate awareness of the ruins and remnants belonging to the supposed virgin land's previous inhabitants made the fact that the wilderness was not empty unavoidable. Not only was it filled with strange creatures and wild men, it was also already replete with specters of their past, and so it became part of the colonizing process in the New World to deal with the spectral presence of the native population. America is initially Gothicized through the specter of its native inhabitants, rendered uncanny, not only due to their otherness, but also the colonial "doublethink," bifurcating the Indian into an entity simultaneously non-existent and threatening. This very contrast is one of the fundamental American dualisms exploited in the Gothic and hinted at in *Coven*.

As previously mentioned, distinct connections between questions of power and ownership and the issue of race and gender are drawn from the very beginning in *Coven*. The first episode ("Bitchcraft") highlights different notions of ownership and oppression. Next to LaLaurie's aforementioned slave-owning and torturing ways, we encounter Madison Montgomery, a young witch and arrogant starlet, whose own sense of privilege and superiority is soon established as her defining character trait. At a college party she flirts with a stereotypical frat-boy and arrogantly tells him that he can be her "slave" for the night, reminding him that "slaves get nothing." We soon learn that the power based on her sexuality of which Madison is so certain is exceedingly fragile, as the boy with whom she was flirting, along with his group of friends, viciously gang-rape her, filming the assault. This scene is an uncomfortable reminder of such real-life scenarios as the Steubenville High School rape case.[10] It also represents an inversion of the accusations against Bastien earlier in the same episode. Madison retaliates, using her telekinesis to kill most of her attackers. In the following episode ("Boy Parts") the eponymous remains of her victims are then reassembled and revived by Madison and Zoe, which is, again, reminiscent of Bastien's hybrid fate. The viewer is invited by these parallels and juxtapositions to ponder questions of bodily integrity, autonomy, and desire in the context both of gender and race.

These various tensions are contextualized on yet another level in *Coven*, namely via its various child-parent relationships. Kyle is being sexually abused by his mother Alicia and Delphine LaLaurie keeps her own daughters in her torture chamber for a year on learning they were conspiring to kill her. Not only is the witches' hyper-religious neighbor Joan an overbearing and abusive mother, but she is a murderess, responsible both for the death of her husband and, eventually, her son. Fathers are ineffective and mostly absent throughout the season. Fiona's and Cordelia's relationship is clearly a very damaging one for Cordelia who suffers from her mother's blatant abuse of her power, both as a parent and as supernatural monarch. We learn that Cordelia's personal hell consists of continuously trying to gain her mother's approval and failing in the attempt ("The Seven Wonders"). The only motherly figure in her life is Myrtle Snow, her mother's rival and member of the witch council. When Cordelia blinds herself in a reverse-Oedipal attempt to regain her second sight in "Protect the Coven," it is Myrtle who returns her eyesight to her. Nevertheless, Cordelia is eventually forced to kill Myrtle in order to free herself and the coven from the "rot" of the past ("The Seven Wonders"). Fiedler writes about the American oedipal "guilt of the revolutionary haunted by the (paternal) past which he has been striving to destroy" (129), and Cordelia is likewise trying to dismantle her mother's legacy of corruption to make a new beginning possible.

This symbolic generational conflict is combined with what Fiedler calls "the essence of the American experience"—the Faustian pact (27). To stay young, healthy, and beautiful, both Marie Laveau and Fiona Goode are not only willing to sell their soul to Papa Legba ("The Magical Delights of Stevie Nicks") but to sacrifice the lives of future generations. Legba, who is usually characterized as a mere psychopomp and messenger between the worlds, is pictured as a Voodoo-Mephistopheles who is able to trick Marie into sacrificing an innocent soul in the form of a new-born baby every year, beginning with her own child. Fiona, on the other hand, need not be tricked and promises to "mutilate [her] own daughter" if it is necessary, in exchange for eternal youth and health. Figuratively and literally, Fiona and Marie are thus attempting to deny life and a place in the world to the next generation. Marie takes innocent lives and Fiona clings on to her throne as the Supreme, planning to kill her successor in order to gain her power and thus add another thirty-odd years to her own reign. This willingness to bargain with the fates of others can, again, be interpreted as an echo of America's past attitude toward the commodification of African American lives.

The concept of "witch supremacy" itself, finally, is another factor in *Coven* that undermines personal autonomy and freedom in a way uniquely tied to American Gothic. We learn that "witches survive only if united under a strong, singular authority" ("Go to Hell") and while the ideas of witch supremacy and white supremacy are never contrasted explicitly, the implications are clear. Not only racial equality but also the democratic principles upon which America is founded are undermined. The villains in old world

Gothic tended to be figures of authority in a patriarchal hierarchy—clerics, aristocrats, and fathers. Being proud to have escaped the bane of aristocratic rule, American sentiment and thus American Gothic gravitated towards different kinds of villain. In *Coven*, however, we seem to return to the concept of a sometimes benign and sometimes malevolent aristocracy against which there is little check. The implications of this return to an almost aristocratic system of arbitrary supremacy reflect "the inherent contradiction of a free republic deeply committed to slavery" (Morrison 49, 50). Goddu reminds us that "Like Europe, America has feudal institutions, a decadent aristocracy, tyranny, and oppression" (18). The American, anti-aristocratic impulse stands in direct contradiction to both slavery and the concept of the Supreme in *Coven*. While Cordelia is portrayed as a benevolent ruler who overthrows the old ways of the coven and opens it up to a new age of transparency and progress, we are still left with the knowledge that the old system abides. Myrtle's aforementioned death serves to parallel Cordelia's reign with Fiona's, who killed her own predecessor in order to gain power. Although it is implied that Cordelia's selfless sacrifices for the coven rendered her deserving of the supremacy, there is no indication that the position is in any way merit-based (or inherited—despite Cordelia having "royal blood"). We have seen that each of the girls could feasibly have been next in line for the rule, including Madison, who is portrayed as a despicable character with few redeeming qualities. As Fiona has demonstrated early on in the season, humans without supernatural abilities are powerless to resist the Supreme's will and so are other witches. While Cordelia's Cincinnatus-like attitude is thus showcasing the potential benefits of a benevolent and all-powerful ruler, the rest of the season has primed us to recognize the Gothic implications of power-imbalances and relinquishment of freedom.

Conclusion

American Horror Story: Coven thus manages to amalgamate a large spectrum of American Gothic elements into a storyline which juggles the issues of power, oppression, and autonomy inherent in the subjects of race, gender, and authority. Staples of the genre, such as specters of slavery and the Salem witch trials are maneuvered in a way that allows a commentary on the very nature of America as an idea. The season ends with Cordelia as the new Supreme ("The Seven Wonders"), having thrown off the fetters of the old rule and established her own council, issuing a public invitation for new students for Miss Robichaux's Academy. "Come to New Orleans," she tells these potential young witches through the medium of television, rendering it not only the new Salem, but the new city upon a hill, ready and ostensibly doomed to repeat the mistakes of its own past.[11]

Notes

1. In works of Southern Gothic the region's people, their personal habits and relationships, as well as the social order they find themselves in, is often portrayed in terms of the grotesque and the macabre. Depictions of decay and poverty are also common. *Freak Show's* human tragedies are reminiscent of such staples of Southern Gothic as Flannery O'Connor's short story collection *A Good Man Is Hard to Find* (1955) and the way in which it makes the grotesquery of the soul the subject of discussion.

2. In his seminal 1919 essay "The 'Uncanny'" Sigmund Freud describes the uncanny as "that class of the terrifying which leads back to something long known to us, once very familiar" (369, 370).

3. In 2013 the body of Canadian student Elisa Lam was found in the Cecil Hotel's rooftop water tanks, and surveillance footage from one of the hotel's elevators showed her behaving very strangely and erratically before her disappearance. While her death was ruled an accidental drowning, the mysterious circumstances accompanying it lent the case, and in association the Cecil Hotel, notoriety.

4. Season One featured the "Black Dahlia" (see Glossary), Season Two Anne Frank as another German import, Season Four had Edward Mordrake (said to have been a man with a second face growing out of the back of his head), and Season Five its aforementioned parade of serial killers, to give just a handful of examples.

5. When we eventually encounter the witches' council, seemingly embodying legislative, judicative and executive power all at once, it boasts one male member, but he is never described as anything but a "colleague," while the other members of the council are "sisterwitches."

6. Misty Day, who is burned at the stake by a religious group in "Bitchcraft," is the exception. Luckily she has the power of resurgence and brings herself back to life.

7. In his book *Without Sanctuary: Lynching Photography in America* (2000), James Allen has collected nearly 100 such images.

8. In the eleventh episode ("Birth") of *AHS's* first season, the indigenous people of North Carolina are mentioned as part of the story surrounding the mysterious disappearance of colonists from Roanoke Colony in the late sixteenth century.

9. Hawthorne himself, of course, managed to overcome this supposed difficulty in order to write his own Gothic stories, such as "Young Goodman Brown" (1835) and "Ethan Brand" (1850).

10. In 2012 a female high school student in Steubenville, Ohio, was sexually assaulted by her peers while she was incapacitated by alcohol. Several of the attackers publicized these acts on social media.

11. The biblical notion of a "city upon a hill" was taken up by John Winthrop in his 1630 sermon "A Model of Christian Charity," which imagines New England as this new city upon a hill, watched by the world.

Works Cited

Allen, James. *Without Sanctuary: Lynching Photography in America.* Santa Fe, NM: Twin Palms Publishers, 2000. Print.

Bailey, Dale. *American Nightmares: The Haunted House Formula in American Popular Fiction.* Madison: University of Wisconsin Press, 1999. Print.

Birnbaum, Debra. "Q&A: Noah Hawley and Brad Falchuk Reap Benefits from Movie Stars' Move to TV." *Variety.* Variety, 12 June 2014. Web. 29 November 2015.

"Birth." *American Horror Story.* Writ. Tim Minear. Dir. Alfonso Gomez-Rejon. FX Network. 14 December 2011. Television.

"Bitchcraft." *American Horror Story: Coven. The Complete Third Season.* Writ. Ryan Murphy and Brad Falchuk. Dir. Alfonso Gomez-Rejon. Twentieth Century Fox, 2014. DVD.

Botting, Fred. *Gothic.* London: Routledge, 1996. Print.

"Boy Parts." *American Horror Story: Coven. The Complete Third Season.* Writ. Tim Minear. Dir. Michael Rymer. Twentieth Century Fox, 2014. DVD.

Crow, Charles L. *American Gothic.* Cardiff: University of Wales Press, 2009. Print.

"The Dead." *American Horror Story: Coven. The Complete Third Season.* Writ. Brad Falchuk. Dir. Bradley Buecker. Twentieth Century Fox, 2014. DVD.

"Devil's Night." *American Horror Story: Hotel.* Writ. Jennifer Salt. Dir. Loni Peristere. FX Network. 28 October 2015. Television.

Fiedler, Leslie A. *Love and Death in the American Novel.* London: Dalkey Archive Press, 1960. Print.

Freud, Sigmund. "The 'Uncanny.'" *Collected Papers: Volume IV.* 1919. Trans. Joan Riviere. London: The Hogarth Press, 1925. 368–407. Print.

"Go to Hell." *American Horror Story: Coven. The Complete Third Season.* Writ. Jessica Sharzer. Dir. Alfonso Gomez-Rejon. Twentieth Century Fox, 2014. DVD.

Goddu, Teresa A. *Gothic America: Narrative, History, and Nation.* New York: Columbia University Press, 1997. Print.

Golden, Richard M. "American Perspectives on the European Witch Hunts." *The History Teacher* 30.4 (1997): 409–426. Print.

Hawthorne, Nathaniel. Preface. *The Marble Faun.* 1860. London: The New English Library Limited, 1961. Print.

Honaker Herron, Ima. *The Small Town in American Literature.* New York: Pageant Books, 1959. Print.

Ingebretsen, Edward J. *Maps of Heaven, Maps of Hell: Religious Terror as Memory from the Puritans to Stephen King.* London: M.E. Sharpe, 1996. Print.

Lowder, J. Bryan. "Why I'm Vibe-Watching *American Horror Story.*" *Slate.* 17 October 2012. Web. 29 November 2015.

"The Magical Delights of Stevie Nicks." *American Horror Story: Coven. The Complete Third Season.* Writ. James Wong. Dir. Alfonso Gomez-Rejon. Twentieth Century Fox, 2014. DVD.

Maurer, Mark. "*True Detective, American Horror Story* and Why the Anthology Series Is All the Rage." *Indiewire.* 12 February 2014. Web. 29 November 2015.

Mighall, Robert. *A Geography of Victorian Gothic Fiction: Mapping History's Nightmares.* Oxford: Oxford University Press, 1999. Print.

_____. "Gothic Cities." *The Routledge Companion to Gothic.* Eds. Catherine Spooner and Emma McEvoy. London: Routledge, 2007. 54–62. Print.

Morrison, Toni. *Playing in the Dark: Whiteness and the Literary Imagination.* London: Picador, 1992. Print.

Pearce, Robert Harvey. *Savagism and Civilization: A Study of the Indian and the American Mind.* Baltimore: Johns Hopkins Press, 1953. Print.

"Protect the Coven." *American Horror Story: Coven. The Complete Third Season.* Writ. Jennifer Salt. Dir. Bradley Buecker. Twentieth Century Fox, 2014. DVD.

Ringel, Faye. *New England Gothic Literature: History and Folklore of the Supernatural from the Seventeenth Through the Twentieth Centuries.* Lewiston, NY: Edwin Mellen Press, 1995. Print.

"The Seven Wonders." *American Horror Story: Coven. The Complete Third Season.* Writ. Douglas Petrie. Dir. Alfonso Gomez-Rejon. Twentieth Century Fox, 2014. DVD.

Wall, Kim, and Caterina Clerici. "Welcome to Gibtown, the Last 'Freakshow' Town in America." *The Guardian.* The Guardian, 26 February 2015. Web. 29 November 2015.

Zinn, Howard. *A People's History of the United States: From 1492 to the Present.* 1980. London: Longman, 1996. Print.

Epilogue
Past Nightmares and Anticipated Horrors

Rebecca Janicker

A murky plume of smoke curves skyward from a lonely homestead in a field of rippling corn. A shadowy trio of figures with gleaming eyes drifts towards the camera. A woman descends a gloomy stairway through which hands stretch out to grab at her bare ankles. A macabre mobile of assorted tools and weaponry hangs suspended above a child's crib as a hand reaches up to seize a carving knife. A cluster of scarecrow like figures lurches across a rural landscape followed by an obscure figure gripping a sickle. A millipede crawls along the length of a woman's scalp and follows the parting of her hair down onto her face. A child's doll comes alive to exhibit darting eyes and an inexplicably bloody maw. The recurring motif that unites these seemingly disparate, though similarly unsettling, scenes is that of a question mark coupled with the number six—?6—a symbol that serves to denote the aura of mystery that worked simultaneously to display and to obscure tangible details of the upcoming sixth season of *American Horror Story*.

A total of twenty-six such fleeting sequences, released throughout the weeks prior to the publicized FX premiere date of September 14, 2016, were all that eager fans had to go on as they awaited the latest instalment of the *AHS* franchise. Lisa Kernan observes that, in furnishing a potential audience with a foretaste of particulars pertaining to narrative and characters, a trailer represents "a body of expectations" as well as "a set of desires" about the anticipated experience to be gained by watching a chosen text (9). The teaser trailer, a notable component of many contemporary promotional campaigns, appears during the early stages of production when little footage is available, and is therefore marked by its brevity (242). In the case of the campaign for Season Six of *AHS*, the visually arresting, tantalizingly brief teaser images

200

described above worked to generate much speculation about the latest twists in store from a franchise that quickly built up a reputation for shocks and scares. However, the 2016 campaign was atypical in its withholding of key details, such as theme and principal cast members, that are usually divulged well in advance. It seems that *American Horror Story* has become sufficiently well entrenched in the viewing calendar to pique interest even in the absence of hard facts and that its audience is confident about the kind of experience that this show will have on offer. Showbiz columnists and social media sites worked hard to fill in the intentional blanks left by the channel and the showrunners, searching for links to past seasons, theorizing about prospective cast members and envisaging the type of setting in which they would be terrorized by any number of threats, whether human or supernatural in origin.

When the premiere aired, the veil of secrecy had to be drawn aside, at least to some extent, and the subject matter of the new season, now branded under the subtitle of *Roanoke*, was finally made known. The first episode introduces the Millers—Matt and Shelby—who relocate to Roanoke in coastal North Carolina after Matt is attacked and Shelby suffers a miscarriage. In a departure from the program's usual mode of storytelling, and with a clear intimation of the troubles to come, their story is conveyed via the framing device of a paranormal documentary entitled *My Roanoke Nightmare*, through a combination of dramatic reconstructions and talking head interviews with the Millers themselves. The scene is instantly set for conflict when the couple falls in love with an eighteenth-century backwoods farmhouse and outbids some hostile local "hillbillies" at the auction ("Chapter 1"). Once ensconced in their new abode, the Millers soon experience a series of disconcerting or outright traumatic events, ranging from home invasions and the subsequent discovery of a creepy home video to a bizarre "rain" shower of human teeth and a disorienting experience for a panicked Shelby in the woods surrounding their isolated home.

Such narrative and thematic elements plainly situate *Roanoke* as a coherent and worthy successor to the preceding five seasons of the horror show. Matt and Shelby's efforts to move beyond a difficult past and make a fresh start show unmistakable echoes of the Harmon family's relocation in *Murder House*, as does the physical setting of an afflicted domestic space. The choice of Roanoke—known as the Lost Colony—as the scenario entails a focus on one of the more enigmatic and disquieting episodes of America's early history and thus follows in the footsteps of *Coven*, with its emphasis on witches in Salem and slavery in New Orleans. Recalling the night that their home was targeted by an unknown threat, Matt's thoughts turn to their antagonistic neighbors and he shares in an interview that because he and Shelby are an interracial couple living in the South, "this kind of hate is something that's always on the back of my mind" ("Chapter 1"). Shelby and Matt's story thus raises issues of race and place, a theme that features in several seasons, including *Coven* and *Freak Show*, as well as evoking the interracial marriage of Kit and Alma Walker in *Asylum*. The depiction of Los Angeles as a city of violence, from which Matt and Shelby flee to embrace a more peaceful, rural lifestyle, appears first in *Murder House* and then finds fuller expression in *Hotel*. All in all, the preliminary events of *Roanoke* tender firm links to the pre-existing *AHS* universe fleshed out over the first five seasons.

Part One of this collection took into account ways in which the *American Horror Story* franchise points up established practices as well as more recent developments in the twenty-first century entertainment industry. Lorna Jowett considered the use of repertory casting in *AHS* and *Roanoke* can be seen to continue in this vein by employing many familiar faces, including, thus far, Sarah Paulson, Lily Rabe, Denis O'Hare and Kathy Bates. Another cast member, Cuba Gooding, Jr., is new to this program but stars as O.J. Simpson in the 2016 spin-off series *American Crime Story*, and thus might well be seen as part of Murphy and Falchuk's repertory company. Here, the talking heads/re-enactment format permits key characters to be played by more than one actor, thus expanding the cast even further. Stacey Abbott analyzed the relationship between *AHS* and the rise in Gothic tourism in the second essay and *Roanoke*'s explicit situation within an authentic and identifiable geographical location has obvious potential for those seeking to extend their onscreen engagement with a horror text into their own lived reality. Through examining U.S. television scheduling practices in the third essay, Derek Johnston considered the importance that the industry places on seasonality. Though it is yet unclear how *Roanoke* will mark the holiday seasons in 2016, *AHS* has repeatedly emphasized Halloween within its narratives. Further, the anticipation surrounding Season Six demonstrates that the program itself is seen as a fixture on FX's fall schedule.

Case studies on issues of representation in specific seasons made up the subject matter of Part Two. Nikki Cox scrutinized the treatment of gender roles and the American family in *Murder House* in essay four and the first episode of *Roanoke*, with its depictions of domesticity and thwarted aspirations to parenthood, makes overt allusions to that season. The fifth essay saw Kyle Ethridge draw on monster theory to explore the much-maligned figure of the witch in *Coven*. Season Six's use of hillbilly antagonists sees the introduction of the "backwoods primitives" trope (Hervey 239), a horror staple that suggests a thematic interest in another type of "monster," similarly employed to convey anxieties about culture, identity and marginalization. Noting that *Freak Show* looks to less supernatural sources of horror than do other seasons, Carl Schottmiller discussed discriminatory attitudes towards so-called "monsters." Such debates, with their potential to reveal much about American history and culture, seem applicable to *Roanoke* thus far.

Part Three comprised a variety of essays on tropes and conventions of the horror and Gothic genres. The seventh essay saw Rebecca Janicker evaluate how the Gothic device of haunting functions in *Murder House*, a season especially noteworthy for its extensive use of supernatural protagonists. Likewise, the past rematerializes to disturb the present in *Roanoke* as Matt and Shelby undergo terrifying encounters with long-departed residents of their home and its environs. Philip L. Simpson explored the Gothic theme of the abuse of power in *Asylum*, describing how corrupt organizations such as Briarcliff may facilitate the mistreatment of vulnerable people by those in authority. As *Roanoke* progresses, it becomes apparent that the Miller's farmhouse has precisely one such dark history—it once housed an assisted living facility run by two sisters who murdered their elderly charges—and that this is far from dormant ("Chapter 2"). Reflecting on *AHS*'s tendencies to push at conventional genre boundaries, Emma Austin posited that the franchise might fruitfully be seen as a postmodern text. Certainly, *Roanoke* continues the pattern of genre blending and takes this one step further by presenting Season Six through the lens of an entirely new genre, namely that of the documentary. Finally, Conny Lippert examined the ties between *AHS* and American popular culture, identifying *Coven* as the season that resonates most deeply with American history and also with key conventions of American Gothic. With its Southern setting and thematic preoccupation with the perils of the wilderness, *Roanoke* pays clear tribute to this Gothic legacy.

All in all, *Roanoke* seems set to follow in the bloody footsteps of its *AHS* predecessors. With its foundation in key genre tropes and alertness to American history and popular culture, *American Horror Story* is a franchise that look ready to keep audiences entertained with its trademark levels of gore and suspense, while also striving to keep them guessing with new twists on its tried-and-tested small screen horror formula.

WORKS CITED

"Chapter 1." *American Horror Story: Roanoke*. Writ. Ryan Murphy and Brad Falchuk. Dir. Bradley Buecker. FX Network. 14 September 2016. Television.

"Chapter 2." *American Horror Story: Roanoke*. Writ. Tim Minear. Dir. Michael Goi. FX Network. 21 September 2016. Television.

Hervey, Benjamin. "Contemporary Horror Cinema." *The Routledge Companion to Gothic*. Eds. Catherine Spooner and Emma McEvoy. London: Routledge, 2007. 233–241. Print.

Kernan, Lisa. *Coming Attractions: Reading American Movie Trailers*. Austin: University of Texas Press, 2004. Print.

Glossary

The "Axeman" of New Orleans
New Orleans was terrorized throughout 1918 and 1919 by an unknown assailant who broke into homes by night and murdered the sleeping occupants. The killer, whose identity remains unknown, was branded the "Axeman" because the bloody nature of the crimes suggested the use of such a violent murder weapon. A letter, allegedly from the killer, was sent to the *Times-Picayune* threatening further violence on March 19, 1919, to all but those with jazz music playing in their homes.

Ted Bundy
Ted Bundy confessed to the killing of more than thirty young women and girls across America between 1974 and 1978, although the true number is suspected to be far higher. The former psychology major would often use such tactics as requests for assistance, e.g., with a feigned injury, to lure his victims before raping and murdering them.

Jeffrey Dahmer
Serial killer Jeffrey Dahmer was active from 1978 until his arrest in 1991. His crimes against his male victims included rape, murder and cannibalism. He achieved notoriety when an intended victim escaped and the police discovered human remains, such as severed heads and an altar made from skulls, in Dahmer's Milwaukee home.

John Wayne Gacy
Following a conviction for sexual assault in 1968, John Wayne Gacy went on to sexually assault and kill upwards of thirty boys and young men in Illinois in the 1970s, many of whose bodies were found concealed under his home or elsewhere on his property. When undertaking charitable work in the community, Gacy would often dress as his alter ego, "Pogo the Clown."

H.H. Holmes
H.H. Holmes, born Herman Webster Mudgett, was a medical doctor, inventor and entrepreneur who constructed the Holmes Castle hotel to accommodate

those flocking to Chicago for the World's Columbian Exposition in 1893. Soon to be known as the "Murder Castle," this purpose-built, mazelike structure comprised such intricacies as false doors, concealed passages, sliding panels and peepholes, all of which facilitated Holmes's goal of killing and disposing of an unknown quantity of victims at his leisure.

Delphine LaLaurie

Madame Delphine Macarty LaLaurie was a wealthy Creole socialite who hosted lavish parties in the fashionable Vieux Carré of New Orleans. In 1834, a fire broke out in the Royal Street mansion in which she lived with her third husband. Subsequent investigations revealed several slaves, mutilated and starving, imprisoned in the attic. LaLaurie's grisly legend endures and the house, reputed to be haunted, is a fixture on ghost tours.

Marie Laveau

The legendary Voodoo practitioner Marie Laveau lived in New Orleans in the nineteenth century. Her work as a hairdresser, combined with her reputed supernatural powers, gave her a degree of social prominence. Laveau's name lives on and her tomb in St. Louis Cemetery No. 1 (which may actually be that of her daughter) is a major tourist attraction in the city.

Dr. Josef Mengele

As an SS officer and medical doctor at Auschwitz during World War II, Dr. Josef Mengele was instrumental in the selection of victims for death in the gas chambers. In addition to these crimes, he gained infamy on account of his sadistic research. With a background in genetics, Mengele conducted extensive and frequently lethal experiments on prisoners, often on twins, as they held a particular source of fascination.

Richard Ramirez

Throughout 1984 and 1985, Satanist and serial killer Richard Ramirez invaded and robbed numerous homes in California, subjecting his victims to violent sexual assault and murdering thirteen people.

Elizabeth Short (aka the "Black Dahlia")

In 1947, the body of aspiring 22-year old movie actress Elizabeth Short, dubbed the "Black Dahlia," was discovered on a vacant lot in Los Angeles. Her murder became notorious for its brutality—Short was severely mutilated and cut in half at the waist—and for its mystery, as the case remains unsolved.

Richard Speck

On July 14, 1966, mass murderer Richard Speck imprisoned eight student nurses in their shared Chicago home, terrorizing and systematically killing the women throughout the course of that same night.

Aileen Wuornos

Aileen Wuornos robbed and murdered at least six men along the Florida highways from late 1989 and into 1990, later accusing them of rape or attempted rape.

The "Zodiac Killer"

From the late 1960s, a serial killer took the lives of an unconfirmed number of male and female victims in Northern California. This person, whose identity has never been established, acquired the soubriquet of the "Zodiac Killer" on sending the local press letters that contained cryptograms and claims of responsibility for numerous murders.

About the Contributors

Stacey **Abbott** is a reader in film and television studies at the University of Roehampton and has written extensively about the horror genre in film and TV. She is the author of *Celluloid Vampires* (2007), *Angel* (2009), *Undead Apocalypse* (2016), and the coauthor, with Lorna Jowett, of *TV Horror* (2013). She is the editor of *The Cult TV Book* and co-editor, with David Lavery, of *TV Goes to Hell* (2011).

Emma **Austin** is a senior lecturer in film and media at the University of Portsmouth, with specific research and teaching interests in horror in popular culture. She has created learning packages on horror for undergraduates and A-level students. She writes on aspects of zombies in popular culture, genre history and specific horror films and has been included in several edited collections.

Nikki **Cox** received an MA in anthropology from California State University in 2015 and is a doctoral student in the Anthropology Department at the University of Oregon. Her master's thesis focused on secular pilgrimage, community, space and place and nonreligious spirituality in nature. Her research interests also include folklore, American popular culture, gender, performance and environment.

Kyle **Ethridge** received a master's degree from the Department of English at the University of Southern Mississippi in 2014 as well as a master's in library and information science at the same institution in 2016. His research interests include Gothic and Victorian literature, queer studies and monster studies. His essay for this collection emerges from work he presented at the 2015 PCA/ACA conference in New Orleans, Louisiana.

Rebecca **Janicker** received a Ph.D. from the University of Nottingham in 2014 and her dissertation was published as *The Literary Haunted House* (2015). She has previously published on the Gothic fictions of Robert Bloch, Stephen King, Richard Matheson and H.P. Lovecraft and she lectures in film and media studies at the University of Portsmouth in the UK.

Derek **Johnston** is a lecturer in broadcast literacy at Queen's University, Belfast. He mostly researches genre histories, particularly relating to fantastic genres and British television. His monograph *Haunted Seasons* covers the history and development of traditions of horror stories as seasonal events in the U.S. and UK. Other research has covered British and American science fiction on film and television, particularly pre–1960s.

Lorna **Jowett** is a reader in television studies at the University of Northampton. She is the coauthor with Stacey Abbott of *TV Horror*, author of *Sex and the Slayer*, and editor of a forthcoming collection about time on television. She has published many articles on television, film and popular culture, and is working on a book examining gender in the new *Doctor Who* universe.

Conny **Lippert** received her doctorate from the University of Bristol in 2015. Her thesis focused on topographies in Stephen King's and H.P. Lovecraft's Gothic works. She earned a master's degree at the University of Nottingham in 2008 and a bachelor's degree at the University of Bayreuth in 2004. Her research interests are Gothic and horror fiction, popular literature and culture and American literature.

Carl **Schottmiller** is a doctoral candidate in the Department of World Arts and Cultures/Dance at the University of California, Los Angeles. He holds an MA in folklore from the University of California, Berkeley, and a BA in English and women's studies from Ohio University. His research investigates social, cultural and political issues concerning representations of queerness in popular discourse.

Philip L. **Simpson** received a doctorate in American literature from Southern Illinois University. He serves as provost of the Titusville Campus of Eastern Florida State College and has worked at the college in other administrative roles and as a tenured professor. He is the vice president/president-elect of PCA/ACA and an editorial board member of the *Journal of Popular Culture*.

Index